*She took the royal fa...
entered Buckingham P......—and the world
by storm when she left it....*

What was life as a Duchess really like for the red-haired, irrepressible Fergie? Royal insider Ingrid Seward, editor of *Majesty* magazine, goes behind the locked doors of the Palace to tell us:

Who was the high-spirited and mischievous redhead who loved—and left—a Prince?

What was life like with a husband absent nine months of the year—and what ever happened to Koo Stark?

When did the honeymoon end and the realities of life as a Royal descend?

Where did Fergie and Diana's most infamous prank take place?

And *how* did Fergie struggle to maintain a private life under constant scrutiny?

A riveting inside look at the life of the Royal Family's most controversial member

St. Martin's Paperbacks by Ingrid Seward

ROYALTY REVEALED (with Unity Hall)
FERGIE

ℱERGIE

*Published in hardcover as SARAH:
THE LIFE OF A DUCHESS*

INGRID SEWARD

ST. MARTIN'S PAPERBACKS

To my husband Ross and our daughter, Arabella

The author and publishers gratefully acknowledge permission to reproduce the photographs in this book. All fees for the use of pictures from the Ferguson family album will be donated to charity.

First published in Great Britain by HarperCollins Publishers under the title *Sarah: HRH The Duchess of York: A Biography*. Previously published in the U.S. in hardcover under the title *Sarah: The Life of a Duchess*.

FERGIE

Cover photographs courtesy Alpha London/Globe Photos, Inc. Credits on front: of Fergie with Diana, Globe Photos; of wedding, David Parker; of Fergie with children, Dave Chancellor; color photograph of Fergie, Dave Chancellor. Credits on back: Fergie on horseback, Jim Bennett; Beatrice pulls Fergie's hair, Alpha/Globe Photos; with Eugenie, Alpha/Globe Photos; with Andrew, Alpha/Globe Photos.

Library of Congress Catalog Card Number: 91-19833

ISBN: 0-312-92855-6

Printed in the United States of America

St. Martin's Press hardcover edition/September 1991
St. Martin's Paperbacks edition/June 1992

10 9 8 7 6 5 4 3 2 1

ACKNOWLEDGEMENTS

I would like to thank the Duchess of York for her invaluable assistance when I set out to write this book and for allowing me access to her family and friends, all of whom gave me their straightforward and honest opinions because she had asked them to do so. In particular I would like to thank Susan and Ronald Ferguson, who have put up with me in their home on numerous occasions over the last eighteen months, and Mrs Barrantes for coming to see me in hospital after I had had my baby daughter. Without Jane Makim's excellent memory and ability to recount a story this book would be a lesser tome. I would also like to thank those at Buckingham Palace who eased my path; namely Geoff Crawford, Jane Ambler, Helen Spooner, Lucy Manners, and Major Bill McLean, who was Equerry during much of the period while I was writing this book.

Among the Duchess's friends I would like to thank all those who gave up their time to talk to me and allow themselves to be quoted in this book; in particular Neil Durden-Smith, William Drummond, Jules Dodd-Noble, Clare Wentworth-Stanley, Clare Greenall, Carolyn Cotterell and Ros Duckworth. Thanks also to Lindka Cierach, Brian Wright and Colin Beckwith.

At HarperCollins Eddie Bell was terrific for supporting the idea in the first place, Carol O'Brien was a brilliant editor, and Amanda McCardie was very encouraging and long-suffering.

Finally, I would like to emphasize that all the views expressed, unless otherwise stated, are mine and mine alone.

CONTENTS

INTRODUCTION

THE DUCHESS OF YORK EXUDES ENERGY. SHE FILLS A ROOM with her presence and, having been taught that, socially, silence must never fall, she pronounces in her well-pitched tones how thrilled she is to be there. Parts of her words are heavily emphasized. 'Absolootly brilliant,' she will say to the assembled company. Smiling broadly, she appears to be totally absorbed in what she is doing. The professionalism which comes from being a member of the Royal Family for the past six years has rubbed off, however, and she turns her neck slightly to look at the clock while simultaneously catching the eye of her lady-in-waiting.

She is open and outgoing, charming and genuinely interested in people. She is elegantly dressed, slim and well coiffured, but not everyone approves of the Duchess's style. In the beginning she was too boisterous, too outspoken and too fresh for a British public that wants its Royal Family in a mould of decorous conventionality. Sarah appeared to be trying too hard. Worse, she seemed to be enjoying herself.

The initial public reaction to her had been favourable. People responded to her charm and humour, to the way she seemed determined to get on with things without surrendering her personality to the strictures of royal life. She insisted on continuing to work, which was deemed commendable. She remained loyal to her old friends, which was admirable. And she refused to throw out her old wardrobe or go on a crash diet, which, initially at least, won her plaudits.

Yet her very success in continuing to 'be herself' was the seed for her later troubles. She appeared to be having too much fun, and the smile that had first enchanted started to irritate.

She was accused of revelling in her position, of being altogether too 'fun-loving', of taking too many skiing holidays ('If only it was tennis no one would mind,' she says). Her dress sense was criticized. She was attacked for 'deserting' her new-born child. Finally, and the worst insult of all, she was called a 'parasite'.

Her grandmother, Lady Elmhirst, had warned that this would happen, that the first wave of affection would be followed by a swell of hostility. There is a long established tradition of picking one member of the Royal Family after another and naming him or her as the current 'bad royal'. It has happened in turn to Prince Philip, Princess Margaret, the Prince of Wales, Princess Anne, the Princess of Wales, and Princess Michael of Kent. That it was inevitable made it no less hurtful.

'I am tough on the outside but I am marshmallow on the inside,' she admits and some of the insults hurled at her have reduced her to tears. The ritual of the 'bad royal' had become very savage indeed.

Adapting to the strictures of royal life is a monumental challenge. It took the Princess of Wales several years and the transition from private person to public property was a painful one marked by tears and tantrums. Sarah, too, found herself caught in the barbed wire of no-man's land between what she is and what she is expected to be. Older, confident in her personality, she was better equipped to deal with these pressures. She is still the warm-hearted, ebullient woman I first met in Switzerland almost a decade ago. She has had the unqualified support of her family and her husband and drawing on her experience and what she calls 'my inner strength', she has faced up to the daunting responsibilities that are hers for life and which she is determined to fulfil.

1

Childhood

SARAH FERGUSON ENJOYED A CHILDHOOD WHICH, IN retrospect, seems idyllic in its comfort and Englishness.

She lived in a 'very big and very white' house in the heart of the golden circle centred on Sunninghill in Berkshire, an hour's drive from London. Her father, Major Ronald Ferguson, called it suburbia. It was anything but. Lowood House is an imposing ten-bedroom Edwardian house set in fourteen acres of garden and woodland. There were sloping green lawns and the long gravel drive leading up from the gate lodge to the main house was lined with rhododendrons and bamboo bushes. Below the drive there was a rose garden where 'everything was identical to left and right' and beyond that graduated lawns fell away, joined by old stone steps. Behind the staff cottage was an old apple orchard and a tennis court and the stables.

The Major and his young bride, Susie Wright, had bought it in 1957 from the wealthy Dupree brewing family. It was conveniently close to the Combermere barracks where Ronald, then twenty-eight years old and a captain in the Life Guards, was stationed. Both husband and wife were well off and well connected. Susie's engineer father owned an iron, coal and steel business in Derbyshire, the Major was from a long line of soldiers, and between the two of them they provided Sarah with a family tree that includes four dukes, three mistresses of Charles II and makes her a fourth cousin of the Princess of Wales.

Both parents were excellent horsemen and during Royal Ascot week the house was filled with guests. Some came for the racing, others for polo played at Smith's Lawn on the Queen's nearby Windsor estate. Sometimes there were so many guests that the overflow had to be housed in a caravan in the driveway and the nursery on the ground floor was converted into an extra bedroom.

The Fergusons did not establish themselves there immediately after their marriage. Shortly after the birth of their first child, Jane, on 26 August 1957, Susie joined her husband at his posting in Aden, leaving the baby behind in the care of her grandmother, Doreen Wright, and a 'typical Scots dragon of a nanny'. The British Empire was in decline and the Union Jack, which had once flown so triumphantly over two-fifths of the world, would soon be lowered in country after newly independent country. But large areas of the map were still coloured red and for families such as the Fergusons, raised in the tradition of imperial service stretching back over more than a century, foreign duty was still expected. Attitudes have changed. When Sarah left Beatrice in England and flew to Australia to spend a few weeks with her naval husband a furore of protest followed her. In the late fifties it was not considered strange to leave a young baby behind in England. Quite the contrary. It would have been considered remiss if Susie, only a year into her marriage, had not joined her husband on his overseas posting – and irresponsible if she had chosen to take her young daughter with her into the heat and disease of southern Arabia.

Nine months later the Fergusons were back at Lowood and at three minutes past nine o'clock on the crisp morning of 15 October 1959, Susie gave birth to Sarah Margaret. The child, like her sister before her, was delivered at the fashionable Welbeck Nursing Home in London's Marylebone. Ronald Ferguson drove up from Combermere barracks to be at his wife's side and reported, in clipped, military fashion, that he was 'thrilled and delighted' with his little girl and 'relieved they were both doing well'.

Jane's first excited memory of her little sister is of 'a great big mop of curly hair. Just curls all over her head'.

When Susie returned from Aden she had employed a charming Princess Christian-trained nanny 'who was wonderful' and stayed with the family for two years before she left to get married. The Fergusons were secure enough financially to be able to employ a cleaning lady, Miss Morton (whom Sarah called Mortie), and a couple, Mr and Mrs Cole, who lived in the lodge cottage at the top of the drive. There were also the various different nannies.

'It was difficult to find the right one,' Susie admits, 'and we did have quite a few, but it wasn't because the children were naughty. It just worked out that way.'

Susie also employed au pairs, one of whom was Ritva Risu who later sold her version of life with the Fergusons to a newspaper. Susie did not like what she read.

Looking back, neither of the Ferguson girls recalls any feelings of jealousy, and there was certainly no favouritism. 'Mum was very good,' Jane recalls, 'and if it was Sarah's birthday she would give me a present too and ask one of my friends to the party and if it was mine she would do the same thing for Sarah, but we did have some mutual friends too.'

The sisters became the best of friends which, despite the distance separating them, they remain today. They were used to being together and when there was no hunting and their father was on military call, their mother took them off to Europe skiing with the au pair or nanny.

'We went every year,' Susie remembers. 'We went to Lenk and to Zurs, Courchevel, Méribel and Verbier.' Sometimes their friends came too. One of her friends, Sally Uniac, was tragically killed and her two children, Camilla and Robbie, came to live with the Fergusons for almost two years and Susie took them all skiing. 'The daughter, Camilla, was about Sarah's age and we all had great fun,' Susie says.

One year they were invited to stay at the family house of one of their Swiss au pair girls, Mary Anne. Mary Anne's family had an old wooden farmhouse in the mountain village of Lenk. Built on stilts, the area underneath the house was protected from the snow and housed the chickens and cows. The two little girls were fascinated to see the animals and birds living under the house and spent hours collecting eggs and helping to feed the cows.

'We went for three weeks,' Susie recalls. 'It was the girls and I, plus my daily, Mortie, whom Sarah adored, and Mrs Cole the housekeeper was another great character. We all went trundling off in the car, driving all the way, full of people, luggage and children.'

Susie may not have been obviously maternal with her children when they were babies but as soon as they started to develop into real little people she took the time and effort to teach them all the things she herself enjoyed.

'I first took Sarah skiing when she was four and Jane was six,' she says. 'Sarah was very brave. She has always been brave, it was the same with her riding. She would ride anything and had no fear. I did everything with them and loved it.'

During the long summer months of childhood the two girls played on the closely cut lawns of Lowood House, and while their parents were with the polo crowd at nearby Smith's Lawn, would give elaborate tea parties for their teddy bears with the dogs acting as extra guests. Sarah was always very imaginative and, as soon as she could talk, amused herself for hours in the make-believe world she and her sister shared.

They would take chicken eggs from the nearby farm, find an old tin and make scrambled eggs on the bonfire at the bottom of the garden, pretending they were at their own grand banquet. In later years they impersonated the riders and horses they saw on television. In their show jumping events Sarah played the flamboyant Harvey Smith while Jane pretended to be the more gentlemanly David Broome. They built scaled-down jumps to add to the fun of the game with Sarah taking the role of Andrew

Fielden, a member of the British team, whose horse Vibutt had a spectacular habit of kicking out its hind legs holding its tail high. Jane preferred Marion Coates and Stroller, her small horse which made the enormous jumps. Whole afternoons were spent in this way. Often it was so quiet the housekeeper, Mrs Cole, used to wonder what the girls were up to until she spotted them on the lawn using part of a washing line for reins.

'It's all right,' she would say. 'They're just playing horses again.'

School seemed an intrusion. At the age of three Sarah followed her elder sister to Mrs Laytham's, a popular kindergarten at Englefield Green which described itself as 'for the children of the gentry'. It is the events at home, however, that provide the most vivid memories.

But if the girls were well-loved and indulged, they were not spoilt.

'I was frightfully strict about manners,' Susie says. 'They were taught to always get up when people came into the room and write thank-you letters. My own mother was brought up very strictly and correctly and I think it rubs off on you.'

Their father, in keeping with his army background, was also a stickler for manners, even in the very young, and his daughters were taught to say please and thank you almost as soon as they could speak. There were times, however, when they were as naughty as any children.

'When something was wrong Sarah would always get the blame,' her mother recalls. 'She'd accept it too. She was a frightfully unselfish child and had a very generous character.'

Jane recalls one summer afternoon when she went into the garden at Lowood and started picking off all the rose heads. Suddenly realizing the trouble she was heading into she hastily stuffed the roses into Sarah's little pockets until they were bursting and petals were showering all over the lawn. Susie saw the two girls from the window and, realizing what had happened, rushed out into the garden.

'I told Mum that Sarah had picked them all,' Jane confesses, remembering how her little sister loyally stood there, with her ginger head bowed, tears splashing down her cheeks, and rose heads tumbling from her pockets. 'She got into terrible trouble and when Mum scolded her and sent her to bed, she went without a word.'

On another occasion when Sarah was eight she was allowed into her mother's big double bed for the afternoon to read her comics and books. 'I was a bit bored,' Sarah told television presenter Sue Lawley, 'and I saw on her dressing table the most beautiful string of pearls and a pair of scissors, and I thought "That's too good to be true", so off I went and chopped each pearl up so they ran all over the dressing table and over the floor and it was completely awful. Mum walked in and her face fell a mile. I was in bed with the covers up to my chin.

'She just looked at me and I said "Please don't stop me riding, swimming, enjoying things with my friends." She said, "Perfect, those are all your punishments. You can't do any of that for a week."'

Then there was the time when their mother was out watching their father play polo and they encouraged each other on and sneaked into their mother's bedroom on the first floor. Their idea was to recruit some extra guests for one of their tea parties and the bedroom was full of their mother's precious and prized collection of teddy bears.

Creeping up the wide wooden staircase and down the long landing, they pushed open the door to their mother's room. Jane was escorted by her favourite koala bear, almost devoid of fur, while Sarah was supported by her stuffed rabbit, who was wearing a pretty coloured skirt. They found the teddy bears, and after consultation with the koala and the bunny, decided to invite them to the party – via the quickest route to the garden, through the window.

One by one they threw the bears out of the window, over the stone balcony and onto the lawn below. Unfortunately, one of their guests did not make it. It became lodged in a mossy patch between the balcony of the two adjacent rooms. And try as they might they were too small to do anything much about it.

'Mum was furious when she came back,' Jane remembers, 'as it was one of her favourite, really old teddies. I think she ended up having to get the gardener to dislodge it for her while we were sent to bed without having had our tea party.'

Such inevitable incidents of childhood apart, Sarah, a Little Orphan Annie look-alike with her pile of hair, was a popular little girl. 'She was always doing something that amused everybody,' her mother recalls. 'She was the most attractive child with enormous great big red, heavy curls that, if you pulled them out, bounced straight back again. She looked top heavy until she had her hair cut.'

Susie was a popular mother, always available for outings and games. 'We seemed to have thousands of children around us,' she remembers. 'I was always doing something barmy in the car – it was in the days before seat-belts – and we had such fun. All their friends loved to go off on an outing with us or do something with us. It was just me and the girls.'

In the holidays both children invited their ever-increasing group of friends to the 'big white house' for parties. Birthdays were a big event and they used to have at least twenty children over. Party clothes have not changed much since then and Beatrice and Eugenie wear some of the little smocked dresses their mother wore as a child. The games, too, are the same. Susie would organize oranges and lemons and pass the parcel, games Princess Beatrice plays today. 'Every time the music stops, she is there trying to unwrap the parcel,' Sarah says.

Sarah displayed the same single-mindedness. 'She was very determined in what she wanted to do and she wanted to do everything,' her mother recalls. 'She was always saying, "Shall we go and do this, shall we go and do that? Come on. Let's go!" She was full of enthusiasm.'

It is a characteristic that could sometimes lead her into trouble.

On horseback it was an asset. Daughters of a cavalry officer and an excellent horsewoman, Sarah and Jane both started riding at an early age. Sarah first sat on a pony shortly after her first birthday and got her own pony when she was only three. Evil-tempered like most Shetlands, the pony was forever trying to unseat his rider, though rarely with any success.

'We were horse mad,' Jane remembers. 'There were two stables at Lowood and an apple orchard where we used to chase our ponies on foot. There was also a wood which was nice and mossy and we used to build jumps there, pretending to be ponies ourselves.

'There was a little track through our wood, which led up the hill and came out onto the drive of Ayesha, the Maharani of Jaipur's house. She was nice to us and we loved walking up to see her when she was getting dressed in her saris.'

The whole family was now settled in this leafy, comfortable world. Their father, his foreign duties over, was spending more time with his daughters. He would play with them for hours, helping them clean out their rabbit hutches and reading them bedtime stories. When they sat on his knee they used to grab his eyebrows, pull them over his eyes and cry, 'Curtains.'

The Major rarely accompanied his brood on the winter sojourns to the Alps – he had had a cartilage removed and did not ski – but every summer he would take his daughters on sandcastle building, bucket and spade holidays to Bognor Regis or Brancaster.

His life was now divided between his family, his army duties, and his polo. He had taken up polo when he was stationed in the Suez Canal zone in Egypt in 1954. By the time his children were born he was established at Smith's Lawn as a protégé of polo enthusiast Colonel Humphrey Guinness, a pre-war polo international. Through polo he met Earl Mountbatten of Burma and this brought him into regular contact with Mountbatten's nephew, Prince Philip. The two men, both five goal players (out of a possible ten) were considered among the best of English players. They got on well off the field as well and Ronald and his wife were invited to Sandringham for shooting weekends during the winter.

Ronald goes to pains to point out, however, that the Fergusons were never particularly close to the Royal Family. They were only ever invited to Sandringham once a year and when he stopped shooting so did the invitations.

'That nearly caused a divorce,' he says with feeling, 'especially as there was an invitation in the pipeline when I decided to give it all up. But it would have been hypocritical to accept that invitation and refuse all the others, so I told Prince Philip I couldn't go. I decided I had no right to take a pheasant or partridge's life so I stopped. I don't regret it.'

Susie did. She was very angry with her husband for making his decision just as their annual invitation to Sandringham was due. She had enjoyed riding with the Queen while the men were out shooting. She liked Sandringham House with its curious mixture of valuable paintings and old-fashioned furnishings. She found the other guests rather more stimulating company than many of her husband's army friends.

During the summer weekends at Smith's Lawn, however, they were still in the privileged position of being on familiar terms with the Queen, Prince Philip and their children. While Ronald was playing polo Susie would stand near the pony lines with her daughters, whose treat it was to feed their father's ponies with sugar after each chukka. Sometimes the royal children would appear and they would play together, but neither Sarah nor Jane has a very clear memory until much later on. Susie remembers some meetings in those early days but, she insists, it was nothing special.

'Our families would meet and naturally the children would play together like any other children,' she says. 'They didn't understand what royalty meant at that age.'

In the early sixties polo was a relaxed affair, very much an interest of the military caste. If everyone really did meet on the polo field, as Susie, much to her regret, would later say, then it would not have taken long to effect the introductions. There were few spectators other than the few true enthusiasts, many of whom had served in India where British officers had first encountered the sport. There were no hordes of cameramen running backwards in a frantic attempt to snatch an 'informal' photograph of the Royal Family at play. Indeed, the only photographer who took a regular interest in the game was the gentlemanly Colonel Voynovichas, the former Yugoslavian cavalry officer who now called himself John Scott. It was Scott who snapped the now well-known photographs of Andrew and Sarah at Smith's Lawn in the pony lines.

Jane recalls the occasion. 'I can remember meeting Prince Andrew and the Queen at polo with my mother and my sister. It was cold and for once we were in really scruffy clothes – I was wearing jeans and a jumper and my hair was tied back and Camilla Uniac was with us. I remember Mum telling us exactly what to say when we met the Queen and I knew it was jolly important for Mum that we should do the right thing. Prince Edward was there too and Lady Sarah Armstrong-Jones.

'We stood in the pony lines and then went to tread in the divots between chukkas. I tried to speak to Prince Andrew, but he was quite difficult to talk to. I remember he wouldn't say much at all, although we both tried hard to talk to him.'

It was 1967 and the future Duke of York, then aged seven, was far more interested in slipping away to play in his mother's car than he was chatting to his future bride or watching the polo. It was not a momentous occasion for either Sarah or Andrew and, had it not been for John Scott's photographs and the subsequent course of events, would now be long forgotten. He was not a fan of horses or riding and still isn't. 'I'm the only member of the Royal Family who doesn't ride,' Andrew says, 'largely because I fell off too many times when I was small.' His wife confirms: 'I don't think he enjoys it very much.'

Sarah and Jane, on the other hand, most definitely did. They were allowed to watch television in the small study off the drawing room on the ground floor. *Batman* was a favourite but it was really horses they were interested in: the Horse of the Year Show at Wembley, show jumping from Hickstead, anything in fact that gave them even the slightest glimpse of something equestrian. Jane recalls: 'When we weren't watching them or riding them or pretending to be them we played with them.'

For Christmas and birthday treats, the Ferguson girls were taken to Beauchamp Place in London to a small basement shop and each bought a model horse called a Julip. The thriving business is still extant today and the lifelike models remain every pony-mad girl's delight. Each breed is represented and can be ordered in the colours of their favourite pony, down to the smallest markings. Stables, saddles, bridles, rugs and grooming equipment are also available, each a miniature duplicate of the real thing.

In 1969 the family moved out of Lowood – it is now an old people's home – and across the county line to Hampshire. For two such horse-minded girls Dummer Down Farm was a delight. Set in 876 acres, it is a mixed arable farm with a herd of Friesian cattle, a flock of sheep, chickens, dogs and, most importantly from Jane and nine-year-old Sarah's point of view, a large yard with stabling for half a dozen horses.

Sarah already knew the house well. The Fergusons had been connected with the village since 1939 when Sarah's grandfather, Colonel Andrew Ferguson, bought Dummer House and its estate. In 1958, suffering from ill-health but not wanting to move out of the area, he sold the big house, the stud he operated near Winchester, and three hundred surplus acres, and bought the farmhouse.

The Colonel died in 1966 and after his widow, Sarah's grandmother Marian whom she always called 'Gargar', had settled into a small cottage along the lane, Ronald and his family moved in. It was not as large as Lowood – it only has eight bedrooms – but it was still a substantial, late Georgian residence. The girls had their own bedrooms (Sarah's, at the top of the stairs, is now used by her half-sister, Eliza) and home life revolved around the large farmhouse kitchen on the ground floor. The scrubbed pine table was the family meeting place and the dining room was seldom used except for dinner parties.

The top floor, with its beamed ceilings and the large rocking horse brought over from Lowood, was the attic bedroom and still is. Today, if both Sarah and Andrew and the children are staying, the attic is used for one of the policemen, while the others stay in the little bungalow Ronald converted into a simple guest cottage. A smaller room off the kitchen was the main nursery where the girls kept their favourite toys and watched the large old-fashioned television or listened to the BBC Light Programme. They were not allowed to watch television until their bedrooms were tidy and all the toys had been put away, and they were encouraged to fold their clothes on the back of the chair each night before they went to sleep.

There were the inevitable inter-generational clashes. It was the late sixties and fashion and manners were changing. Bob Dylan, the Beatles and the Rolling Stones were topping the charts, Twiggy was billed as the 'Face', colour television had just begun, everything was 'swinging' or 'dodgy', and Sarah loved saying, 'See you later Alligator'. The Major did not always approve. He liked his daughters to dress like young ladies, not refugees from Chelsea, and was always urging them to wear pretty little dresses. They seldom did.

'We loved clothes,' Jane says, 'but because of the farm and the ponies we usually wore jeans, which Dad hated.'

'I was a bit of a tomboy,' Sarah remembers. 'Mum was always trying to make us wear dresses, but we never found time to put them on.'

The move to Dummer coincided with a career change for their father and the Major was seeing a lot more of his children. Having failed to impress at Staff College, and with his prospects of promotion thereby limited, he decided – with considerable regret – to resign his commission in the Life Guards, and turn his hand to running the estate and playing polo. One of the cavalry's top players, Ronald Ferguson owned eight polo ponies whose upkeep was barely covered by his modest army pension. To supplement his income he later took a three-day-a-week job as a public relations consultant with the London firm of Neilson McCarthy. It was horses, however, that were the major focus in the Ferguson household.

Jumps were built and the children's ponies were housed alongside the polo ponies in big loose boxes in the yard.

In those days the sisters did everything together. 'Neither of us led the other,' Jane insists. 'We got on so well and we both liked doing the same things.'

Another variation of their game of make-believe was to imagine the farm dogs to be horses. They would take them to the gardener's woodshed and construct stables out of wooden boxes. They would exercise them as if they were thoroughbred race-horses, leading them around the yard and bringing them buckets of water and the scraps of food they had secreted from the kitchen.

'One day we were playing with the two dogs and we got called to do something,' Jane recalls. 'We left one dog in the box as he was in the middle of being "groomed" – and promptly forgot about him. After a couple of hours I was wondering where Kerry was and remembered he was still in the box! Poor dog, he was so glad to see us he was shaking all over with relief.'

Other misadventures followed. In the games they played Sarah was the 'ideas' girl. Says Jane: 'She always made it fun, she had such a good imagination.'

One of their favourite pastimes was 'catch' which they played on their bicycles around the garden and farm. One would hide, the other counted to fifty then set off in pursuit on her bike.

'One day,' Jane recalls, 'we were playing on our bikes in the lane by the farm. We had been playing all afternoon and as it was about four o'clock and winter and the sun was going down, it was getting dark. I went and hid down the lane. I waited while

Sarah counted to fifty, expecting to hear her searching for me any minute. But I heard nothing. What had happened was that she'd ridden into a strand of barbed wire which had cut her right across the chest. Eventually I saw her walking down the hill, pushing her bike with blood seeping through her clothes. She was so brave, all she said was, "I think I've cut myself."'

The injury was serious. She had come down the gravel drive, round the corner and had only seen the barbed wire at the last moment. Unable to stop, she had skidded under the wire which had caught her across the chest and gashed her open.

'It was really nasty and we had to rush her off to the hospital,' Jane remembers. 'She was quite accident prone, you know – and she still is. But she never made a fuss – and she still doesn't.'

Still determined to avoid any jealousy developing between the pair, Susie continued to be rigorously even-handed in the dispensation of gifts.

'I was rather extravagant,' Susie remembers, 'but at the same time they did enjoy it and I wanted them to have everything I hadn't been able to.' If one received a Sindy doll so would the other (and both ended up in the farmyard mud when they fell out of the cardboard box bicycle side cars they had made for them). As they grew older these double presents were almost always something to do with horses – bridles, grooming equipment, head collars, show bandages. They had help to put them on.

'I had a marvellous Australian girl groom called Binny,' says Susie (who, it happened, was the cousin of Alex Makim whom Jane would later marry). 'Binny and I would bundle the horse box up with six horses and go plodding off to something. We were always either organizing gymkhanas at home or going to them.'

Sarah was developing into an excellent horsewoman. Susie was impressed by her determination and did everything she could to encourage it.

'She had a marvellous little pony who was about thirteen

hands high – a Welsh cross thoroughbred,' Susie recalls. 'She had to really ride him, as he was thoroughly naughty and wanted his own way. Sarah wanted hers too and was determined to win a rosette with this stubborn little pony, but it was difficult as he always picked one jump to stop at during the day. It was very frustrating as you never knew which one it was going to be.'

At the Eden Vale show Susie was chatting to Fred Winter when Sarah rode by, pink with angry frustration.

'Mr Winter,' she said. 'I don't know what I'm going to do with Herbie, he keeps stopping at one jump and I never know which one it is going to be.'

Winter gave his advice. 'Just thwack him,' the great trainer said. 'It won't hurt him, but it will let him know who's boss.'

Sarah went into the first jump, pulled out her whip and struck the pony's rump. It worked. Herbie roared around.

After the round the young rider trotted over to her impromptu coach and said, 'Mr Winter, you're very clever, you got Herbie going.'

It was the beginning of an effective partnership. Herbie became a top class hunter and the pair went on to win the Peterborough Show together.

If Sarah was good in the saddle she was not over keen on the work required to get there. On a typical occasion Jane, her mother and the girl groom were working in the stables preparing the ponies for a show when Sarah poked her cheeky face round the door on the pretext she wanted to help.

'All right, all right,' Susie said knowingly, 'we don't need you, go and do something else. Everything's ready, everything's organized. There is only one thing you have to do and that is remember to bring your riding hat.'

'Yes Mum,' the ten-year-old said and skipped back into the house, delighted to be let off the disagreeable task of grooming and plaiting the ponies. She became so absorbed in a book she was reading that it was several minutes before she heard her mother shouting for her that they were ready to leave. She made it into the yard just as Susie, Jane and the girl groom were loading the last of the ponies into the horse box. Sarah climbed in and they drove off. Just as they were turning into the main road, a plaintive voice was heard from the back seat. 'Mum,' came the cry: 'I've left my hat behind.'

Her mother says: 'That was what she was like but you couldn't get cross as she was so sweet.'

Ronald Ferguson recalls a similar incident when he drove Sarah to a meet a few days later.

'I drove her there and unloaded the pony. It was a very cold day and there was a biting wind. I turned to get back into the box when I saw this little figure sitting bolt upright on her pony waving like mad and shouting. I couldn't hear what she was saying, so I went back to where she was. "Where are my gloves Dad?" she said – as if it was my fault. So I dutifully went back to the horse box and, sure enough, there they were on the passenger's seat. I retrieved them feeling rather pleased with myself and took them over to her. She put them on, then pulled a face and said, "Dads, why haven't you warmed them up for me?" Although I never spoiled the girls they obviously got used to some very high standards of parental care!'

Sarah agrees. 'I was quite difficult. I think my parents had to really keep control over me. But Mum was fantastic, she was very enthusiastic about everything we did. She insisted we go to all the gymkhanas. She was a super horsewoman.'

Her mother in her turn insists that it was Sarah's enthusiasm that got them all going. 'She was a tremendous companion,' Susie recalls.

Mother and daughters also went fox hunting together, 'and when we did,' Susie says, 'you wouldn't see her for dust.' The girls hunted frequently in Warwickshire where their aunt, Susie's sister Brigid Salmond, lived and one day when Sarah was staying she was invited out cubbing. Like all field sports it has its own esoteric rituals.

'She was very little,' Susie recalls, 'and riding a pony called

Bubbles. The hunt killed and she was bloodied because she was the first person to reach the fox after the huntsman. She was given the fox's brush and was absolutely thrilled. It was a great honour.' The initiation ceremony was performed by the late Duke of Beaufort, the legendary foxhunter and close friend of the Queen who was always known as Master. (When the Princess of Wales shot her first stag at Balmoral the stalker likewise daubed her face with its blood.)

It was competition that really caught Sarah's interest, however, and her bedroom at Dummer Down Farm was soon filled with rosettes and cups. She was even allowed to take time off from school to practise her riding before big events such as the Royal Windsor Horse Show and Hickstead. She became such an accomplished rider that her parents began to wonder if she might take up showing and eventing professionally. Sarah, however, didn't enjoy the dressage, an essential part of showing. It was the thrill of the cross country courses that excited her.

She was trained by top rider Dick Stillwell, who improved her jumping to such a standard that she was able to compete over the professional course at Hickstead in the All England Schools Championships on a horse called Spider.

'He called her Ginger Top,' Susie remembers, 'and every time she won any competition she used the money to buy Spider a new bandage or a new rug. It was always a present for Spider.'

Sarah was developing into an extrovert, open-hearted young woman, but with a mind of her own. As she got older so her relationship with her sister started to change.

'We were also both quite strong,' Jane says. The two girls still got on well together but Sarah was becoming more assertive. 'I tried to be the bossy older sister, but Sarah didn't respond. The older she got the bossier she became. I think we get it from Dad. Mum wasn't bossy, but she was a great organizer and we get that side of our characters from her.'

There was nothing Susie enjoyed more than arranging tennis and swimming parties, entering her daughters riding competitions, planning ski holidays, and ordering such events as the family Christmas, a traditional and important celebration in the Ferguson household.

The girls helped deck the tree in the drawing room with decorations stored in old cardboard boxes with the name of their old home, Lowood, written on the top, and every year Ronald Ferguson would organize a 'surprise' visit to a theatre or pantomime in London. To make the day more exciting he would not tell Susie or the girls where they were going to have lunch or what they were going to see. He would meet them off the train. They would try and listen to what 'Dads' was telling the taxi driver, but he never let them hear, enjoying the subterfuge.

'When we had finished lunch,' Ronald remembers, 'I would deliberately walk the wrong way down the pavement so they didn't guess and sometimes I would go straight past the theatre to confuse them even more. They would shout, "It's here Dads, it's here" . . . and I would say, "No, it's not" and walk on past.'

Sometimes he would pretend to have a stiff leg and would limp along the pavement dragging it behind him, all the while keeping a straight face. It embarrassed Jane who used to plead with him to stop. But Sarah loved it and would egg him on.

'Do it more Dads,' she used to call. 'Do it more.'

On Christmas Eve Sarah and Jane hung their father's shooting socks, the largest they could find, at the ends of their beds. 'We used to choose them the night before and have a fight over who was going to have the biggest one,' Jane recalls.

When they were little and living at Lowood they would try and stay awake to see Father Christmas arrive. Downstairs, beside the fireplace in the large drawing room, a bottle of beer and some tangerines were waiting for him, along with some carrots they had taken out of the larder for his reindeer.

By the time they moved to Dummer they were old enough to know that the person in Saint Nicholas outfit was actually their mother. But still Susie went through the routine of getting into the old Father Christmas costume they kept in the dressing-up box and tip-toeing into the bedrooms where her daughters, playing their part, would pretend to be asleep.

'I remember the noise of the presents crackling in the stockings as Mum put them in and putting my foot down the bed to see how heavy the stocking was,' Jane says. 'Sarah and I used to wake up really early and open all our presents. She would come into my room or I'd go into hers and then we'd both go into Mum and Dad's room.'

Then it was downstairs for breakfast before the whole family – both Sarah's grandmothers spent Christmas at Dummer – attended morning service at the local church. There were still more presents, piled high in the long drawing room on the sofa or chair each girl had been allocated, but they had to wait to open them.

Once back from church Susie would check the turkey in the kitchen while the grandmothers would lay the table in the dining room and Sarah and Jane excitedly got in everyone's way. They were not allowed to go in the drawing room until everyone was ready and had to queue up outside the door until they were all assembled. As soon as the door was opened, they rushed in and pounced. They always saved their parents' presents to the last. For the most understandable of childhood reasons – because they were always the largest.

As they always had been, the presents were always matched. If Jane got a saddle so did Sarah. 'Sarah and I were always comparing presents,' says Jane, 'but Mum was very careful to make sure we had similar things. They might have been different colours, but one was never bigger than the other.'

All together, counting those from grandparents, godparents and some of the Major's well-heeled polo friends, Jane and Sarah received up to twenty gifts each year. The girls were not allowed to lose sight of the generosity behind the giving, however. Susie made sure that after each present was opened they wrote who it was from and what it was (though, in the excitement, the who and the what sometimes got confused).

It was then into lunch. After the main course of roast turkey with all the trimmings the family would cross arms and pull crackers. Paper hats and little gifts showered over the floor and Jane and Sarah would read aloud the jokes, not quite understanding them. Once all the crackers had been pulled and everyone was festooned in paper hats, they were allowed to leave the table and go and play with their new toys.

While the women were clearing the table Ronald Ferguson would show the girls how their toys worked or how to put them together. Sometimes he would insist that his daughters watched the Queen's Christmas message, though, as Jane recalls, 'We didn't really understand it.'

Thank-you letters came later and they were almost always made to write them on the day – something Sarah still does.

'Sarah is a marvellous letter writer,' her mother says. 'She always was.'

If the weather was cold they were allowed to sit and watch the 'Christmassy things' on television. If it was clear they were allowed outside to play.

'It was,' says Sarah, 'the most perfect childhood.'

The idyll was about to end. The Christmas of 1972 was the last the Fergusons would spend together as a family.

2

Schooldays

After sixteen years the Fergusons' marriage had run its full course.

The Major had come to take his wife for granted or appeared to which, to Susie, came to the same thing. The outward appearances of a contented, comfortable union were maintained but the relationship was no longer what Ronald believed and Susie pretended it was.

It was a change Jane and Sarah hardly noticed at first. Their friends did. The riding and swimming parties became more infrequent and instead of having their playmates over at Dummer all the time, the girls found themselves spending more and still more time at other people's houses.

When Susie dropped Sarah off at the home of Clare Steel (later Wentworth-Stanley) in nearby Little Froyle, she no longer stayed to help them with their riding but would drive off to spend the day at the Fergusons' flat in Chelsea.

'I remember her mother was always dropping her over to us,' Clare remembers. 'It meant very little to me at the time and I think Fergie liked coming to us as it was such a happy home. But I didn't go to Dummer much.'

This unsatisfactory situation came to its emotional head during a holiday on the Ionian island of Corfu in the summer of 1972. Among the house party guests was professional polo player Hector Barrantes, a powerful, handsome Argentinian with large hands, rumpled face and a distinct dimple in his chin. A year younger than Susie and eight years younger than her husband, he had been born without wealth into an Argentinian military family. Unusually in the rich man's world of polo, that lack of money had not been a fetter to his career. He had not started working with ponies until he was fifteen years old and did not play his first game of polo until he was twenty-eight, but he was on his way to becoming arguably the finest breeder of polo ponies in Argentina and, with a handicap of ten, he was numbered amongst the sport's elite. Susie fell in love with him and he with her.

It was a vulnerable time for both. Hector had just suffered the most appalling personal tragedy. He had badly fractured his right leg in a car crash outside Buenos Aires. Louisa, his wife of fourteen years, was also in the car which was being driven by Hector's sister. Louisa was eight months pregnant. She was killed and the unborn child died with her.

The polo set rallied round and persuaded the reluctant Hector to join Ronald and Susie and a party of friends, including trainer Fred Winter's daughter, Philippa, on the trip to Corfu, where they all shared the rented Villa Petra.

Susie's life with Ronald, the only man she had any experience of, had not been unhappy. There had been a few early problems: when she was a young bride of eighteen, for instance, Ronald used to spend hours talking to his mother late into the night. The moment Susie plucked up the courage to explain to her strong-willed mother-in-law how the situation upset her, Lady Elmhirst assured her it would never recur. Strong she might be but unfair she wasn't, and Lady Elmhirst was anxious to ensure Susie settled down and enjoyed an enviable, country-oriented lifestyle centred on dogs, horses and children.

Materially she wanted for nothing. Her children had given her cause for maternal satisfaction. And though the Major's decision to give up shooting pheasant had taken them off the

Sandringham house party invitation list, she enjoyed a fulfilling social life. Emotionally, however, she was bored.

Ronald's bluff military persona belies a personality that can be both charming and considerate. At the same time he can be something of a stubborn loner. He became so involved with polo – he had just agreed to become Prince Charles's polo manager as well as continuing his job at the Guards polo club – that he failed to notice that his lively wife was drifting away.

'We met Hector playing polo,' Ronald Ferguson says dismissively, brushing the incident away with calculated indifference as if it were a fly on one of his polo ponies. 'We went on holiday to Corfu and he was there too. That is when it all started, I suppose.'

It was. The atmosphere was tense. The Major was gruff. Hector and Susie spent their time laughing and joking together. Everyone in the house party could not help but notice what was happening.

To schoolgirl Sarah, however, Hector Barrantes was still just a name on a polo team list. Her only concern at the time was the thought of leaving Daneshill, the school near Basingstoke she had gone to as a weekly boarder when she was ten, and all the friends she had made there.

By her own admission she was not the most academic of students. She was not pushed. Amongst her parents' set there was little pressure for young ladies to be highly educated and few of Sarah's friends went on to university or even wanted to. Theirs was a ladylike progression culminating in a cooking or secretarial course, travel, and then a job with an understanding boss willing to give Friday afternoons off, before they married and settled down into motherhood, just as their mothers had done before them.

Given the limit of that horizon, Sarah did reasonably well. She excelled at sports and was popular with her school contemporaries. Unlike her sister-in-law, the Princess of Wales, she was considered a successful pupil, eventually gaining six 'O' levels and rising to be joint head girl. The emphasis, however, was always more on manners than matriculation.

Miss June Vallance, the head mistress, saw it as her duty to provide a home away from home for her young charges. 'I liked to make sure they had a happy and relaxed childhood,' she says. 'Adult life lasts a long time and can be very hard.'

The day began, in the Gordonstoun manner, with an early morning run. Breakfast was followed by morning prayers in a big barn which doubled as the school gymnasium. At meals the girls were made to sit up straight. If they did not Miss Vallance would put a ruler down the backs of their dresses.

They were allowed to watch *Top of the Pops* on television and the girls would dance to the records (Neil Diamond's *Song Sung Blue* was a favourite dance number of Sarah's).

Fellow pupil Clare Steel recalls that Daneshill, housed in a Jacobean house in the town of Old Basing some twenty minutes drive from Dummer 'didn't have a school atmosphere at all. It was lovely.'

It was certainly a happy time for Sarah, and the friends she made there are still amongst her closest. They included Clare, now married to Lloyd's broker Nick Wentworth-Stanley, and Conservative councillor's daughter Lulu Blacker, now the headmistress-cum-owner of a kindergarten in Fulham.

'We became known as the Terrible Threesome,' says Clare. Miss Valance, as one would expect, placed great emphasis on good manners. That included showing respect for your elders by obeying the rules. If Lulu, Clare and Fergie – she was given the nickname at Daneshill and it stuck – chose to bend them, they had to be punished. The penalties were hardly severe, however, and usually amounted to nothing more than a brief enforced separation of the offending troublemakers. Miss Vallance believed in discipline without force and being made to stand outside the classroom or being exiled to another dormitory were the usual punishments.

'If we weren't together we weren't naughty,' Clare shrugs. 'It was the obvious cause of any problem.'

The trio shared the same dormitory during most of their time there. It was aptly called the Billiard Room: the girls were packed like snooker balls into eight beds and four bunks. There were, of course, midnight feasts, and endless talking after lights out. Joining in were Pandora Delevingne, daughter of Royal Academy of Arts President Jocelyn Stevens, Nicki Begg and Sarah Mann. One entry in Clare's diary of the summer of 1972 reads: 'Fergie put baby powder all over Mann. Fergie had to move to room eight.'

Another entry reads: 'Put red felt pen on Fergie's hair. Lulu was sent out of science by Colonel Holmes and I got a note saying, "Hi ya Fergie" confiscated.'

The chief troublemaker was not Sarah, but the high-spirited Lulu. Clare remembers: 'Lulu was the ringleader and Fergie and I were the followers, always getting into trouble while Lulu usually managed to get away with it.'

There were childish scrapes with teachers. Sarah once squirted water over Miss Davenport, who supervised the early morning runs. And she waged a running battle with the French mistress, Mrs East, who, to Sarah's child's eye, was always picking on her. She in turn went out of her way to irritate Mrs East and disrupt the class.

The French mistress had a habit of rubbing her hands together and rolling her tongue around in her mouth and when she was annoyed she would do it hard and fast, causing the class to dissolve into giggles. Sarah was particularly adept at mimicking this mannerism and Mrs East could hardly fail to spot her tormentor.

'Would Sarah Ferguson please stand up and leave the classroom,' became a regular cry. Some good must have come out of all this, however, as French became one of Sarah's better subjects.

The lessons were held, not unusually at a school of this kind, in what Clare remembers as 'sort of Nissen huts. It sounds dreadful and if I went back today and they still had them I would be horrified. But they were warm and clean.' In Sarah's memory, though, academic activities were overshadowed by the sport. In the large grounds was an unheated swimming pool, and several hard tennis courts which were used for netball in the winter. Hockey was also played in the winter term; tennis, cricket and rounders in the summer.

Clare, Lulu and Sarah were all good at games and they formed a formidable rounders team, something which still amuses them when they meet today.

'It was our great claim to fame,' Clare remembers. 'I was bowler, Lulu was backstop and Fergie was first post.'

It had been intended that Sarah would continue in this happy manner through to the end of her education. In 1972, however, Miss Vallance's brother, who had a financial interest in the school, decided to sell the house and move the school into smaller premises. The senior school where Sarah was due to go was closed. Another school had been found and that meant examinations.

Says Clare: 'I don't remember Fergie being brilliant but she was bright enough not to worry. She passed.'

At the end of term the girls put on a puppet play for the whole school. It was a great success and they celebrated by going for an undetected midnight swim, an almost nightly occurrence in those final days. When the last day of term arrived, there were tearful farewells. Sarah even gave Mrs East a leaving present. 'Gosh, I was unhappy,' Clare wrote to her diary.

It was the end of the Terrible Threesome. Lulu and Clare went to St Mary's, Wantage. Sarah, meanwhile, was sent to Hurst Lodge in Sunningdale.

It was an unusual choice for the sports-minded Sarah who, by her own admission, might well have benefited from a stricter discipline than 'progressive' Hurst Lodge provided. But it was the summer of 1972, and the developments in Corfu were about to strain her parents' marriage to breaking point. Her sister, Jane, was already there and, in the interests of continuity, it was decided that Sarah should go there too.

Hurst Lodge was founded during the war by Doris Stainer, sister of Leslie Howard (the actor of *Gone with the Wind* fame). It was originally a ballet school, but when it was forced out of London by the German bombing, Miss Stainer had enlarged the curriculum to include English, French and deportment. By the time Sarah arrived the then headmistress, Celia Merrick, had improved the academic base to include sciences, languages, history and geography, while still maintaining its tradition of dance. Because of Miss Stainer's connections and the school's location close to several major film studios and the showbusiness-favoured areas of Ascot and Sunningdale, Hurst Lodge had a tradition of pupils drawn from the film and entertainment business and many of the girls were the 'daughters of'.

Florence, daughter of French movie star Jean-Paul Belmondo, was a pupil. So was Emma, daughter of director Bryan Forbes and actress Nanette Newman (Emma, now living in Los Angeles with her actor husband John Standing, saw Sarah when she was on an official visit to Los Angeles in 1988; they 'were hauled out for the "famous Brits cocktail party"'.) Other contemporaries included actress Aimi McDonald's daughter Lisa, the late Peter Finch's daughter Samantha and comedian Ted Rodgers' daughter Fenella Heron, who later shared the head girlship with Sarah.

It was, everyone recalls, 'a happy place' of a hundred pupils, half of them day girls, the other half weekly boarders like Sarah, housed in a half-timbered mock Elizabethan mansion. There was not a great deal of academic pressure. Discipline was fairly lax and Sarah was fairly naughty.

'I was like every child at school,' she remembers. 'I enjoyed being naughty and hated being caught.'

Sarah seldom was. She had learnt from Lulu. 'I put dye in the lavatory system and glue on the teacher's chair,' she recalls.

Miss Perkins was the maths mistress and as anything to do with geometry or algebra confused Sarah ('Maths was not my best subject,' she admits) she would endlessly plot new ways to distract the class, thereby ensuring that the lessons went more quickly. It was at her suggestion that a group of girls squeezed glue on the unfortunate teacher's chair and waited in anticipation for her to sit down. Miss Perkins' suspicions were alerted, however, by the giggling in the classroom and the damage inflicted was only slight.

'I managed to be out of the way when the teacher came into the room and never got caught,' Sarah confesses.

In keeping with the school's tradition, the pupils were taught dance, but if they were not ballet fans they could concentrate on modern dance or sport. Sarah did both, excelling at tennis, netball and swimming and taking modern dance lessons with her friend 'Flo' Belmond who was also in the six-bed Pink dormitory.

All the dormitories were named after colours and Pink was always the rowdiest, with pillow fights and late night feasts.

Gradually, though, Mrs Merrick's method of bringing the best out of her pupils by making them make their own decisions started having its effect. Sarah, the girl whom one school report had described as 'slapdash, stubborn and headstrong', started to assume responsibility.

She was popular, particularly amongst the young girls. She became captain of netball, a prefect and eventually joint head girl. She dismisses the honour. 'I was so uncontrollable they had to make me head girl so I would start behaving.'

That is not the way her contemporaries remember it. Says Lisa Mulidore: 'Everyone looked up to Fergie. She was a great source of strength and fun. She was a great head girl because we all liked her.'

With the responsibility came the privileges. With the other seniors Sarah was allowed to live apart from the main school building in a wooden annexe overlooking the swimming pool. They had the use of a small kitchen where they could make cups of coffee and tea and 'masses of white buttered toast' and a sitting room with its own television set. Mrs Merrick's philosophy was that if she gave the girls her trust they would respond accordingly. In Sarah's case she was proved correct; she acknowledges that, by the end, she 'worked quite hard and was becoming more responsible by the minute'.

In counterpoint, the improvement at school was weighted against the unhappiness at home.

Susie was spending more and more time in the London flat, miserably trying to deal with the dichotomy of guilt and compassion. Ronald Ferguson remained at Dummer, morose and dejected. Both grandmothers stoically tried to keep things together and would look in to offer what help they could. Susie's mother, Doreen Wright – the girls called her 'Grummy' or 'Dar' – wisely never took sides. Ronald's mother Lady Elmhirst who lived across the road in Dummer village spent much of her time in the kitchen at Dummer dispensing sound advice to her son, who would not listen.

Susie was desperate. But Ronald, feeling hurt and betrayed, was not in the mood to make life easy for his wife. He would start divorce proceedings, then halt them, refusing to believe or accept that she wanted to marry Barrantes. Hector, meanwhile, refused to live with Susie until she was a free woman.

Jane and Sarah were caught somewhere in between. They were supportive of their father, understanding of their mother whom they both adored. Looking back over the wreckage of her parents' marriage Sarah says: 'It would be awful for them to go on living together if they were at each other's throats all day.'

It was another two years before the situation was finally resolved, however, and if anyone alluded to her parents' unhappiness Sarah would quietly turn away.

'She was always very sensitive about what people thought and about their feelings,' says Clare Steel. 'She got easily hurt by things.'

Yet considering all the upset engendered, Sarah handled the situation with remarkable maturity – probably, as she would later explain, because she had no alternative. Her school work continued to improve. And, like all teenagers, her interests started widening. She started talking about boys.

There were school dances with boys from Radley and Wellington, not remembered as the greatest of successes. Only soft drinks were served, the boys spent most of their time sneaking outside for cigarettes, and the girls gathered in corners to giggle. The prettiest girls intimidated the gauche young men and usually ended up as the wallflowers. Sarah was not shy, but she was still at an awkward age, preferring to imagine herself with dashing Nicky Henson, whom she had seen in a production of Shakespeare's *The Taming of the Shrew*, than with one of the callow youths on offer. A school outing to the Bloomsbury had been organized to see the play which was on the 'O' level English syllabus and the blond, blue-eyed actor had made a considerable impact on the schoolgirls. One noted in her diary: 'Fergie and I have fallen in love with Nicky Henson.'

Some of the girls had brothers at Eton College which was quite near and any letters that arrived with that particular postmark were pounced upon. The morning post was laid out on a table for the whole school to see and any girl whose missive was sealed with the letters SWALK (sealed with a loving kiss) would come in for a barrage of envious teasing.

Sarah was forever falling in and out of love – or so she told everyone, though few of the objects of her passions realized in what affection they were held. When she did make friends Sarah, like Jane, was slightly nervous of asking the boy home. With their mother away they had to deal with their father's sometimes eccentric ways on their own.

'Dad used to embarrass us,' Jane recalls. 'He was always coming downstairs in his dressing gown and being frightfully bossy. If we were having lunch and Sarah and I were sitting around the kitchen table with our friends he'd say, "Come on, hurry up and clear away!" It used to drive us mad. That's probably why we didn't have many people home to Dummer – we imagined he put them off!'

During the holidays or on weekends the girls were sometimes allowed to go to parties. But their father was always very strict about the time they returned home. He would leave his bedroom door open about three inches so he could hear them coming in.

'We'd always miss the top two steps on the stairs because they creaked,' Jane recalls. 'But we seldom got the better of Dad.'

In the mornings over breakfast Ronald used to continue his teasing.

'And what time did you get back last night?' he would say to the girls and any friends who had been invited to spend the night. 'I heard the stairs creaking with more than two pairs of feet.'

Both girls would blush – it was acutely embarrassing to the teenagers to be teased in front of their guests like that and they would squirm with discomfort.

'It was character building I suppose,' Jane says, without conviction. 'And Dad gave us lots of advice about our boyfriends. He'd always voice his opinion and we'd listen – most of the time.'

The Fergusons had agreed that the girls would be happier in the familiar surroundings of Hampshire with their ponies and dogs and their grandmother nearby, so the Major was now the head of what was in effect a one-parent family. Always organized himself, he now had to take on the extra responsibility of organizing the house. He had staff to help, but they too had to be organized. His missed his wife though he would not admit that at the time.

'Dad hated a mess,' Jane says. 'He started loading and unloading the dishwasher and washing and drying up. He also became rather good at cooking. His speciality was cheese sauce – without lumps – and scrambled eggs. Eventually we got sick of having it every single night and took over ourselves.'

Once they had done their kitchen duties, Sarah and Jane would retreat to the little bungalow in the stable yard which their father had converted into a more sophisticated play room for them. There they would listen to Neil Diamond and Don Maclean records on their old record player, 'a real cheapy – you pulled the arm back and it clicked', and spend hours recording their favourite songs on the double-reeled tape machine their mother had left behind.

Sometimes their father would come in to see what they were doing. He would fling open the windows, declaring in a loud voice, 'It's far too steamy and hot in here, why don't you all go and play outside.' The girls would 'die' with embarrassment and whisper to their friends not to take any notice.

For Sarah a practical consequence of her parents' marriage break-up was that she had to look after her pony herself. She missed having her mother around at weekends to drive her to horse shows and organize her pony. She also missed the encouragement and condolences Susie had always given her. 'I had to do all the work which took away some of the enthusiasm I had,' she admits.

'Mum' was only a phone call away in London and always anxious to help, but that was not the same as having her at home and on constant call. In order to cope with the situation she simply blocked out any unpleasant thoughts that came into her head. It was her way, her only way, of dealing with the situation.

'We were too young to fully comprehend what was happening,' Jane says. 'I was fifteen and Sarah was thirteen and we were both at Hurst Lodge where we had all our friends and Dummer was our home. It was stability. We had enough around us to overshadow what was really happening. I think it affected us more when we got older and really understood what had happened.'

School certainly helped. Mrs Merrick, the headmistress, remembers the situation well and insists: 'The separation had remarkably little effect on Sarah. This was really due to her parents; they made sure it had the minimum effect on their daughters.'

'We both got closer to Dad,' Jane says. 'He was our support. He learned to cook very quickly and we'd all go into the kitchen and burn the bottoms of the saucepans.'

When Jane left school – Sarah still had another two years to go at Hurst Lodge – she continued her studies at Queensgate College in London, where she studied History of Art and improved her Spanish and French. During the week she lived with her mother in the Fergusons' flat in First Street, Chelsea, returning at weekends to Dummer Down Farm to be with her father and sister. She remembers: 'I used to spend the week with Mum in London and come home at the weekends and spend them with Dad. It was chaotic, but never once did Dad try and put us against Mum or Mum put us against Dad. We never felt any resentment for either of them.'

In the transfer of roles common to such situations the girls felt that it was up to them to look after their father. 'Dad was so unhappy,' Jane recalls. 'We realized he desperately wanted Mum to come back even after six months had passed. He just adored her I suppose. It made us feel guilty. Both of us at one time or another thought the break-up might in some way be our fault. We knew it wasn't but we couldn't help thinking perhaps . . .'

In the spring of 1974, when Sarah was fifteen and Jane seventeen, the Fergusons were finally divorced and Susie went to live with Barrantes in the Sussex village of Iping outside Midhurst. Divorce was no longer quite the dirty word it had been. But for a woman to leave not only home and husband for a foreigner, but also her children, was inevitably the subject of comment. There had been moments when Barrantes had doubted the wisdom of continuing the relationship. Susie may also have entertained misgivings but this was a consuming passion. It was the biggest single force in her life and she was determined to find a way.

Susie's way was to leave behind everything she loved most – her children, her home, her dogs. Her only concern was for the happiness of her children and Hector, who, for all his romantic looks and charm, balked at the role of homewrecker. Many of the possessions she had collected over the years stayed at Dummer with the children. Even the large leather bound photograph albums she had so painstakingly compiled over the years were left in the sitting room cupboard. She took nothing to remind her of her marriage and she made few demands on Ronald. She could have fought for custody of the children, but she did not want to cause further disruption at such a crucial stage of their education or to remove them from all the familiar things they knew and loved.

Susie points out: 'Sarah was fifteen when I left. Fifteen, not thirteen. She was very sensible. We were very close and she was totally supportive of what I had decided to do.'

She acknowledges that 'it meant changing things. But until the Falklands War Hector and I spent four months of the year in England, so it wasn't as if Sarah was never going to see me again. From the end of 1974 until 1982 we came over for the polo season and Sarah spent six months with us in Argentina one year and three months another.'

In July 1975 Susie Ferguson married Hector Barrantes at Chichester Register Office. Sarah liked her stepfather and was delighted for her mother.

'It was so good to see her so happy,' she says. 'I think life is there and you've got to take it with both hands.'

3

Life with 'Dads'

WITH SUSIE GONE AND TWO TEENAGE DAUGHTERS TO LOOK after, Ronald Ferguson set about rebuilding his home life.

'I turned myself over to Jane and Sarah completely at week-ends,' he recalls. 'It was their time, not mine.

'I was determined not to let the circumstances of the situation affect them in any way at all. I think I built up a bond discussing things with my daughters that a mother normally would have done. I used to make sure everything was ready for them when they came back from school and I wouldn't allow them to think I had better things to do. I tried to build up a relationship with both of them and the present relationship we enjoy is a result of those days.'

But Dummer is a large house and Ronald, organized and house proud though he may be, is not one of nature's 'pinafore men'. He missed the freshly arranged flowers in the hall and the feeling of bright domesticity his wife had generated. A recipe of burnt saucepans, scrambled eggs and cheese sauce (even without the lumps) was not an entirely satisfactory substitute.

A housekeeper, he felt, would provide the solution but, as Jane recalls, 'we didn't make things very easy for them as we didn't want to be told what to do by someone we didn't know,' and the turnover was quick.

Eventually the Major put an advertisement in *The Times*. It read: 'If you are a dog lover, a driver, a reasonable cook, have a sense of humour, like the country and like children, apply. If you are any or all of the above please ring . . .'

Over thirty women of varying shapes and sizes turned up at Ronald's Neilson McCarthy office just off Berkeley Square in Mayfair. None fitted. They wanted weekends off, or wanted their boyfriend to stay at weekends. 'I wanted nothing of that for the girls,' he says. 'It was very important for me.'

Just as the Major was giving up hope, the telephone rang again and a girl called Ros Runnell introduced herself on the line. Her interest had been aroused by what she calls the 'eye catching' advertisement and she told Ronald she more or less fitted his requirements. She was twenty-three, had done a secretarial course, spent time in Australia, but was not really trained to do anything.

'When he spoke to me,' Ros remembers, 'he said his wife had left him for a ten goal polo player and he was only five goals' – as if by explaining Barrantes' handicap the Major had explained everything.

'I liked the sound of her,' Ronald remembers. 'And when I met her I knew she was the right one. She was clean, tidy and smart, so I hired her on the spot.'

Ros, who had been living with her mother in Sussex, went to Dummer Down Farm to lunch where she met both Sarah and Jane and Ronald's mother, Lady Elmhirst, who dropped in 'accidentally on purpose'. She took to the girls at once, especially to Sarah who she remembers as a 'perfectly normal teenager'.

She also liked Lady Elmhirst and Lady Elmhirst liked Ros, an attractive, capable girl with dark hair and large green eyes and it would soon occur to Ronald's mother that here might well be a replacement for the departed Susie.

That was most definitely not in her terms of employment, however, and while she admits that she found the Major 'terribly attractive', it was the atmosphere at Dummer that attracted her to the job.

'It didn't feel like a job at all,' she recalls. 'When the Fergusons like you they embrace you and you become one of the family.'

The girls were well adjusted and the work load was not especially hard. The wonderful Mrs Mac came in every day to prepare lunch for everyone – the girls, Ronald, the girl grooms – which they ate sitting around the kitchen table. If Mrs Mac was not around Ros prepared the simple food the family favoured. Steaks and salads, shepherd's pie, fish pie, or toad in the hole, that typically English dish of sausages and batter baked in the oven which Sarah considered her 'number one favourite' dish.

'If we could have ham, salad and mayonnaise we'd be quite happy,' Jane remembers. 'We weren't allowed Coca-Cola, tomato sauce or ketchup, except for treats. But we didn't mind at all. All we really liked was mayonnaise. We would have had it all the time if we could, but it was strictly a lunchtime thing.'

In the evenings Ronald and Sarah liked eating supper in front of the television set in the sitting room unless the grandmothers were there, when they would all revert to the kitchen again.

Susie's mother, Mrs Wright, dropped in most weekends to arrange the flowers her son-in-law had so missed.

'When Mrs Wright came to stay we had wonderful kitchen suppers,' Ros remembers. 'We used to mob Ronald up, teasing him and pulling his leg. It was riotous just being at home with the family. We all shrieked with laughter. We never had intellectual conversations – we were far too busy being rude to each other!'

She formed a close relationship with Sarah, who treated her as an older sister. 'She used to call me Rastus – she still does – I have no idea why, but she'd shriek through the house "Rastus", and I would reply "Yespers". It was silly, but it was a happy time.'

Friends started calling in again, Flo Belmondo amongst them, and Sarah was enjoying her young life. 'I think, as Mum wasn't there, I had to grow up quickly and learn responsibility,' Sarah says. 'At fifteen it was a question of getting on with it.'

She talked about her mother openly though, as Ros says,

she never went into the details of the break-up of her parents' marriage.

Mother and daughter still kept in close touch and Sarah would often spend the night with Susie at the house in London.

Late one night the Major received a telephone call from the police informing him that the property had been bombed by the IRA. Jane, who was doing a typing course at Queen's Secretarial College and happened to be staying there that evening with Mrs Cole, the Fergusons' housekeeper from the Lowood days, telephoned a few moments later to say, 'I'm OK Dad, but I think you had better come up to London.'

On the drive up the motorway he was stopped for speeding. His explanation impressed and instead of a fine he was given an escort of police outriders to Chelsea.

'When I saw the house the entire front had been ripped off,' he remembers. 'Jane and Mrs Cole had been watching television in the basement sitting room, but had decided to go upstairs to bed. If they hadn't the blast would have killed them.'

The bomb had been intended for the house across the street, the residence of a Matron from Holloway Prison where some IRA suspects were being held.

'I decided there wasn't much I could do that night in the way of organizing repairs, so having made sure Jane and the housekeeper were all right I decided to go to bed,' Ronald continues. 'But when I went into the bedroom, I discovered half the wall had been ripped away and was exposed to the elements.'

Undeterred by the inconvenience, the Major put on his pyjamas and climbed into bed and went to sleep – with half the wall hanging down the front of the house.

He was not so relaxed when it came to the subject of his elder daughter's romance, however.

Jane had developed a crush on one of the farm hands – a rangy Australian named Alex Makim. Makim had come to Dummer Down Farm through his cousin Belinda Coy, who had helped Susie look after the horses. His sister Sally was doing her grand trip through Europe (a tradition amongst young Australians) and called in on her cousin, followed shortly by Alex, who was anxious to learn polo and willing to do anything around horses. At twenty with longish sunbleached hair and a floppy moustache, he cut a romantic figure in Jane's youthful eyes, and with her sister she spent hours in the yard teasing him about his Australian accent and the funny way he used words. He was unlike any of the boys she had met and she was soon infatuated. Sarah was not slow to see what was happening and would wander around the yard loudly humming the Donny Osmond hit, 'Puppy Love'.

The Major did not approve of Jane's attachment. Susan Deptford, the future Mrs Ferguson, had just arrived on the scene and she recalls: 'Ronald wasn't worried about Sarah at all. He worried about Jane. I can remember terrible tears and her begging him, imploring him, to let her go out to Australia. He was being sensible, trying to tell her to live in England for a bit first as she'd only just left school.'

He sent her to Kenya to stay with her maternal uncle, Brian Wright. She had been introduced to a host of suitable young men, but when that failed to take her mind off the man she had set her heart on, he reluctantly allowed her to fly to Australia and stay on Alex's farm, Wilga Warrina, in New South Wales 'to see what she was letting herself in for'.

She returned to regale her sister with exotic tales about the Australian outback. The house, she said, had an outside loo and a corrugated iron roof that leaked. North Star, the nearest town, had fourteen pubs, was twenty miles away, and looked like the setting for a Western. It had been spring in New South Wales and lambing time, which involved the castration of the young rams. Jane told Sarah how Alex had thrown a pair of testicles at her – in fun – and that she had not flinched. Sarah was horrified. She decided her sister must have gone mad.

'Because I was so young I was adaptable,' Jane claims. 'If I did it now it would be a culture shock, but then it was a terrific adventure and I was very excited.'

On matters connected with his own romantic life the Major was considerably more circumspect. He became known to his polo cronies as the Monk of Drummer. Always reserved, he became almost a recluse after Susie left him which only accentuated the impression of aloofness – some would call it arrogance – that he can convey.

'Once you have seen him larking about with the dogs and the children you know he is not like that,' Ros says, 'but that unfortunately is a side to him which people don't often see. He is shy and he hates parties – because he doesn't drink he never relaxes at them.'

Sarah and Jane, determined to cheer him up, encouraged him to find himself a girlfriend 'but they were pretty quick to tell me if they liked them or not,' the Major remembers. 'By dinner time on Friday they knew and if they didn't like them they were usually back on the train by lunchtime on Saturday.'

One girl who passed the weekend test was attractive blonde Susan Deptford. She had met Ronald at a cocktail party given by Victor Law, one of his friends from his army days, and he had asked her out to dinner. Sue was living an active social life and refused. She already had a date.

Victor Law, who remains a good friend, was determined to get the two together, but it was to be another six months before he managed to organize an evening when everyone was free. At the time Sue Deptford was sharing a Chelsea flat with her friend, Elizabeth Beale. Victor persuaded them to give a dinner party. Ronald, who was 'feeling very sorry for himself' agreed to come, but when he reached the bottom of the stairs in the Cheyne Walk flat, nearly turned round and went home again. Sue, who was employed cooking directors' lunches during the day, was preparing lamb with garlic. He had smelt the garlic wafting down the stairs – and he hated garlic.

'As I enjoyed doing the cooking, Victor and Liz used to call me Helga the au pair,' Sue explains. 'When Ronald arrived they said, "Have you met Helga? She's the au pair", and that became the joke of the evening.'

The Major survived the garlic and the following day sent 'Helga' a large bunch of red roses and a card on which was written the word 'WOW'. Sue was enchanted. Liz told her not to be carried away, that Ronald Ferguson probably sent red roses to every girl he met.

He didn't. And when Sue telephoned to thank him, he asked her and Liz to come and stay at Dummer for the weekend of the local Hampshire Hunt Ball.

'It was the first time I had met Sarah,' Sue remembers. 'Liz and I were giggling like a couple of schoolgirls when she opened the door. She looked so sweet with her short bubbly haircut, she must have been about thirteen or fourteen.'

The teenaged Sarah was fascinated by what she imagined were two very sophisticated Chelsea girls. She bombarded them with questions and followed them up the stairs to the guest bedrooms. As they unpacked she stood there, asking them where they got all their clothes, what they were going to wear for the dance and what did they do in London.

'She kept looking us up and down,' Sue remembers. 'She was fascinated and she obviously hadn't met many London girls of our age.'

A small vase of flowers had been placed beside each bed, together with a bottle of mineral water and a basket of fruit and biscuits. The whole house was immaculate and filled with large vases of flowers which Grummy had arranged. When Sue and Liz had washed and changed they went downstairs to the drawing room where they drank champagne and chatted to the other guests around the log fire. It was, Sue found out later, the first dinner party Ronald had given since Susie had left and everything had been prepared in her meticulous style.

Sarah acted as a waitress, carrying the vegetables and clearing away the glasses. 'She, Grummy and Ronald were a little team looking after us,' Sue recalls. Ronald was obviously proud of his daughter, though he did keep issuing her with instructions – to clear away the glasses and then be sure to remember to turn down the beds after they had left for the Ball. Sarah took her father's orders with cheeky grace.

'She was terribly excited,' Sue recalls, 'and kept giggling and saying, "Isn't Dad an old bore?"'

In the morning Sarah helped the Major take the tea trays in to their guests. She asked them what they wanted for breakfast. What she really wanted to know was what the dance had been like and 'Did Dad dance with you?'

'She obviously wanted to know which one of us her father had his eye on,' Sue recalls.

Both grandmothers had been in and out of the house throughout the weekend and just before she left to return to London they asked Sue how serious she was about Ronald, which struck the future Mrs Ferguson as a little premature though it did confirm that the Major had not had many young women down to stay.

After that weekend Sarah encouraged her father to take Sue out again. Ronald wrote to her and told her how much Sarah had liked her and said how attractive she was. Sarah helped her father compose the letter, an illustration of the relationship he had worked so hard to forge with his younger child.

'I felt sorry for Ronald, the way on Sunday night she would tell him things she needed for school, like a new pleated skirt, and he would worry if her shoes were clean,' Sue says. 'They were the sort of things a woman should be doing and I felt for him.'

Sue was already a little in love with Ronald. The Major was equally taken with Sue. But first he had a slight embarrassment to sort out.

'What I didn't realize was that my mother had secretly been matchmaking between Ros and myself,' the Major says. 'I had no idea and when I discovered I was furious. I wouldn't have any part of it.'

The idea of starting a relationship with someone who happened to be living under the same roof was, he felt, quite wrong and might undermine the security and family unity he had tried so hard to create. It was for those reasons that his courtship of Susan Deptford, the daughter of a well-to-do Norfolk farmer, progressed at an old-fashioned pace.

It was some time before Sue paid her next visit to Dummer. They had dinners in London instead. And only gradually did she start to get to know his two daughters. 'They seemed,' she says, 'so enthusiastic and happy.' They, conversely, had decided to be awful to their father's girlfriend.

'They were of an age to be like that and I think she had a rough time,' Ros remembers. 'She tried so hard to make everybody happy and almost killed herself in the process.'

Jane, who had been in Kenya during the weekend of the Hunt Ball, remembers their first meeting. 'I answered the doorbell of our place in First Street and then stood behind the door so she couldn't see me. I said "hello" very frostily. I looked her up and down and was very aloof.'

That evening Ronald was going to a dinner party in a London restaurant with Prince Charles's architectural *bête noire*, Peter Palumbo. Before, whenever he was asked out, he used to take Jane with him and she was decidedly put out to find herself replaced at her father's side. Sarah was more amenable but, egged on by Jane, decided she could be just as unpleasant.

The next time Sue came to Dummer for the weekend 'we gave her the once over, looked her up and down and tried to pick faults in her,' Jane recalls. 'It was difficult because she was so nice.' But not impossible for two young girls grown used to being the centre of their father's attentions and with their minds set on mischief. They noticed that the initials on her luggage were S.R.D. and decided to construct a nickname around them. They could not think of anything until Jane had the idea of reversing the initials to D.R.S. and with a whoop of laughter they came up with the name 'Drisle'.

Sue refused to be defeated. She liked the girls despite their adolescent petulance. She admired Ronald for maintaining the happy atmosphere and was impressed that Grummy appeared fond enough of her former son-in-law to help him make the house look nice for a girlfriend's visit.

'I've always been loyal to Ronald,' Doreen Wright says. 'I liked him from the beginning when he came home with Susie and lay on the end of my bed chatting as if he had known me all his life. He's always been good to me.'

Like Ros, Sue found the Ferguson family 'great fun'. She sensed that if she was not too pushy the girls would eventually accept her and she treated them as younger sisters, not like a potential stepmother. 'I never reprimanded them over anything,' Sue admits.

She joined in the family sport of teasing Ronald about his old-fashioned ways and 'ganged up' against him when they all wanted to do something he did not.

'One important thing I learned early on,' Sue says, 'was that once Ronald had made up his mind about something he didn't go back. He was too dogmatic, too black and white.'

This was illustrated when Sarah wanted to go to a party but when she asked her father he gave her a categoric 'No'. Her disappointment upset him, but having once forbidden her, he insisted on sticking to his decision. Playing the part of both mother and father had made Ronald over-protective and sometimes unnecessarily strict.

'I told him to think about things first, then he wouldn't have to go back on his word,' Sue says. 'I got round him gradually and eventually he agreed to let Sarah go to the party.'

Sue started taking Sarah shopping and was instrumental in persuading Ronald to let his daughter have the clothes she wanted, not the ones he wanted her to have. She sometimes drove her back to school on Monday mornings in her bright yellow VW Beetle, and during the drive they would discuss 'anything and everything', from her pony and the dogs to her lack of boyfriends, to Jane's romance with Alex.

Sarah would tell her Ferguson family anecdotes. Ronald's favourite Jack Russell terrier, Mr Bugs, had been knocked down in Windsor Great Park and was sent spinning across the road; Ronald rang Ros and told her to draw the curtains in his bedroom and place a rug on the bed as Mr Bugs was concussed (it is the kind of story guaranteed to wet Susan's always emotional eye).

Another thing Sarah felt she was able to discuss with Sue was her mother. When Susie was away on Hector Barrantes' ranch in Argentina, Sarah would say how she longed for her to come back. 'Mum's so much fun', she would say. 'And so beautiful.'

To the twenty-eight year old Susan Deptford, Susie Barrantes seemed to have everything. 'When I first met Ronald he was always talking about Susie,' Sue admits with characteristic honesty. 'He told me she had incredible energy and drive and in all the years they were married, he had never seen her put her feet up and do nothing.'

Susie, however, was in the past. Sue was the future and on a polo trip to California, he proposed to her on a Santa Barbara mountain top.

'It was very romantic,' Sue remembers. 'He had bought the ring at Garrards and carefully hidden it until this moment when he produced it from his pocket and put it on my finger.'

Their host Michael Butler (who produced the hit musical *Hair* and was the brother-in-law of Geoffrey Kent, one of Ronald's polo playing pals) provided champagne for everyone in his ocean-side home. Sue and Ronald sat on cushions and toasted their future together. Ronald promptly rang home to break the news.

'I telephoned and Ros must have answered as I told her,' Ronald remembers. 'But as soon as I said it I knew I had made a mistake – not for Ros, but for Sarah and Jane. It is one of my deepest regrets. I should have done it some other way. It was a shock to all of them, including Ros, but it was Jane and Sarah I was concerned for.'

Back in the sitting room of Dummer Down Farm house there was a stunned silence. 'It was a shock for me and the girls too,' Ros remembers. 'They didn't feel threatened, but it was quite a surprise. I remember trying to make the place look nice for them to come back to and I put some daffodils in a vase in the hall and forgot to put water in them so when I came down in the morning they were all dead.'

As Ronald and Sue drove from the airport he asked her to remove the engagement ring he had so romantically placed on her finger. She asked why.

Ronald tried to explain that in some complicated way he was letting Jane and Sarah down by putting his own happiness first. Sue listened with understanding – and went ahead and ordered her wedding dress from Bellville Sassoon. It was not until the November of 1976, however, that they were married.

There were a few familial dramas to get out of the way first. On the polo field that spring Sue came face to face with Susie Barrantes for the first time, never the most comfortable of experiences for either woman in such a situation. But it passed without incident or aggravation. 'She was very sweet and friendly,' the second Mrs Ferguson recalls.

Sarah, meanwhile, was facing her 'O' levels. 'She used to get terribly het up about her exams,' Ros recalls.

Sarah eventually passed six – English language, English literature, art, geography, maths and biology. But although she had enjoyed her time at Hurst Lodge, a school with more emphasis on academic qualifications might have suited her better. Sarah, despite what she says about her academic potential, had been quite capable of achieving more at school but she needed pushing.

The only thing that Sarah was really concentrating on that final summer of school was her sister's impending marriage. The Major, reluctant to lose his older daughter to a distant land and a life very different from the one she had been brought up to, but keen to ensure her happiness, had at last given his consent. The date was set and the arrangements made as Sarah was saying goodbye to her schoolfriends, holding her last midnight feast, and enjoying her last midnight swim. She had no real regrets about leaving Hurst Lodge as she had when she left Daneshill. Life beckoned and there was the excitement of Jane's wedding to look forward to.

She had been asked to be a bridesmaid and she was, wearing a long square-necked dress, edged with blue. The flowers, the music and the reception for two hundred in a marquee on the front lawn of Dummer Down Farm had been organized with all his customary military precision by Ronald Ferguson, aided by Jane.

And on 26 July, exactly a month before Jane's eighteenth birthday and a year and a day after her mother's marriage to Hector Barrantes, the wedding took place in the twelfth-century All Saints parish church of Dummer.

It was a splendid affair befitting the daughter of a former officer in Britain's most elite cavalry regiment. Ronald gave away the bride. His former wife, Susie Barrantes, was there. So was his future wife, Susan. Alex's parents, over from the outback of Australia, mixed in with the Fergusons' rather grander polo playing friends.

As she was leaving, the new Mrs Makim threw her bridal bouquet to Sarah as they had planned. As Sarah caught it, a guest in the crowded marquee yelled out, 'When are you going to find your Prince Charming, Sarah?'

Ten years minus three days later, on 23 July 1986, she had.

4

London

SCHOOL OVER AND WITH AN ADULT WORLD WAITING TO BE discovered, Sarah decided to travel.

It was an ambition common to most of her friends and she had more opportunity than most. Her sister was in Australia and was anxious for her to come and visit. Her friend Clare Steel, now Wentworth-Stanley, invited her to holiday at her parents' home in Nantucket on the Eastern seaboard of America. Her mother offered an even more exotic locale.

When Hector Barrantes wooed Susie Ferguson he asked her if she truly loved him, 'and when she said yes, I told her, "I'm going to take you to live with me at the other end of the earth".' Sarah decided to follow her mother to the pampas of Argentina.

Her father bought her the air ticket. Sarah was now nearly seventeen years old, but with Jane gone the Major had become particularly protective towards his spirited younger daughter. The night before the flight he telephoned the airline to say that he was bringing his daughter to Gatwick airport in the morning and that she was flying to Argentina as an unaccompanied minor.

'She was livid with me,' the Major remembers and she had a point. 'She had to wear a card around her neck saying she was a minor.

'On the drive to the airport she ranted and raged and used words an unaccompanied minor shouldn't even know! When I handed her over to the air hostess she walked away without even a backward glance.'

Hector and Susie were waiting to meet her in Buenos Aires to drive three hundred miles to the south-west across the great prairie to the township of Trenque Lauquen, a hundred miles from where they would settle permanently.

Susie was still settling in and that involved her in long periods of unaccustomed silence. There is a large and long established English community with its own schools and clubs in Buenos Aires. Out on the pampas, however, only a rough and guttural dialect of Spanish is spoken and as Susie recalls: 'My whole life changed drastically because no one there except Hector spoke English and I didn't speak Spanish and he would not translate for me. He was quite right, of course, as it forced me to absorb the language,' just as Hector had had to do when he first arrived in Britain.

It was not the easiest of language courses – 'I love to talk,' Susie says – but it worked and Mrs Barrantes now speaks Spanish so well that, if she happens to take an unwelcome telephone call, she can convincingly pass herself off as Lilianna the maid. Sarah seemed to have little trouble overcoming that language barrier, however.

She enjoyed life on the ranch where the Barrantes spent the Argentinian winter looking after their four stallions, two dozen mares with foals, thirty-four polo ponies and sundry dogs. Unable to have a family of their own – after losing a third child when Jane and Sarah were very young Susie had had a hysterectomy – the Barrantes had lavished their affection on their pack of eight pet dogs which included Basset hounds, Irish wolfhounds and Jack Russell terriers, a breed the Fergusons had long favoured.

The Barrantes were intent on building their own polo centre to breed, raise and train their own ponies and Sarah liked accompanying her mother on bone-rattling rides in Hector's pickup truck looking for suitable properties. There was the pleasure of riding some of the world's finest polo ponies. 'She was one of the most natural riders you could ever hope to find and Sarah became so expert she could make a horse do anything she wanted,' Susie says. Crossbred from thoroughbred stallions and native Criollo mares descended from the horses brought over by the Spanish conquistadors, the ponies are awesome in their pace and manoeuvrability and they provided an exciting test of Sarah's ability.

She lost weight and got on very well indeed with the ranch hands who would whistle at her when she was out riding. She responded to the attention.

'It was very good for her and she adored it,' her mother remembers, though her sister, far away in Australia, was rather keen that she should find herself a steady boyfriend.

There is no doubt that the time she spent in Argentina matured her. She found her mother's company stimulating and Susie took the time to explain how Hector's love and commitment had brought her great happiness.

'When you're happy you've always got more to give, not only to your partner but to everyone,' Susie says. 'I told this to Sarah and it is something she has always remembered.'

After six months it was time to leave the open spaces and the big skies and the freedom of South America behind and return to England. It took her a while to readjust.

She was enrolled at Queen's Secretarial College in South Kensington and she did not find the course stimulating.

Dummer had inevitably changed. During her absence, Susan and the Major had been married (at the Chelsea Register Office with Ronald's mother, Lady Elmhirst, and her own father, Frederick Deptford, standing witness). Susan was now busy turning the farmhouse into a home of her own in readiness for the child she was carrying. With the London home sold, and Dummer just out of comfortable commuting distance, Sarah moved into a London flat with a cousin, Ros Bowie.

It was all a bit tedious after Argentina. She did not want to become a secretary but her family told her, as families do, to stick at it because it would enable her 'to get a job anywhere in the world'.

Ancient typewriters – of the sort that seemed purposely built to catch on the edges of a young woman's nails – were used for teaching, the keys carefully covered to stop the girls cheating. Cheating, of course, was something of a tradition for the two hundred pupils at the college. They considered themselves sophisticated girls and learning to type was a labour which they were only doing because their parents made them. All they really wanted was to have fun and being confined to a classroom in the centre of London when so much was going on was simply 'too much'.

But instead of sensibly getting on with the job and finishing it as quickly as possible, energies were channelled into finding ways of avoiding the boring work. It was quite simple. Typewriter keys were uncovered. And shorthand could be copied from the person next door. All the class needed was a couple of dedicated pupils to crib from.

Sarah was certainly not one of those. She and her new found friend Charlotte Eden, daughter of the former Tory MP, Lord Eden of Winton, were amongst the worst culprits. They sat at the back of the typing class and giggled.

At lunchtime everyone went to the café across the road and ordered platters of spaghetti bolognese while they discussed their plans for the weekend. Sarah had not yet got into the social scene of London and spent many long evenings in the flat or at the cinema with girlfriends. She often wrote to her sister in Australia complaining that she was depressed and alone.

Such moods of Byronic gloom seldom lasted. It only took one telephone call or invitation to cheer her up again. One weekend she returned to Dummer to announce excitedly that she had met some great people. 'She suddenly found a circle of friends and her life completely changed,' Sue remembers. 'She was in a crowd of her own age and things just took off.'

Socializing became far more important than the tedium of

the shorthand, typing and book keeping taught at the college, and Sarah and Charlotte, like most of the other girls, spent most of their days looking forward to evenings and weekends. It was 1977, the year of the Queen's Silver Jubilee celebrations, and London was bustling with tourists. The Arabs were arriving in large numbers and they were to be seen on the streets or sitting in their flowing robes on the pavements around the secretarial college.

Cocktail parties in shared flats or houses formed a large part of the social life and weekends were always in the country, either at Dummer, or in large house parties organized around someone's coming out dance (the Deb Season was no longer the grand affair it had been when Susie Barrantes made her social debut, but there were still enough parties and balls to keep a well-connected girl entertained).

When Sarah completed her nine-month course it was hardly surprising that she and Charlotte Eden ended up sharing the dubious distinction of coming joint bottom of their class. Sarah left with shorthand of ninety words per minute and a typing speed of thirty-nine.

'We were dunces at shorthand and typing,' Charlotte confirms. Sarah's report was not as bad as it might have been, however. It read: 'Bright, bouncy redhead. She's a bit slapdash. But she has initiative and personality which she will use to her advantage when she gets older. Accepts responsibility happily.'

That summer Sarah was invited to Nantucket to stay with her former school friend, Clare, whose parents kept a summer house there. A fashionable island near Boston, Nantucket is much favoured by the sailing set. To the two teenage girls it was a summer paradise. They could laze around all day, sun bathing and watching the preppy American boys on the beach. 'We did a lot of giggling,' Clare remembers. They went sailing with Clare's brother Tim, on whom Sarah developed a slight crush. In the evenings there were beach barbecues and, failing all else, twenty-four hour American television.

It was Sarah's first trip to the United States and she liked everything about it. 'She was very easy going,' Clare remembers. 'You never felt you had to entertain her. She was happiest in a pair of old jeans, just mucking around and she'd join in with everything.'

Back in London Sarah and Clare started moving in the same set. It included David Waterhouse, who would later become a close friend of the Princess of Wales, bloodstock agent Angus Gold, Laura Smith-Bingham and her brother, Kim.

Before Sarah started going out with Kim Smith-Bingham she had enjoyed some mild flirtations (one with the very dashing cavalry officer, Michael Corry-Reid, from whose family the Fergusons had rented the villa on that ill-fated trip to Corfu) but Kim was her first regular boyfriend. He was two years older and comparatively more sophisticated than Sarah.

The Smith-Binghams are a prosperous Oxfordshire family. His father, Charles, who was separated from Kim's mother, was involved in horse racing as an owner and a consultant for the British Bloodstock Agency.

Kim had first met Sarah in South America where he went to work as a ranch-hand after leaving school. 'She was one of the only English people around,' he recalls, 'but I hardly saw her and didn't really meet with her until much later through my sister Laura.'

Like many of the crowd Sarah was mixing with, Kim had worked in the City. He was charming and affluent and, at over six foot, an attractive young man, albeit with prematurely thinning hair. He sent her flowers and their dates would vary from dinners at the Ritz and Annabel's nightclub to an outing to the latest movie followed by a Chinese meal. Sarah enjoyed the theatre and sometimes persuaded Kim and a party of friends to go to the latest show before a late night supper in a Soho restaurant. When they stayed in, Smith-Bingham would cook spaghetti and they would watch television.

'We never lived together but we did spend a lot of time

together,' Kim has recalled, adding, 'We were too young for people to have thought of us as a long-term couple.'

Sue meanwhile had produced her first child, a boy named Andrew Frederick John, at the Royal Hampshire County Hospital in Winchester on 7 September 1978 and Sarah was delighted with her half-brother. Sue enjoyed her visits to Dummer with Kim. 'It was such a contrast to me as I was wrapped up in the baby and she used to keep me in touch.'

Her father was not so keen. He decided that a trip to Australia to visit Jane and Alex might help Sarah forget about Kim, and with this in mind he organized one.

'Of course she didn't forget about him,' Ronald says, 'but we did have an interesting time.'

The Australian outback was certainly that. The Makims lived in an L-shaped wooden house with a corrugated iron roof set in 8000 acres of bush close to the New South Wales border with Queensland. Wilga Warrina – aboriginal for house amongst the trees – was little more than a shack shaded by blinds and hung with nets to keep the flies out. In the summer the temperature would regularly reach one hundred and twenty degrees Fahrenheit. When the rains came, if they did, the red dust turned into a mire and the house leaked and every available dish and bowl would be laid down to catch the drips. There were snakes and flies and red-back spiders for whose poison there was no antidote.

What entertainment there was was correspondingly rustic. There were evening barbecues which went on into the early hours and when one of the revellers fell into the fire in a drunken stupor and started roasting, the Makims' neighbours roared with amusement. The Major preferred to sit watching re-runs of *The Two Ronnies* on television.

An evening out was a major expedition. One night the family went to dinner at a neighbouring farm. After several miles the Major, his six foot two inch frame crouched uncomfortably in the back seat of Alex's Jeep, asked how much further they had to go. 'Over the hill,' Alex replied. The 'hill' turned out to be over a hundred miles away, making a round trip of two hundred and eighty miles altogether.

'Sarah and I couldn't believe it,' the Major recalls. 'We looked at each other and started laughing and we couldn't stop. The thought of being stuck in the car for hours while being driven on a bumpy track was not our idea of fun.'

While they were there Jane celebrated her twenty-first birthday. There were three hundred guests who motored in from hundreds of miles around. 'It was good fun but Dad was a bit shocked,' Jane recalls. 'He went to bed and got up at two or three in the morning to go to the loo. When he came back five minutes later there were two people in his bed. He roared: "This is my bed. Get out".'

When there weren't any parties or people or the occasional polo match, the sense of isolation could be oppressive. The nearest town with a store was North Star and that was twenty miles away. Sarah and the Major always volunteered to do the shopping and one day spent six hours there, so anxious were they for company.

One day Sarah and the Major went out to tend a horse's hoof that had become septic. As they set off down the dusty track Sarah noticed that her father was walking in a most peculiar way.

'What are you doing, Dads?' Sarah enquired.

'I'm doing the Australian walk,' he replied. 'I'm looking up for the falling bats, down for the snakes, and brushing my face to get rid of the flies.'

Worse than the flies was the outside lavatory, known in Okker as the 'dunny'. It attracted frogs which in turn attracted snakes. Jane remembers: 'I was in there once when I thought I saw a frog coming round the corner. All I could see was the head. It got bigger and bigger and I thought it must be a blue-tongued lizard. The next moment I realized it was a snake and I jumped on top of the loo screaming so loudly it slithered away.

'I can't stand snakes. They are terrifying – slithery and

revolting. Sarah has the same fear. She hated the flies, too, but the dangerous spiders didn't worry her.'

Sarah was pleased for her sister who seemed very happy with her husband and the life she had chosen for herself. However, as much as she enjoyed the horses and the riding, the outback of Australia held no particular attraction for the younger Ferguson girl. But it had been an experience and before she set off on the long journey back to Sydney and the flight home she wrote 'Pretty fair dinkum' in the leather visitors' book (a touch of Home Counties refinement Jane had brought out with her from England). Loosely translated, that meant that she had quite enjoyed herself.

Once back in the more familiar surroundings of Hampshire, Sarah was tempted to settle into the convivial atmosphere of Dummer and concentrate on her riding. But as her father explained, she either had to dedicate her life to horses and riding or go to London and get a job. He was certainly not prepared to keep her. He would buy her a second-hand car and supplement her income with a small allowance, but he assured her she would have to work.

'So I gave up riding and went to London and worked,' she said.

'It was a big decision,' her mother recalls. 'She was a very good horsewoman. But if you have a horse you have to be responsible for it and come home every weekend. When children are in their late teens they can't make up their mind if they want to go out every night or have a horse. Sarah knew she would never make a champion rider, as she hated dressage – an essential part of competing, so she made the right decision.'

Sarah's first foray into the world of commerce was to find a temporary job working for Flatmates Unlimited, a flat-sharing agency in the Old Brompton Road. Wendy Stewart-Robinson, the boss of the company, which included a domestic and baby-sitting section, was expecting her first child and was in urgent need of extra help.

'We were in a state,' Wendy remembers. 'We found some names through the bush telegraph and one of them was Fergie.'

The job, which was only supposed to be for a couple of weeks, lasted for three months. She used the time to look around for something permanent. She wanted a proper job and the idea of working in public relations appealed, even if it meant starting as a secretary. She asked her father who was working in PR himself at the time to help. The Major spoke to his friend Neil Durden-Smith who had his own company with a staff of twenty-five and offices in Knightsbridge.

Durden-Smith Communications was situated in an old mansion block on the corner of Sloane Street and Basil Street. The office was open plan interspaced with several private rooms. It was in one of these that Sarah found herself being interviewed by Neil Durden-Smith, who owned and ran the business. A former sports broadcaster married to television presenter Judith Chalmers, he is an affable man who subscribes to the notion of working hard – and playing hard too. He had a large circle of 'chums' with whom he did business over long lunches or cocktails. He was successful – his clients included BMW, Trusthouse Forte, Seagrams, Guinness and the jewellers Mappin & Webb and Garrard – popular and good company and Fergie, as everyone called her, very much wanted the job she had been called in to apply for.

'She was quite nervous and self-conscious,' Neil remembers. 'She was on the short list with a couple of other girls who were very competent, smart and well groomed. She was a complete contrast, but she was terribly keen. She was honest, explaining to me that she had never had a proper job before, but wanted to learn. I rated that very highly.'

The job was the position of secretary to one of Neil's account executives, Sarah Mason Pearson, who worked on the Mappin & Webb account. Unable to make the decision between the three girls, she asked Neil to see them all and help her make a choice.

'I told her that two of the girls had it all, but personally I would go for Sarah Ferguson. She had the personality and although she needed training I thought she would give one hundred and twenty per cent to any job she went into. I said I would go for that extra twenty per cent and give her the job.'

Told that she had been hired, Sarah immediately telephoned her father. He, in turn, telephoned Durden-Smith to ask him 'to teach her everything you know' and insist that she be shown no favouritism. Durden-Smith reassured him on both counts.

Sarah was due to start her new job in the New Year. By way of introducing her to the company, her new employer invited her to the annual Christmas party. A man of style, Durden-Smith never needed an excuse to celebrate and asked his staff to report to the office the morning after their annual cocktail party with their passports in their hands. They had no clue where they were going, but knowing their boss, guessed it would be something rather special. It was.

'I told everyone to report to the office at 7 a.m.,' Neil remembers. 'It was the first time Fergie had met most of the people and there she was at 7.15 in the morning with directors, account directors and secretaries, chatting as if she'd known them all her life.'

When Neil announced to the assembled revellers they were to be taken to lunch in Paris, a cheer went up, drinks were downed and everyone climbed into the waiting coaches laid on to take them to Heathrow airport, where they found to their dismay the engineers on a wildcat strike and fog closing in.

Durden-Smith was not about to let something like a strike or adverse weather ruin his Christmas lunch. He 'went to see someone at Heathrow and he managed to help and we got on the penultimate aircraft to get off before the fog closed in'. When they all finally boarded the aircraft there was another small problem – the bar was closed as they were still attached to the pod.

Durden-Smith, anxious not to let the spirit of the party

evaporate, went up to the flight deck and spoke to the pilot. 'I told him we were all very thirsty and could he do anything about it?' Neil recalls. 'He was a good chap and he organized for the bar to be opened and by the time we took off for Paris all the champagne had been drunk.'

When the slightly intoxicated group arrived in Paris they were over two hours late. But the intrepid Neil had contacted the restaurant from the aircraft and informed them of the delay so that when they arrived at the Perroquet Vert (the Green Parrot) in Montmartre they were still welcomed.

'She was only twenty but Fergie was managing very well,' Neil remembers. 'She entered into the spirit of things, listening to all our after-lunch speeches and in-house jokes with a big grin on her face.'

The party did not break up until well after 6 p.m., by which time the carefully laid plans began to go awry. They dashed to the airport only to discover the fog had finally stopped all flights out of Paris.

'I rang the Hotel de la Tramoie on the Champs Elysées,' Neil remembers, 'and asked them if they had rooms for thirty people. Luckily they did and we all decamped to the hotel.'

The party continued into the night with Neil announcing that anyone who didn't go on to the Crazy Horse – the famous Parisian nightclub where the girls dance semi-naked – was a 'Piker'. Sarah went and together with Durden-Smith and some of the more resilient of the group, watched the cabaret, danced and drank through almost to the following morning.

It was a wild and captivating beginning. But the job would also involve a lot of hard work and Sarah would later say that the time at Durden-Smith Communications, 'taught her everything she knows about PR and a lot about people'.

Public relations work suited her. She has, according to Durden-Smith, 'a natural gift of getting into people's psyche' and, like her mother, is able to converse with anyone about almost anything. It was her liking for conversation, however, combined with her active social life that caused her a few initial problems.

Every morning Sarah would cycle to work arriving at the office breathless, but just on time. Leaving her bicycle in the large reception area (everyone else would padlock theirs to the railings outside) she would be at her desk with thirty seconds to spare. Within minutes the telephone would be jangling with eager callers – not business connections but friends anxious to discuss the previous evening's events and the coming night's activities. She deftly got rid of the early callers by whispering, 'I'll call you back later', but as the day wore on Sarah's list of callers grew and her subterfuge lessened. It was annoying to those around her and one of the other secretaries, a young girl called Helen Hughes, went to Durden-Smith and told him that they were all getting a bit fed up with the incoming and outgoing calls that had nothing whatsoever to do with business.

Durden-Smith called Sarah into his office and told her there were too many personal calls. She apologized and said, 'Right, I'll sort it out.' And the telephone stopped ringing.

She bore 'the goody-goody who spilt the beans' no ill-feeling. Today Helen Hughes is one of her close friends and one of her ladies-in-waiting.

Nor did she mind being told what to do. She was eager to learn. Her typing and shorthand, so dismal when she left Queen's, were improving. She started arriving early for work. And after the caretaker had complained about the 'girl with the red hair, who was in such a hurry, she just leaves her bike for everyone to fall over', she started padlocking it to the railings outside the office.

'She had tremendous stamina,' Durden-Smith recalls. 'She was very headstrong when she came and didn't quite realize the workings of a company which has its own rules, but she welcomed being put right.'

Durden-Smith's hunch about Sarah was paying off. When she was involved with a client nothing was too much trouble. If she was at a party and she saw someone standing alone she would detach herself from whoever she was talking to and look after them. 'She has a great memory for names and was brilliant at introductions,' Neil recalls. 'I used to call her my party star.'

Life at Durden-Smith Communications was not all parties, of course, and Sarah worked hard on several accounts under the auspices of Peter Cunard who remembers her as someone who never involved herself in office politics, never lost her temper and always had a cheerful word for everyone. She sometimes did the wrong thing or forgot things, but never with disastrous results.

She did once cost the company rather a lot of money when she was working on the Seagram account, however.

'They had a national angling competition,' Neil remembers. 'And they needed a special trophy for it. So Fergie organized it with Mappin & Webb, who were also clients. Unfortunately for us she got the order wrong and ordered a sterling silver trophy instead of one made from silver plate. It cost the company a few bob, I can tell you, but the anglers were very happy.'

During the eighteen months Sarah worked for Durden-Smith they became good friends. She had persuaded him to give her friend Charlotte Eden a job in the company, which proved a popular move amongst the staff. They liked Charlie Girl, as Durden-Smith nicknamed her. She was enthusiastic with an outgoing personality, qualities he particularly admired in Sarah, who was at her best when there was a crisis and would work from seven in the morning until midnight if necessary.

As Durden-Smith recalls: 'She was the one who said, "I'll do that Neil, I'll sort it out, just leave it to me". And off she'd go and do it. It was a challenge to her.'

Just about everything was a challenge to Sarah. Her tremendous stamina allowed her to lead an active social life, work hard and all on the minimum of sleep.

'She'd switch on a reserve tank,' Neil says. 'When there were one hundred things to do and only time to do ninety-five, she was the person who would stay late and get in early. She gave life one hundred per cent all the time.'

She still spent many of her weekends at Dummer, arriving with her blue VW piled with dirty washing. If she did not go she still got her washing done. As her father remembers: 'I received a telephone call from Sarah one Friday night, telling me there was a parcel from London arriving at Basingstoke station and could I go and fetch it from the Red Star office. When I asked her what it was she informed me it was her dirty washing!' Ronald soft-heartedly drove to Basingstoke and fetched the parcel.

Both the Major and his wife liked having her home. Sue, pregnant for the second time, liked hearing about the Chelsea life she had left behind and Sarah was now enjoying.

She would also talk to her about Kim Smith-Bingham, with whom she was still involved. She was now flat-sharing with one of his friends, Angus Gold, who lived in a two-bedroomed apartment in Prince of Wales Drive, opposite Battersea Park. Every day Sarah would leave her car outside the flat and bicycle to work across Battersea Bridge into Sloane Street. If Kim came to fetch her from work, she would leave the bike padlocked to the railings and jump into his car for an evening together. But their dates were becoming too infrequent for her liking. Smith-Bingham had moved to Verbier in Switzerland where he was selling skis and clothes and renting equipment.

When he was away Sarah kept herself busy. After work she and Charlotte would go to local wine bars – to Motcomb's in Belgravia or round the corner to the Rib Room at the Carlton Tower Hotel (which had a happy hour when the drinks were half price) and discuss their plans.

'Fergie always liked these gatherings,' one of her office colleagues, Judy Regis remembers. 'But she was incorrigible and couldn't stay still for long – she always seemed to be going to about five different drinks parties in an evening.'

But she missed her boyfriend. 'It was blissful when she was with Kim,' Sue recalls, 'and terrible tears and dramas when she couldn't see him.'

She would often spend hours with her grandmother,

'Grummy' Wright, pouring out her problems. 'She's like a wise old owl; everyone with any problems goes to Grummy,' Sue confirms.

At the end of the year she was due to visit her mother and stepfather in Argentina again. And as Neil was in the process of selling Durden-Smith Communications, she suggested that Charlotte might like to join her for a Christmas on the pampas.

Charlotte jumped at the idea and suggested they move on afterwards and travel through the rest of South America. Sarah agreed.

5

Bachelor Girl

FOR ALL MAJOR RONALD FERGUSON'S INSISTENCE THAT HIS younger daughter should get a job and earn her own way, work or, more precisely, a career was not yet at the top of Sarah's agenda.

She was young and there were good times to be had. She had enjoyed working for Durden-Smith Communications – and with a boss who flies you to Paris for a party on your first day, who wouldn't? But she was also going to enjoy her travels through the New World.

It was, she recalls, one of the most exciting periods of her life. She kept a daily chronicle of her youthful adventures. She still has the diary tied with a blue ribbon in her apartment in Buckingham Palace.

Charlotte and Sarah set off in the autumn of 1980. The first entry, written in her neat, rounded hand in a vivid green ink, is dated shortly after her twenty-first birthday. There were good-byes to be said first, of course, and the girls' departure from Durden-Smith Communications was an excuse (not that Neil ever needed one) for a farewell party with champagne toasts. In celebration of her birthday her father gave her a cocktail party for one hundred and fifty guests in the Crystal Room of the Berkeley Hotel in London. She had declined his offer of a dance at Dummer, saying that she would rather have the money for the trip; and a couple of weeks later they were on their way.

They were met, as Sarah was on her first trip to Argentina, at Buenos Aires airport by Hector and Susie and they drove straight to the Barrantes' new 4000-acre ranch.

Hector drove fast along the two-lane highway, his foot hard to the floor with only the occasional deceleration for a wandering cow or when they passed through one of the small towns that dot the pampas. Four hours and four hundred miles later they turned through the wooden gates at El Pucara (it means Fortress in Spanish). The only contact with the outside world was by crackling radio telephone and the nearest town, Tres Lomas, was twenty miles away.

Hector had converted a hundred acres of this flat land into a polo field and exercise area for his ponies and surrounded it with hundreds of saplings to protect it from the winds. The house was set back a mile from the road at the end of a drive lined with willow and cactus and spruce trees. Almost anything will grow on this abundant, seemingly inexhaustible plain where the twelve foot deep top soil is so fertile that it is cheaper to buy more land than fertilize what you already own and the gauchos slaughter a cow just to eat its tongue.

Sarah and Charlotte rode the humid prairie, worried about the mosquitoes, and helped Susie move into her new A-framed home. Sarah learned the rudiments of Spanish in its gruff Argentine version.

And there were the ponies to admire. Hector Barrantes had started with little. He was now on his way to becoming probably the best breeder of polo ponies in Argentina. And Argentinian polo ponies are the best in the world, commanding prices of up to £30,000 an animal.

Introduced by the British in 1876, the sport ranks second only to soccer in the Argentine sporting calendar and as many as 40,000 people attend the Argentine Open in Buenos Aires.

Barrantes' 'valiente' ponies were almost invariably part of the winning team.

The secret, Hector explained, is patience. The ponies (a misnomer: a pony is a horse under 14.2 hands, while the average height of polo 'ponies' is 15.1 hands) are not confined to stables but are turned out year round. They play every day for six hours and in between are schooled by the 'domadors', the ranch hands who do the breaking-in. It is a long process. While other breeders often sell their ponies at the age of four or five, Barrantes kept his – and at the last count he had three hundred and fifty horses including a breeding stock of sixty-two mares and seven stallions – until they were six or even seven.

'I'm in no hurry,' he said.

The girls were. After a Christmas celebrated in the traditional English manner (even in the heart of the pampas Susie maintained the homely English tradition of three meals a day, fresh flowers and pretty curtains), they set off by rackety bus to drive to Iguaza Falls to see the most magnificent waterfalls in South America and then north to Rio de Janeiro.

Using the *South American Handbook* for reference, they stayed at cheap but comparatively safe lodgings on the overnight stops en route. By the time they got to the Falls, however, on the borders of Argentina, Paraguay and Brazil, 'we had run out of money,' as Charlotte recalls, 'so we slept in the bus station on the benches, surrounded by throngs of peasant women with their children and chickens.'

They had their onward bus and airline tickets, but they did not have enough cruzeiros left to buy even a corn on the cob from one of the maize sellers. Resorting to their wits, they took advantage of the South American habit of providing small pieces of cheese and olives with every drink. They walked into the nearby hotel, 'trying to look as prosperous as possible', as Charlotte says, asked for two glasses of water, 'scoffed' the modest tapas and then ran off to catch the bus.

It had been an exciting adventure in a continent where single women are looked on as easy prey. The murder of tourists was common enough to warrant a warning in the *South American Handbook*, as do the travellers' more commonplace hazards of pick-pockets, false arrest, beggars and robbery.

'I wouldn't do it today but it was great fun then,' Charlotte says.

They survived and after staying with friends of Major Ferguson in Rio, they flew on to the United States and headed for the ski resorts of the Rocky Mountains. Says Mrs Barrantes: 'I had a great friend in Squaw Valley so Sarah and Charlotte went to stay there and work for a while,' looking after children, waiting on table in a cafeteria, cleaning the immaculate 'log cabin' chalets and skiing the crisp, dry, easily negotiated high altitude snow in between times. Then it was back across the continent to meet up with Hector and Susie in Palm Springs.

They finished up in Louisiana on the Gulf of Mexico. After the corrugated, rutted shambles of Latin America, and the clean-limbed freshness of the mountains, the musky neon nights of America's jazz city were overpowering. 'The most worrying time was walking around the back streets of New Orleans. We definitely thought we would end up being mugged,' Charlotte says.

That summer back in England they regaled their friends and family with the edited highlights of their trip. They had been away for almost six months. In their absence Susan Ferguson had given birth to another child, a daughter called Alice, who was born while Sarah was in Argentina. She telephoned her with the news and asked her to be a godmother. Babies do not particularly excite Sarah. She prefers them from a year upwards. But she did find her little half-sister with her dusting of blonde hair 'terribly sweet' and spent a while helping her stepmother around the house at Dummer.

With her funds now all but exhausted there was no chance to linger, however. A job and a flat had to be found and a faltering romance – she was still involved with Kim Smith-Bingham – continued.

The accommodation part of that common equation was easily resolved. Back on the London social circuit she encountered Carolyn Beckwith-Smith whose mother was an old friend of Susie Barrantes. 'We met at a cocktail party and I happened to mention that if she was ever looking for somewhere to live she should give me a call,' Carolyn recalls. 'Amazingly she said, "How about now?" and she practically moved in then and there.'

A very attractive blonde, Carolyn had her own home in Lavender Gardens, a street of terraced houses in Clapham. Only ten years before, the area had been a respectable but decidedly working-class suburb on what had been scathingly called 'the wrong side of the river'. Soaring property prices, however, had driven the younger generation of Sloanes out of their traditional territory and there had been a mass migration across the bridges from Belgravia and Chelsea into the hitherto uncharted regions south of the Thames. With them came the bistros and flower shops, design centres, fabric shops, picture framers, and other such services deemed essential for civilized living and by the time Sarah moved in, Clapham was secure as a forward post of urban respectability.

The flatmates got on well together. Carolyn has a sense of humour to rival Sarah's – it is said she once put sneezing powder in her stepfather's omelette. Artistic and Bohemian, she had worked for interior decorator Nina Campbell, managed Edina Ronay's clothes shop in Liberty's in Regent Street, and was a close friend of dress designer Lindka Cierach. All would figure prominently in Sarah's future.

At the time she was working as a make-up artist and used to show Sarah different ways of doing her hair and making up her eyes.

Carolyn continues: 'Fergie was very tidy, immaculate in fact. She wasn't a great Hooverer or ironer but everything in her room was always very tidy. She can't stand a mess.' They employed an Indian cleaning lady to do the dusting and polishing and the sitting room was always full of fresh flowers – freesias and roses were Sarah's favourites – and the walls were hung with oil paintings.

'We didn't entertain much, we didn't have time,' Carolyn remembers. Both were living active social lives, 'and it was a question of who was last in and was it too late to wake the other up. If we had a bad time we would cheer each other up.'

Her domestic arrangements settled, Sarah now had to get down to the more substantial task of finding herself a job; she answered an advertisement in *The Times* for a personal assistant cum secretary to William Drummond, an art dealer with premises in Covent Garden.

Drummond – lanky, sandy-haired, chain smoking, always moving, and possessed of an engagingly droll wit – recalls his first meeting with Sarah. 'When she arrived I told her I couldn't even see her as I had such a terrible hangover. You can imagine all that mass of red hair when you are hung over. It was rather like having to look straight into the sun.'

He knew nothing about her and she was just one of thirty applicants, jobs in art galleries being very sought after by young girls from Sarah's background. A couple of days later, while wandering through Covent Garden, Drummond encountered a colleague in the art business who told him how fortunate he was to have Sarah Ferguson joining him. He was slightly taken aback as he had still not made up his mind which of the thirty he was going to hire. That chance remark decided him.

'I thought, "That's the right spirit", and made up my mind immediately,' he says.

For Drummond, an expert in rather obscure eighteenth-century oil paintings and drawings, a prerequisite of the employment of a secretary was that she did not know too much about his speciality. 'That allows you to get on with playing with your pictures while they do all the nasty things,' he explains.

For Sarah part of the job included taking Drummond in hand. She made him morning coffee. She tried to feed him up;

because he was too engrossed in his work to bother to organize his own lunches she would fetch him sandwiches from Maxwell's, the snack bar across the road ('She was a handsome eater herself – when she wasn't starving herself,' he says). She tried to make him cut down on his smoking. She became friendly with his wife and children and would help him select their Christmas gifts.

'She also remembered everyone who came into the gallery, what they had bought, and their names. It was quite a gift and she was a great person to have around,' he says.

Like Durden-Smith before him he noticed how her social life sometimes conflicted with her work but, being easy-going, he chose to disregard the amount of time off she took – or the telephone bills she ran up. There were some telephone calls even Drummond could not ignore, however.

'It eventually came out that she was a friend of the Princess of Wales and I suddenly realized that many of the phone calls she had were from her,' the art dealer says. Diana was pregnant at the time and suffering badly from morning sickness.

'She never spoke about it but I think Sarah used to help her keep her morale up by having lunches with her,' Drummond observes.

One evening Sarah accompanied the Prince of Wales to dinner at the Savoy and to the theatre to see Barry Humphries' alter ego Dame Edna in a performance *An Evening's Intercourse*. The outing was recorded in a newspaper. 'Sarah was incensed,' Drummond remembers, 'because they had called her father a millionaire landowner. "I can assure you", she said, "that he's not a millionaire!"'

Drummond's esoteric world of eighteenth-century art was a long way removed from palaces and polo. He knew nothing of the comings and goings of the Royal Family or Sarah's connections. 'I eventually discovered that Major Ron and Prince Charles were great polo muckers and made men-ish noises together,' he says.

Despite their different interests Drummond and Sarah became

good friends. She introduced him to Mrs Barrantes, and mother and employer made comment on Sarah's lack of interest in clothes. He complimented Susie on her daughter's abilities.

'She was a self-reliant, confident person – people who ride horses and crash about the place have to be,' he says. 'And she certainly wasn't backward about coming forward.'

Sarah eventually left the gallery because she wanted to spend more time in Verbier. She wanted to ski. She was also following her heart. During her time with Drummond she had finally ended her relationship with Kim Smith-Bingham and had started walking out with Paddy McNally. She found Drummond her own replacement, her old school friend Clare Wentworth-Stanley.

'I had a whole gang of rather nice, pretty girls come to me through her,' he says. 'Clare, Charlotte Eden and then Amanda Pirry.'

Drummond eventually closed his gallery in Covent Garden because of the rise in rents and now works from an apartment in St James's which is crammed with fine art. He still sees Sarah – 'I never called her Fergie' – for the occasional lunch or dinner.

'In the picture of her life I am of very little importance but the fact that she went out of her way to keep in touch is very much to her credit. She would often ring me up to see if there was anything she could do.' At his request, she became patron of the Dulwich Picture Gallery near where he went to school. 'I am delighted and flattered to think I might have given her a knowledge of pictures, something which must be useful in a family like that,' Drummond wryly remarks.

The extra time Sarah was spending in Verbier did not add up to a full time move, however. She kept her room in Lavender Gardens and the teddy bear she had carried around with her since she was a child kept guard in her absence. To help pay the rent she took a series of part-time jobs.

One was with a video company called RSVP with head-quarters in Kensington High Street. There she became involved with making an advertising video for Harrods with Sheridan

Morley. The theatre critic and playwright remembers her as fun and efficient. She did some temporary work for Durden-Smith. 'She breezed in like a breath of fresh air,' he says. 'She'd go skiing at weekends but she'd always be there at 9 a.m. on Monday morning, ready for anything.'

Her former employer was now running a company called Sports Sponsorship International and was involved in the proposal to set up the Rugby Union World Cup. There were shades of the fishing trophy to Sarah's involvement.

The day before the Australian Rugby Board were due to meet, Durden-Smith received a call from the secretary in Sydney saying that they had yet to receive the proposal. Neil asked Sarah if she remembered posting the document. She said she did and produced the post book to prove it. The proposal had indeed been dispatched – but by sea mail.

She also did some work for a friend, Jules Dodd-Noble who was setting up her own Noble House company which specializes in providing a wide range of office services. 'She was always the one who wanted to help,' Jules says.

'One day I was frantic. I had to do a quote for equipping an entire kitchen for one of my clients and they wanted it by the end of the day. So I took Fergie up on her offer of help and asked her to go to Peter Jones and write down every single thing in the kitchen department and price it. She spent the entire day there and produced every single item written out neatly with the price beside it.'

In April 1984 she finally found a more creative outlet for her talents. Richard Burton was an elegant former racing driver turned publisher of fine art books. Educated at Wellington public school, his savoir faire and Savile Row suits so impressed one observer that he felt moved to describe him as 'straight out of John Buchan – the essence of the English gentleman'.

After·suffering sixty-five per cent burns in a near fatal crash at Reims – 'Jackie Stewart organized a plane and had me whisked into the Burns Centre at East Grinstead where I spent three months while they put me back together' – he gave up the fast lane and went into driver management. Jackie Stewart, Jochen Rindt and Chris Amon were the best in the world at that time, and as they were all living in Switzerland he moved there too.

That had led to an excursion into European property developing and finally, when he came to realize the quality of Swiss printing, into publishing. He was looking for someone to run his London office and Paddy McNally, whom Burton knew from his racing days, suggested Sarah. They met and the two got on well.

It turned into a profitable five-year relationship which survived into her marriage. She was involved in a text book on the Impressionists entitled *The New Painting* which sold 155,000 copies and grossed almost $6 million. She was instrumental in putting together veteran politician and former MP Sir Robert Cooke's last work *The Palace of Westminster*.

Burton recalls: 'I asked Sarah to look around the Houses of Parliament, then put together an author, photographers, designers and get the thing moving. She organized it. It was her baby, she got it together.'

More projects were planned. They were not to be. Caught on the wrong side of international currency fluctuations, Burton was forced to wind up the company and moved to California to try and resuscitate his fortune selling fine art reproductions. The work had certainly suited Sarah, however. She had been paid well, and by the end was earning over £20,000 a year.

It also enabled her to spend almost as much time as she wanted in Switzerland. And Switzerland meant Verbier.

6

Verbier

Verbier, the French-speaking resort in the Swiss Alps, had long been a favourite with a certain crowd of brash, extrovert English skiers. By the early 1980s it was also acquiring a certain social cachet. In those days Gstaad and St Moritz were still considered the most fashionable of resorts but they were rusting with age and conventionality. Verbier was cheaper. The runs were more challenging. And, no small consideration to a group of Englishmen with money, contacts and a single-minded intent on having a good time, the girls were younger and generally prettier.

They decided to move their playground from Gstaad and set up their winter base across the mountains in Verbier. In the group was the witty and immensely charming Paddy McNally who very quickly established himself as the king of the mountain in a large chalet overlooking the town.

Down the hill, literally and – in the Verbier context – socially, lived Kim Smith-Bingham. Sarah, still in the flush of her first love, would join him for weekends and holidays at his home, Les Grands Mots, an attractive two-bedroom, two-bathroom second floor flat with a small kitchen that led into a sitting room with a corner dining table, a fireplace, and a wooden balcony with a less than picture postcard view over the apartment block's car park.

Sarah spent her days on the slopes. She was an expert skier. 'I love the mountains,' she says.

Smith-Bingham was employed in the boot hire section of the ski service shop.

'She would ski every day while I was working,' he recalls. 'She's very good, up to black run standard.'

She did not lack for companionship. As in any resort, the regular skiers who have homes and roots in the place very quickly get to know each other and Verbier had become a winter staging post for many of her friends. Lulu Blacker holidayed there. So did Kim's sister Laura, who is now married to wine merchant Johnny Goedhuis. Everyone socialized together.

'It was great fun,' says Smith-Bingham, recalling his time there with Sarah. 'We'd go out to restaurants or see friends.' Kim introduced her to Paddy and sometimes they would walk up the hill to his chalet, Les Gais Lutins, which he shared with London property developer David Elias.

An invitation to dinner at the 'Castle', so nicknamed for its size, was the hot ticket in the small town. A steep flight of snow-covered steps leads to the front door, which opens into a largish hallway, used to keep boots and skis. Up another flight of stairs is a sitting room with an adjoining kitchen and dining area. It is attractively decorated in the local style with wooden windows and walls, brightly covered sofas and a large open fireplace. On the walls of the hallway and the games room downstairs hung collages of photographs of holidays past. From the looks on the faces of the photographs everyone was having a good time.

Upstairs twenty people can squeeze around the long pine second-floor dining table and the conversation revolves around money, gossip and girls. Any new girl in town is teased unmercifully by Paddy. No one is spared. One night Paddy concentrated his wit and considerable charm on the vivacious redhead. The older man became a great friend of Sarah. She would tell him of the problems she was having with Smith-Bingham.

'Paddy became a shoulder to cry on,' Sue Ferguson recalls. He lent a mature and sympathetic ear and started inviting her up to the chalet, with or without Smith-Bingham. Despite the age difference – he is twenty-two years Sarah's senior – Sarah was very taken with McNally.

The youngest of four sons born to a former Wing Commander doctor in the RAF, McNally had become a racing driver and made money out of his interest by writing for *Autosport* magazine. He then moved on in the high-octane, high-finance world of Grand Prix racing and he started working for Philip Morris's Marlboro, the major commercial underwriters of Formula One, arranging sponsorship deals for such top drivers as Nikki Lauda, Alain Prost and James Hunt.

He had made a good marriage to Anne Downing, daughter of a very rich Monte Carlo-based former racing driver. They had two sons, Sean and Rollo. In 1980 Anne died of cancer. By then the McNallys were separated and the despair and remorse generated by her death led to a rift between Paddy and his in-laws which has still not been healed. Ken Downing has only bitter comments to make about his former son-in-law.

But for all the Downings' misgivings, McNally proved himself a caring father to his two boys. Through a combination of hard work and his Irish Catholic charm Paddy, who in his youth was described by a member of his family as 'harum scarum', was also well on the way to becoming a very rich man in his own right. He set up his own company and under the auspices of Bernie Ecclestone, the organizer of Grand Prix racing, took charge of the placement of the advertising hoardings around the world's Formula One circuits – a deal which would make him a millionaire.

By the time Sarah came on the scene he was established as the leader of a crowd of glamorous and well-heeled rapscallions who knew how to work hard and play hard.

Sarah became numbered amongst the guests. He clearly found her attractive and asked her to join him on one of his motor racing trips. It was the beginning of a four-year love affair and the end of her relationship with Smith-Bingham.

'When we split up it was simply a question of each starting to live a different lifestyle,' Kim says. 'We developed different ideas about what we wanted to do.' He insists: 'Fergie and I were too young to think of anything permanent.' For her it was rather more intense than that.

'It was very serious and they were very keen on each other,' Carolyn Cotterell remembers. 'Your first romance is always a bit of a shock. You don't know what's hit you when you're mad about somebody.'

By the end, however, there had been too many separations and too many tears. Says Carolyn: 'Like all those romances it is the hardest – you don't quite know when the end happens or how to end it. She had been through so many heartaches that when the end came it was almost a relief because she didn't have to hang on for the next call.'

Major Ferguson was not displeased when Sarah told him that she had finally split from Smith-Bingham. He had not wholly approved of the relationship – Kim's City career had not taken off and his move to Verbier had been precipitated in part by unhappiness at work. He liked Paddy, though he presciently predicted that the relationship would never come to anything. But that did not matter at the beginning.

When McNally came to London, Sarah invited him round to Lavender Gardens for drinks.

'She asked me afterwards what I had thought of him,' Carolyn recalls. 'Sarah never made comments like that without me being alerted. I think he was amused and amazed at her because she was so different from anyone else he knew.'

By the middle of 1982 Paddy and Sarah were what is known in Hollywood as 'an item'. She was fascinated by the fast-lane lifestyle of sobriquets and insobriety Paddy introduced her to.

Life at the 'Castle' was fun. During the holidays and on the weekends there were always at least three or four couples staying and the telephone was in constant use – so much so that a meter was attached and guests were asked to write their names in a book when they made a call. Everyone in the set had a nickname. Elias, co-owner with Paddy of the eight-bedroomed 'Castle', was known as Wiggy. Nigel Pollitzer, adopted son of a wealthy industrialist, was called the Rat or Ratty. Businessman John Bentley, whose asset stripping of companies in the early 1970s had earned him wealth and political odium, was Bentles. Property man Olivestone was Olive, while the now Lord Mancroft was always Beano. McNally was known as Toad, a reference to his ability to get on with the right people. There were dinner parties almost every night, with more people arriving afterwards for drinks and back-gammon. Cooking was the responsibility of the chalet girls and nothing to do with Sarah (for which she was most grateful).

Sarah was an excellent hostess, always making sure everyone had drinks and taking care of any newcomers. When dinner was served Paddy took his place at the head of the long pine table with the most attractive girls in the party on either side and Sarah seated somewhere in the middle. This careful placement ensured the conversation kept flowing in both directions. Sarah's skilled small talk was invaluable to Paddy. If there were any important business contacts to be entertained, they were seated next to Sarah who made it her job to make them feel welcome.

No night in Verbier was complete without a visit to the Farm Club discotheque, situated in the basement beneath the Hotel Rhodania and run by Italian brothers Giuseppe and Stefano. The decor was bucolic; the prices were not. Paddy held court at his permanent table in the corner and heads always turned that way as ice buckets were unceremoniously emptied over heads and £50 bottles of Russian vodka were sent crashing to the floor in the crush and the excitement. No one minded – the greatest insult that could have been levelled at the McNally crowd would have been to call them boring. The combination of strong spirit and thin mountain air had a strange effect on almost everyone and the nights became days with people dancing through until dawn.

Sarah danced too but spent more time chatting with the girls.

Sarah's engagement to Prince Andrew would place those antics under a harsh spotlight of scrutiny and malicious hints were dropped. One magazine suggested that there was allegedly more 'snow' inside than there was outside. But those mountain recreations were never as louche as the popular tabloid press sometimes chose to invent. McNally, a conscientious father and respectable and successful businessman, was most particular on that score. He said: 'I have a strict house rule that no one who has anything to do with drugs is allowed to stay with me.' And drugs were never Sarah's speed. The good times were generated by nothing more nefarious than the heady atmosphere and buckets of iced vodka.

'It was rather exciting for her,' Carolyn says. But Sarah's relationship with McNally, as friends noted, was never very relaxed. 'She wouldn't take things casually at all,' Sue Ferguson says. Like her sister Jane, who claims that Alex Makim was 'a mother and father to me', Sarah was looking for an all-embracing emotional support.

Paddy guided her and did his best not to encourage her too much. He was extremely fond of Sarah but he had no intention of settling down and marriage certainly was not included in his plans. That did not suit Sarah. She did not want a casual relationship. When she fell in love she did everything she could to please the object of her affections. His friends became hers, their problems her problems. She would leave little notes and presents for Paddy when she went away and everything she did was designed to bring them closer. For her it was all or nothing and, given that approach, it was inevitable that there would be moments of tension.

The demands of McNally's work did not help matters. Because of her own job commitments Sarah was not able to travel to every Grand Prix and sometimes she would not hear from him for several hurtful days at a time. 'That made her edgy,' Carolyn recalls. 'Then she might get a telephone call in the middle of the night when Paddy was having a party and she had been asleep in bed for an hour or two.'

It was certainly not all gloom and insecurity, however. The pair got on very well together most of the time. They laughed a lot and took obvious pleasure in each other's company. McNally visited Dummer and Sarah got to know his parents. The teasing never stopped – at lunch at one or other of the restaurants high in the mountains Paddy would sometimes shout: 'Ferrrrrgie, what about your diet?' and hide her plate. But in that set everyone teased everyone else and, working to that peculiarly English notion that you only make fun of the people you care about, she took it in the spirit it was intended.

Most importantly, she got on extremely well with McNally's sons, the centre of his life as Becky Few-Brown points out. Once a chalet girl at the 'Castle', then Sarah's successor on the arm of McNally, now the Marchioness of Blandford and future Duchess of Marlborough, she said: 'With Paddy his children always come before his girlfriend . . . before anything.'

Sean was then eleven and Rollo eight and Sarah involved herself in their young lives. She bought them presents and took them to the local store to help them choose their videos. She took them skiing.

She was a magnificent sight on the slopes. She was dressed in the height of the latest ski fashion (aided by her discount at the ski service shop where Smith-Bingham still worked). One year it was a light shiny blue suit, the next the 'Davy Crockett' cap – in fact a fur headband made by a girlfriend and a piece of fur she had bought in an antique shop in the King's Road in Chelsea. With Paddy's encouragement she became skilled on powder, skiing's most challenging skill. 'Kim was what we call a piste-basher. It was Paddy who taught her to ski powder,' remembers Clare Greenall, whose brewery heir husband Peter owns the chalet in Klosters where Prince Charles has often stayed. Naturally athletic and always determined – the word that sums her up best – she was completely fearless as she tracked her way down the virgin snow, throwing up arcs of powder snow in her wake.

'I just adore the freedom of the mountains,' she says. 'It's like taking off your coat. You just get to the mountains and suddenly you're there and I get a sort of buzz from them. If I am away too long, I feel a real need to get back.'

Sarah never actually set up home in Verbier. It was only a winter resort and she still wanted to find a worthwhile career for herself and that meant London. But she flew out at every opportunity. The Christmas of 1983, for instance, was spent in the traditional Ferguson way with Santa Claus outfits and funny paper hats at Dummer with her sister Jane who was over from Australia. But the following day she was on the near empty flight back to Switzerland.

Christmas was fun at the 'Castle'. The house guests were limited to very close friends and people with children of companionable age for Rollo and Sean. It was all very relaxed. People sprawled over the sofas while the children watched videos on television. Sarah skied in the afternoon. In the evening, as other people started arriving, she set to, still in her ski clothes, dispensing the drinks – vodka and bitter lemon was the favourite that year – before taking the boys off for their bath.

The New Year revels were even more extravagant. The Swiss celebrate the night to the full, and the 'Castle' crowd joins in with wholehearted enthusiasm. McNally always throws a party, turning the large basement ping-pong room into a dining area festooned with balloons, streamers and masks decorating the walls. Becky Few-Brown, who was then working as a cook for former world champion racing driver Jackie Stewart, had come up from Geneva to help with the preparations. There were thirty guests including Sarah's schoolfriend Lulu Blacker and after dinner everyone put on the masks and danced to sixties pop songs. Sarah, dressed in tight black leather trousers and a frilled white blouse, was part of the fun and covered herself and everyone else with streamers. At the stroke of midnight there was cheering and singing and a lot of kissing. Then, intent on starting the New

Year as they had ended the old, everyone decanted down the hill to the Farm Club and carried on until six in the morning.

There was little skiing done the following day – just making it up to the Carrefour restaurant for lunch was achievement enough for most of the guests. Sarah was one of the very few who did make it out onto the slopes. A New Year beckoned and she wanted to get on with life.

By Easter she was on her way. A meeting with Paddy's old motor racing friend, Richard Burton, led to her being offered the career opportunity she was looking for. She accepted and in April 1984 went to work as his London acquisitions editor.

She was very excited about the job. She was looking forward to the challenge. It gave her responsibility and professional freedom and, very importantly, a valid reason to travel backwards and forwards between London and Switzerland. That, she believed, would allow her to spend more time with Paddy. In fact it was to set her on a course that would indeed lead her into marriage – but not with McNally.

7

Andrew

WHEN THE BUCKINGHAM PALACE FOOTMAN LOST HIS TEMPER and sent Andrew scudding across the corridor with a well-aimed slap, it was no more than the little prince deserved.

It might have happened sooner. It could be argued that it would have been to the boy's good and everyone else's advantage if that exercise in instant and unarguable discipline had been repeated. If the footman had finally had enough then so too had a lot of other people. Put bluntly, the Queen's second son was a terror.

His antics went beyond the usual boisterousness of childhood. His sister Anne had been determined and self-willed. Charles, his elder brother and future king, had had his childish moments of moody ill humour. But under the stern regime of Nanny Lightbody displays of royal temperament had been contained and, if necessary, punished by early bed and no supper. Charles was smacked for sticking his tongue out at a crowd and for putting ice cubes down a footman's neck. And when Anne once refused nanny's orders to put a sweater on, her father spanked her.

Charles was never allowed to revel in the position that had come to him by birthright. When he was a little boy he once asked a secretary, 'Where are you going?' She replied: 'I'm going to see the Queen.' 'Who's she?' Charles asked. 'Your mother,' the secretary answered. 'It was as if I'd given away the secret of Father Christmas,' she said later.'

No such restraints seemed to apply to Andrew. He certainly knew who his mother was – and who he was.

He hid 'whoopee' cushions in chairs. As soon as he learned to tie his own shoe laces he set about tying together the laces of the palace guards as they stood rigidly to attention at their posts, unable to take evasive action.

'We used to play football along the passageway and every now and then a pane of glass got broken but I don't think we ever broke a piece of Meissen or anything like that,' he says. And if he had he probably would not have cared.

It is also suspected that he was the culprit who put bath foam into the swimming pool at Windsor Castle.

It was not so much the exuberance of these boyish pranks that mattered, however. It was the manner in which they were played. Andrew was just a little bit spoilt.

He was born opportunely at the end of a period which had seen Prince Philip subjected to severe public and Parliamentary criticism. In the summer of 1956 he went to Australia to open the Olympic Games. He then went cruising through the South Atlantic aboard the Royal Yacht *Britannia*, not returning to Britain until the following year. There were whispers of a severe rift in the royal marriage, rumours that found their way into American newspapers. Buckingham Palace issued a denial which was duly reported in the British newspapers – along with the stories that had provoked it in the first place.

The gossip continued in the months that followed and was only finally given the rest it deserved when it was announced that the Queen, who had taken this public discussion of her marriage in her regal stride (in public at least), was expecting another baby.

'People want their first child very much,' Prince Philip has observed. 'They want the second almost as much. If a third comes along they accept it as natural, even if they haven't gone out of their way for it.'

There was a ten-year gap between Anne, the Queen's second child, and Andrew, her third. Nanny Lightbody had gone, to be replaced by the altogether more benign Mabel Anderson and ideas about how to bring up children had undergone a sea change. The influence of America's child expert, Dr Benjamin Spock, had extended even as far as the royal nursery and reason had replaced the rod.

Andrew, like his brother and sister before him, was brought down to his parents' bedrooms to say good morning and they looked into the nursery at tea and bath time, time permitting. But there was a lot more time available now. The Queen had been on the throne for eight years when Andrew was born and she was settled and confident in her royal duties. On 'Mamba' Anderson's days off she would take personal charge of the nursery, romping around with motherly lack of inhibition, teaching him to read and count. When he was a little older she allowed him into her sitting room to play while she was going through the official government papers delivered in their boxes every day – a privilege denied his elder siblings.

Nor was Prince Philip quite the severe paternal task master he is sometimes painted. He did not, he insists, impose his views.

'It's no good saying, do this, do that, don't do this, don't do that . . .' he has said. 'It's very easy when children want to do something to say no immediately. I think it's quite important not to give an unequivocal answer at once. Much better to think it over. Then, if you eventually say no, I think they really accept it.'

There were not many 'nos' in Andrew's young life. Like most parents, the Queen's and Prince Philip's theories about bringing up children had been tempered by experience and Andrew enjoyed a far more carefree infancy than either Charles or Anne.

He was also spared the public appearances the elder children had had to endure. In a conscious reversal of the policy they had adopted with Charles and Anne, the royal parents decided not to pamper to the public's seemingly insatiable appetite for information about the young prince. There were no photo calls; apart from appearing in the official pictures taken to mark the Queen Mother's sixtieth birthday, Andrew was rarely seen.

That in itself presented a problem. As Philip later explained, referring to Andrew and Edward: 'You cannot have it both ways. We try to keep the children out of the public eye so that they can grow up as normally as possible. But if you are going to have a monarchy you have got to have a family, and the family's got to be in the public eye.' Because Andrew wasn't, the more scurrilous of the Continental press concluded that he must be deformed. He wasn't – quite the contrary – but he was excused the formative pressures of constant public exposure.

It was an interesting experiment in royal child rearing – and one fraught with hazards. Cosseted in a palace with an indulgent mother, a kindly nanny, a retinue of servants to command with the snap of his tiny fingers, without the steadying authority of a father who was often away on business, mixing only with the most carefully selected of playmates, Andrew's natural high spirits frequently crossed the boundary into high-handedness.

He was not always popular with the Palace staff, who sometimes saw him as an arrogant nuisance. It was a judgement that was to dog him into adulthood. As the Queen herself has admitted: 'He was not always a little ray of sunshine.'

To widen his experience, Andrew joined the 1st Marylebone Cub Pack. In practice that meant the Cub Scouts joining him in the grounds of Buckingham Palace to learn to tie knots and light fires.

At the age of eight he was dispatched to prep school – not to Cheam where Charles had been so unhappy, but to Heatherdown which happens to be conveniently close to Windsor. 'He will receive the same treatment here as all the other boys,' headmaster James Edwards insisted. And so he did – up to a point. His physical energy made him a 'natural boss'.

Andrew could still be rude when the mood so took him, however. Most of the Palace employees simply put up with it, confining their protests to the servants' quarters. One footman did not. When Andrew started being cheeky he lost his temper and hit the young prince hard enough to knock him off his feet. He then promptly handed in his resignation.

The matter came to the attention of the Queen. She refused to accept the resignation. She said that her son had probably had it coming to him, that he deserved it, and that the footman was on no account to be punished for Andrew's bad behaviour.

It should have been a chastening moment in Andrew's young life. If it was it was not immediately apparent and it was a still rumbustious youngster given to moments of irritating pomposity who followed his elder brother up to Gordonstoun.

There had been long and not always amicable family discussions as to the advisability of sending Andrew to that spartan school on the windswept coast of the Moray Firth.

Charles, sensitive and unathletic, had not taken well to the organized heartiness of the Gordonstoun regime. He had made few friends (and boys who made sociable overtures were jeered at by their contemporaries for 'sucking up'), had failed to make any of the school sports teams, and had been the butt of several well-worn jokes (such as at breakfast when someone would pick up his jar of marmalade, point to the By Appointment warrant on the label and say, 'Oh, Mummy approves').

The Queen Mother had not been in favour of Gordonstoun. Her family had always sent its sons to Eton and she felt that if her grandsons were to be educated at school rather than by the private tutors of royal tradition, then Eton offered the most rounded of educational choices. It is within walking distance of Windsor Castle, its facilities are of an exceptionally high standard, it is large enough to cater to even the most esoteric of enthusiasms and, as the alma mater of nineteen of today's thirty dukes, Eton also happened to be full of 'people like us', a not unimportant consideration to the Royal Family.

As usual, however, Philip got his way. He had been one of Gordonstoun's first pupils after the German educationalist Kurt Hahn fled the anti-Semitic ravages of the Third Reich and set up his school in Scotland dedicated to the principle that 'there is more in you' – that only by challenging youngsters to do what they did not believe they were capable of can the 'whole person' be developed. It is a theory Philip wholeheartedly subscribes to and it led to his founding the Duke of Edinburgh Awards. Eton, he argued, was for the socially privileged, unlike Gordonstoun which insists on community work as part of the curriculum and always takes in a quota of local children at greatly reduced fees (so does Eton, but only on the basis of academic excellence). Eton is also too exposed – the boys have to walk through the town to get from one class to another and it would have been ingenuous to have expected the Press to resist that temptation. Gordonstoun, on the other hand, is remote and inaccessible.

So Gordonstoun it was, first for Charles, then for Andrew. The school was never as tough as legend has it. The morning run rarely amounted to more than a gentle two hundred yard canter while the quick cold showers were preceded by a long hot one. And it was a lot softer by the time Andrew got there. Shorts had been replaced by long trousers. The daily Training Plan no longer included compulsory press-ups. Central heating had been installed 'and the swimming pool was heated to seventy-five degrees', the headmaster, John Kempe proudly declared. So much for the cold shower mentality.

The greatest change of all, of course, was that Gordonstoun had gone co-educational. In Charles's day any boy who dared form a relationship with a local girl ran the risk of expulsion. Now the romances were in-school.

Andrew quite enjoyed his time there. Like Charles, he took to acting, though with nowhere near the same startling brilliance. Charles played Macbeth, Andrew appeared in the farce *Simple Spymen* and as Lucifer in an alternative production backed by heavy metal rock music of Marlowe's *Doctor Faustus*. 'He had a strong, dominating voice that made him ideal for this,' one fellow cast member recalls.

He excelled at rugby, hockey and cricket, was a good squash and tennis player, and an excellent skier.

Academically he was not outstanding. He failed all but one of his 'O' levels first time round and, like Charles before him, went off to spend some time in the old Commonwealth before moving up to the Sixth Form. Lakefield College, seventy miles from Toronto in Canada added breadth to Andrew's experience. Adherents to the Gordonstoun system of self-reliance, Lakefield placed great emphasis on outdoor activities. Students spent much of their time fishing, playing ice-hockey (Andrew had taken the precaution of taking some lessons before he went) and outward bound-style expeditions into the wilderness of the North-West Territories ('bloody wet' was the Prince's verdict on the three hundred mile canoe trip he made through the black fly-infested hinterland of the Canadian north).

It is clear Andrew had a good time in Canada. The two terms he spent there were an ideal break for an athletically-inclined boy of his age from the rigours of exams. They also added to his developing reputation as a ladies' man.

At Gordonstoun he had enjoyed schoolboy flirtations with several fellow pupils; Jenny Wooten, Cally Oldershaw and, most notably, Kirstie Richmond.

In Canada he had a romance with Sandi Jones, the blonde daughter of a retired Colonel. Once back in Scotland he picked up where he left off. He renewed his acquaintance with Kirstie, the daughter of a widowed nurse, who was invited to weekend at both Sandringham and Buckingham Palace. He became friendly with Clio Nathaniels, the daughter of a Bahamas-based architect.

Not all the Gordonstoun girls were smitten, though. One attractive red-headed contemporary cruelly dismissed him as 'a man with a big bottom who laughed at his own jokes'. But he was generally popular with the opposite sex.

He was not so well regarded, however, by many of the boys. This was not entirely his own fault. Like all the royal children he was a victim of his own position. Under the system founded by

Kurt Hahn, titles are never used – pupils are all addressed by their surnames. Charles, however, was always called Charles and Andrew was called Andrew – titles in themselves.

Supposedly egalitarian Canada further complicated the issue. Terry Guest, the headmaster of Lakefield, recalled: 'Our main worry was what the hell we were going to call him. So we had a staff meeting and came up with a scheme. The boys would call him Andrew, the staff would address him as Prince Andrew, the governor would call him Sir, and the chairman of the governors alone would give him Your Royal Highness.'

The Queen and Prince Philip had insisted that Andrew was to be treated 'like everyone else'. He obviously wasn't. Helicopters arrived on the school lawn to fly him away. Aeroplanes of the Queen's Flight waited at the nearby Lossiemouth airbase to fly him down to London for the wedding of his sister. There was a detective always in attendance. There was a barrier between him and the other boys right from the start. It should not have mattered. Charles had faced the same problem and by the end of his time at Gordonstoun had learned to overcome it by the simple method of getting on with life and not standing on ceremony.

Andrew was not so adaptable. Sorting through the comments made by his contemporaries, it is clear that Andrew knew who he was – His Royal Highness Prince Andrew Albert Christian Edward, third child and second son of Queen Elizabeth II – and let everyone else know it too.

One fellow pupil called him just another poor little rich kid who 'didn't know whether he wanted to be a prince or one of the lads'. When assistant headmaster David Byatt asked a class what they planned to do when they left school, Andrew is alleged to have replied: 'It's all right for me – I've got a job to go to already.' It is hard to find any words of unqualified praise in the reams of recollections of his fellow pupils.

He made the outward gestures of joining in. He sneaked off to the wilderness behind Gordonstoun House to join some of the 'shades' for a clandestine cigarette even though he himself did not smoke. He wore Charles's old school sweaters – the height of Gordonstoun chic. He proudly wore a kilt, another bit of Gordonstoun peacockery. But in the final analysis Andrew was just a little too 'stuck-up' for his own good.

He made head boy of his house, Cumming House, but he was never made head boy (or Guardian as it is called) as his father and brothers Charles and later Edward were.

Nor were his examination results all that his parents might have hoped for. He eventually gained three 'A' levels, in History, English and Economic and Political Studies, but only with the lowest E grades. It was enough, however, to secure him entrance into the Forces. There was no discussion about that. He had been absolutely right when he had said to Byatt that he had a job to go to. As Andrew himself points out: 'What else could I do given the fact that I am a member of the Royal Family?'

There was talk of him joining the RAF. He had acquired a taste for flying as a member of the Air Training Corps at Gordonstoun, had learned to glide at the age of fifteen, and had done a parachute course at Number One Parachute Training Centre, RAF Brize Norton, three years later, earning his wings with a series of one thousand foot descents from a Hercules (on the first jump he got his feet twisted in the lines but managed to kick himself free).

In the end, though, he followed family tradition and joined the Senior Service, following his great-grandfather, grandfather, father and elder brother to the Britannia Naval College at Dartmouth.

At the age of twenty-one he qualified as a helicopter pilot and joined 829 Naval Air Squadron flying Sea Kings off the aircraft carrier HMS *Invincible*. He also developed a sailor's eye for a pretty face.

As the second son, he was not bound by the same restrictions as Charles and was able to mix with girls from a wider social spectrum. He dated Carolyn Seaward, the 1980 Miss United Kingdom, and entertained her to candlelit dinners at his apartment in

Buckingham Palace. He dated model Gemma Curry, carried on seeing Kirstie Richmond and Clio Nathaniels, took out actor Michael Caine's daughter, horsewoman Nikki, and courted Royal Ballet dancer Karen Paisey.

Andrew's relationships could end abruptly. When a romance was over, telephone calls were not put through.

One person whose calls were returned was Koo Stark. He was introduced to her early in 1982 by Ricci Lewis, former wife of Mayfair hairdresser Leonard and by then the companion of Charlie Young, one of the few real friends Andrew made at Gordonstoun.

Koo, the daughter of a minor Hollywood film producer, Wilbur Stark, is petite, charming, intelligent, capable of looking after her own interests, and was considerably more experienced than Andrew.

When Andrew met her she was living in Belgravia in the basement of a Chester Square house owned by Scodina Dwek, former wife of a professional backgammon player Joe Dwek, who went on to become an advisor to international financier Sir James Goldsmith.

Andrew introduced her to his family and they accepted her as they found her — for the intelligent, well-mannered young woman she is.

There were other and potentially far more dangerous clouds gathering on Andrew's horizon, however. In April, two months after he began his affair with Koo, the Task Force set sail for the Falklands. Britain and Argentina were in a state of undeclared war — and Andrew, stationed aboard the frontline carrier HMS *Invincible*, was ordered into battle. It was to prove the turning point in his life.

At the controls of his helicopter Andrew had proved himself a competent and conscientious officer. In the mess, however, the same old difficulties had come to light. He was still uppity, still always the prince, never quite mucking in the way he was expected to. It is said that when a senior officer walked into the mess one evening Andrew cheerily informed him, 'You can call me Andy.'

'And you can call me Sir,' the officer coldly answered.

The story may be apocryphal. The fact that it was repeated by so many naval officers is a measure of the regard, or the lack of it, in which he was held at the time by some of his shipmates.

But war is its own leveller. It makes no provision and takes no account of background or status. When the gunfire is real all men are frightened. Bravery is learning to cope with that fear. The adventurous become wary, the brash subdued, and the self-effacing discover sources of courage they never knew they had. Life is given new perspective and just to be alive is perspective enough – for a prince can die just as easily as an able-bodied seaman. Instantly, if he is lucky; messily, painfully, if he isn't.

'I was frightened, absolutely,' Andrew has recalled. 'Everyone was frightened, I'm almost certain. I think to a large degree if you're not frightened then you make a mistake. It is never more lonely than during the moments when you are lying down on the deck with missiles flying around and you are on your own.'

There was no question that Andrew would not accompany his ship into the combat zone. The Queen insisted: 'Prince Andrew is in the Navy and I am sure that he will fulfil whatever duty he is given.'

He was co-pilot aboard a Sea King helicopter flying decoy to the Exocet missiles the Argentinians were determinedly launching at the *Invincible*.

'The idea is that the Exocet comes in low over the waves and is not supposed to go above a height of twenty-seven feet,' he explained. 'When the missile is coming at you, you rise quickly above twenty-seven feet and it flies harmlessly underneath – in theory.' In practice it is terrifying.

His most harrowing moment was watching from the air the sinking of the supply ship *Atlantic Conveyor* by an Exocet intended for the *Invincible*. 'It was horrific. At the time I saw a 4.5 shell come quite close to us. I saw my ship, *Invincible*, firing her missiles.' The Prince's Sea King rescued three survivors.

On 14 June the Argentinian forces surrendered. Two days later Andrew landed in Port Stanley. Asked, 'Bet you wouldn't have missed the experience for the world,' he had the maturity to reply: 'I would have avoided it if I could. So would any sane man.' He was one of the lucky ones and he knew it – out of the 28,000 Britons who had sailed into action, 255 had died and 777 had been wounded.

Andrew acknowledged: 'I think that when I first came out, people were asking, you know, would I actually stay here until the end. I'm jolly glad I stayed here. I'm jolly glad I came here. I've learned things about myself that I never would have learned anywhere else. There were no favours for me on board because I was a prince. My life will change drastically now.'

He returned to Britain a hero, and renewed his acquaintance with Koo Stark. After a three-month tour with the ship back in the waters off the Falklands, he flew her off under the names of Mr and Mrs Cambridge for what he imagined would be a holiday of blissful relaxation on the Caribbean island of Mustique where his aunt, Princess Margaret, has a home. Travelling with them was journalist cum painter Jossy Grey and John Hatt, travel editor of *Harpers & Queen* magazine. When Andrew had invited Jossy and Hatt to join him, Hatt replied that he could not afford the air fares. That was promptly taken care of – the Queen paid. Jossy and Hatt are still friends of Prince Andrew and joined him at his thirtieth birthday celebration in the private room at Annabel's. Time, however, was running out for Koo.

The Caribbean holiday did not turn out to be the relaxed interlude everyone had been looking forward to. Andrew's life, from the point of view of how he approached it, had indeed changed. The public's idea of what a prince should do – and more particularly, whom he should be doing it with – had not. Newsmen spotted the couple on the flight out and photographers and reporters chased the pair day and night. Back in London the sleazy video shops were inundated with orders, and Koo's past in soft porn films was raked up. The tabloids had a field day and even the normally restrained BBC television news screened an excerpt from one of her films at the end of their Nine O'Clock News bulletin.

Prince Edward sprang to his brother's defence. He said: 'He came back from that holiday more drawn, more tired, than he did from three months at war. I think to treat someone who's just come back from serving his country like this is despicable.'

The Queen was upset, her husband furious and it was the beginning of the end of the affair. Telephone calls were no longer returned and Andrew disingenuously started insisting to his friends that there had never been anything in the relationship anyway, that it had never been anything more than a brief flirtation.

Shortly afterwards he found himself back in the Caribbean with the *Invincible*. The warship called in at Barbados. On shore leave Andrew met baronet's daughter Vicki Hodge. Vicki, a top model in the sixties, happened to be a little short of money at the time and the story of that brief encounter found its way into a Sunday newspaper. (It is interesting to note that Vicki made around £25,000 while Koo, who has never spoken about her friendship with Prince Andrew, has collected over £500,000 in various libel awards.)

Andrew admitted shortly afterwards: 'I am more cautious than I used to be.'

8

Romance

IT WAS IN THE SUMMER OF 1985 THAT SARAH FERGUSON received the invitation that would set in train the events that would quite literally change her life and for ever. It was sent, as is the form on such occasions, by the Deputy Master of the Royal Household, Blair Stewart-Wilson, and it requested the pleasure of her company at the Queen's house party at Windsor Castle during the week of Royal Ascot.

Sarah knew she was going to be asked. Her acquaintance with the Princess of Wales had developed into a close friendship and while the Windsor party is very much the Sovereign's private gathering, she enjoys the company of younger people and naturally enough sought the guidance of her daughter-in-law when she came to draw up her guest list.

Sarah was an obvious choice. The right age, the right background, and already on familiar terms with the Royal Family.

But if Sarah was excited by the prospect she was also a little nervous. Until twenty years ago Ascot house parties were stiff and exceedingly formal affairs, with guests invited for the entire week and every evening a white tie and tails affair. In keeping with the other changes in royal life, it is all rather more relaxed these days. The guests come and go and one or perhaps two nights is the usual length of stay. Dinner jackets have replaced full evening dress and the younger members of the family are encouraged to invite their own friends.

'Informality' is a comparative term, however, and even the most confident and usually self-assured of people can find themselves intimidated by the esoteric rites of royal procedure. Guests have to be quietly forewarned, for instance, to bring all the toiletries they are likely to require. Soaps are provided but as the Queen, like many ladies of her generation, never washes her own hair, something as simple as shampoo might be difficult to obtain; Windsor house parties work to a full schedule and the agenda does not allow for impromptu visits to the local chemist.

Clothes present another worry. It is considered ostentatious to arrive with dozens of suitcases. That means packing carefully with one eye on fashion and the other on England's changeable weather which can render an outfit ridiculous when the temperature drops to fifteen degrees overnight and the rains start lashing in. The secret, so seasoned guests point out, is interchangeability, with hats, gloves, shoes, handbags and tights co-ordinated with frocks of different weights.

It also helps to have a hint as to what the Queen might be wearing. Some years ago the Duchess of Sutherland appeared at the top of the staircase on her way into luncheon – to be greeted by the sight of the Queen at the bottom wearing the identical outfit. By the rules that dictate such matters, one of the women had to change – and with regal good manners it was the Queen who did the changing.

Given the differences in age and style, that was not a social hurdle Sarah was likely to encounter and, had there been any likelihood of a clash with Diana, then the two friends were capable of sorting it out beforehand. And as Carolyn Cotterell says: 'Sarah had led quite a jet set life so she had plenty of suitable clothes.' And if she didn't – and although Sarah and Carolyn, in all the years they shared, never once exchanged a skirt or frock as flatmates often do – then she could always borrow from the Princess, as she later did.

Having Diana on hand to show her the ropes also helped. 'And besides,' Carolyn recalls, 'she's a strong character who has a lot of confidence. Whereas I might be fazed by it all she wasn't.'

Even so, she was a trifle apprehensive when Paddy McNally drove her down the M4 to Windsor and let her off at the Castle's private entrance where she was met by a footman who took her luggage and one of the Queen's ladies-in-waiting who led her down seemingly endless corridors and upstairs to her room. There she was assigned a personal maid who did the unpacking, hung everything up and took away the clothes she felt needed pressing.

On the bedside table was a small card embossed with the Queen's cypher giving a list of the mealtimes and a table placement showing who was seated next to whom at lunch and dinner. The first thing that Sarah noticed was that she would be seated next to Prince Andrew.

That was not quite coincidence. They were the same age, unmarried, had known each other vaguely since childhood and, in Diana's mind, would make a well-matched pair at the dining table. The Princess, an incorrigible romantic, may even have been trying her hand at a little matchmaking, though to suggest that Diana was deliberately trying to marry off her brother-in-law overstresses her role in the events that followed. There was a note on the bedside table saying how the various guests would be arriving at the racecourse, either in open-topped carriages or in the large black Daimlers hired for the week. When Sarah walked into the Green Drawing Room at exactly a quarter to one for pre-lunch drinks no one – not Diana, and certainly not Andrew or Sarah – even considered the possibility that the following year she would be sitting in the carriage alongside the Queen Mother.

Sarah was already spoken for – and the man she was going out with had only just dropped her off – while Andrew was a serving naval officer with romantic interests of his own to be getting on with. The only obvious bond between them when they walked into the State Dining Room was an ambition to enjoy themselves, as best they could, in the time available.

Ascot lunches are quick and, by Royal standards, fairly simple. The women are already in their Ascot dresses, the men in morning coats. Protocol decrees that guests must divide their time between the person on either side and everyone has to be out and at the race track by two o'clock. An alignment of mood and emotion can render time irrelevant, however, and in less than one hour Sarah and Andrew had discovered a great empathy.

'We were made to sit next door to each other at lunch,' Andrew recalls.

'Yes,' Sarah elaborates. 'And he made me eat chocolate profiteroles which I didn't want to eat at all. I was on a diet.'

Andrew had playfully told Sarah to pile her plate high with the sticky chocolate pudding, promising that he would have some too. When it came to his turn to be served he waved it away. He recalls: 'I didn't have it so I got hit. It started from there.'

The rest of the day was spent at the races, popping in and out of the Royal Box, wandering through the Royal Enclosure. Sarah and Diana laughed and giggled and made remarks about the more outrageous outfits on display. And where Sarah went, Andrew went too. After tea – held at the back of the Royal Box at a long table that seats fifty – the Press and the television cameras stationed on a first floor balcony overlooking the entrance to the Royal Enclosure finally spotted the pair as they made their way past to the Paddock. They took little notice. Sarah was not out of Andrew's usual model girl mould and most reporters went no further than to record that he was in the company of 'Ronnie Ferguson's daughter'.

Only the *Sun* newspaper went for the romantic jugular. Under a headline announcing 'Andrew's Ascot Filly' it cheekily declared that 'the stunning Sarah had already left her mark, tell-tale flame-coloured hairs on the shoulder of his suit' – a remarkable feat of observation from the Press balcony.

But the *Sun*, as it turned out, was right. As Carolyn Cotterell recalls: 'When she came back from Ascot there were stars in her eyes. She was bowled over and didn't even know what was happening.'

Neither of Sarah's previous romances had been particularly rewarding or, eventually, very amusing. Paddy's work was now taking him away a lot and she often found herself going to cocktail and dinner parties on her own.

'I wouldn't say she was unhappy all the time,' says Carolyn, 'but I wanted her to be happy all of the time. When I could see that things weren't falling into place I longed to be able to say something . . . but you can't live someone's life for them.'

Sarah's friends agreed. There was a general consensus that she deserved a more settled relationship than the one McNally could offer her. They advised her that her affair with a high flyer like McNally was unlikely to end in marriage. Shortly after she started working for Richard Burton she had turned up unannounced at McNally's apartment in Lausanne. He was tired and less than pleased. It was not the reaction of a man who was looking for any permanence in his life.

There was still some life left in their romance, however. They continued to see each other for the next few months, McNally taking pleasure in his girlfriend's notoriety. She joined him on holiday in Ibiza at the hilltop home of Michael Pearson, son and heir of shipping and newspaper (the *Financial Times*) owner Lord Cowdray, and appeared in excellent spirits, water skiing, wind surfing, playing the fool and swimming in the pool which had a picture of Kali, the Hindu goddess of destruction, painted on the bottom by Willie Feilding, the artist cousin of the Earl of Denbigh.

Like the Verbier set, the Ibiza crowd is fast, sophisticated and possessed of a wit that can at times be biting. Millionaire Roger Middleton came down from Verbier for the summer. Popular Belgravia doctor Tony Greenburgh was a frequent guest at Pearson's luxurious eyrie, as was Lloyd's underwriter Rupert Deen and baronet Sir William Piggot-Brown's former partner Mim

Scala, a laid-back Sixties figure whose grandfather was the first winner of the Irish Sweepstake.

The Pearson crowd was McNally's crowd and, divorced from his first wife Fritzi, Michael was just starting his courtship of former MP John Cordle's daughter Marina.

Sarah and Marina became friends. They remain so now that Marina is married to Pearson and settled back in England with two children; Sarah is godmother to Emily, the youngest. The future Mrs Pearson was not party, however, to the romantic developments stemming from that luncheon at Windsor Castle. Who is going out with whom and why and for how much longer provides a bedrock of conversation in Ibiza as in Verbier as in any society. But when one of the parties involved happens to be a member of the Royal Family a code of silence takes hold. Girls who are quite happy to discuss openly their relationships with anyone else suddenly become tongue-tied when a prince enters the frame as if, by merely mentioning the name, the spell will be broken. Which it often is – the Prince of Wales, in his courting days, unceremoniously dropped several otherwise suitable young women after they made the mistake of mentioning their friendship with him.

For almost six months Sarah kept quiet about the nascent relationship with the Queen's second son.

'I don't think she knew and I don't think he knew quite what was happening,' Carolyn says.

The only person it seems who did was Princess Diana. The two women had met after polo at Cowdray Park, the estate in West Sussex owned by Pearson's father. Diana and Charles were in the early stages of their courtship and after the polo he took her back to the nearby Barrantes' home. Sarah happened to be there and while Hector and Charles discussed ponies and Susie hurried about making the tea, they started chatting. Their rapport was immediate and understandable.

Their backgrounds are similar. Diana is the daughter of an earl while Sarah numbers several dukes in her pedigree. They had interests and friends in common. The stratum of British society to which they both belong is close knit and interdependent. The friendships made at school provide the nucleus for later life and if people do not actually know each other, they are likely to know of each other. Sarah's great-aunt Jane, for instance, had married Sir William Fellowes, the Queen's long-time land agent at Sandringham, and Sir William's son Robert, now the Queen's private secretary, had married Diana's eldest sister, Jane.

Diana's brother, Viscount Althorp, has made reference to a further connection between the Spencers and the Fergusons. He claimed during a television interview with the NBC television network in the United States on the day of Sarah and Andrew's marriage that Ronald Ferguson had once proposed marriage to his mother, now Mrs Shand-Kydd.

'Absolute rubbish,' the Major insists, but the veracity of the tale is immaterial. To Diana, locked in her rarefied stratosphere, Sarah was 'one of us'.

Sarah had certainly enjoyed a more adventurous youth than Diana who came 'straight from nursery school' into marriage, as Charles's former valet, the late Stephen Barry, once caustically remarked. She had travelled and mixed freely and easily with people of different nationalities. She had worked for her living – she had an allowance, but as her father points out, only a 'very small one'. When Diana first met her she had experienced only one serious love affair – with Kim Smith-Bingham. Diana was around to see her be emotionally tempered by another – McNally.

If Sarah became 'streetwise' as her father succinctly put it, she still remained what she had always been – friendly, eager to please and to put people at their ease. There is no 'side' to Sarah – what you see is what you get – and Diana responded to her openness and her straight-talking enthusiasm. They became 'BFs' – upper-class slang for best friends – and Sarah was invited to the Royal Wedding the following year.

And when the new Princess of Wales found herself smothering in the claustrophobic cocoon of palace life, Sarah was one of the people she looked to for encouragement and support. She was a way out, a window into the carefree world of young, uncomplicated London life.

They started seeing a lot of each other. When Sarah went away she wrote. When she was back in England, 'Sarah was always batting off to have lunch with her,' Durden-Smith recalls. And sometimes in the most unroyal of places – the public cafeteria at the Harvey Nichols department store across the street from Durden-Smith's offices was a great favourite.

'We became very very good friends,' Sarah confirms.

Another close friend of the Princess's is her brother-in-law, Prince Andrew. She has known him since they were children together and used to share nursery teas at Sandringham. Diana was one of the children who lived on the estate who was invited to the Royal Family's New Year's Eve parties; she remembers dancing with him and kissing him under the mistletoe. The cook at Althorp, her father's country mansion, remembers teasing Diana because she did not have a boyfriend and Diana replying that she was saving herself for Prince Andrew.

As it turned out Diana saved herself for his elder brother. But she remained close to Andrew and the two used to amuse Charles (and sometimes irritate him) with their enjoyment of boisterous jokes and constant chatter.

The Queen used to complain that she had no control over her second son and would delegate the task of getting him to do what was required to Charles, who in turn would complain that he did not have any control over him either. But after the Falklands War a bond of respect grew between the two men. Andrew started introducing his girlfriends to Charles, and although he still preferred to do most of his entertaining in his own rooms at Buckingham Palace – much to the chagrin of the staff there who were used to having the time free – he became a not infrequent weekend visitor to Highgrove, the Wales' country home in Gloucestershire. And, after the encounter over the profiteroles, and with Diana's enthusiastic encouragement, Sarah

Ferguson started featuring ever more prominently in his plans.

It was a courtship that had to be conducted when and how opportunity allowed. He was a serving naval officer stationed at Portland. He had certain royal duties to perform including a visit to Canada. He had also become involved in photography and now had a book of his own work to promote.

Under the tutelage of the late Norman Parkinson and his Filipino–American printer, Gene Nocon, and with a lot of encouragement from his one-time girlfriend, actress turned photographer Koo Stark, photography had developed into Andrew's principal hobby. He took the trouble to learn the rudiments of black-and-white printing from Nocon. He enjoyed the artistic challenge. He made full use, as photographers often do, of the excuse it gave him to meet a host of very attractive young models and actresses, some of whom would appear in his book.

His relationship with Sarah was well on its way by now. But it was still a long way off a public announcement and the book, with its pictures of pretty girls that dovetailed neatly in with his reputation as a ladies' man, provided a convenient smokescreen.

He was interviewed on BBC Radio 4's *Woman's Hour* programme by Sue MacGregor. An experienced professional, she cannily left the question about his private life until the end.

Andrew replied hesitantly: 'I think there have been some people who jump to conclusions about girls. If I take a girl out to dinner I may never have met her before and if they take a photograph of me and it appears in the papers the next day, they tend to jump to conclusions rather more swiftly than perhaps they should.'

MacGregor then asked him if he would be looking for someone who would make a good naval wife. He assured her he had not had time to think about it.

'But,' he added, 'if I do find somebody then it is going to come like a lightning bolt and you're going to know it there and then. So it'll happen.'

Several years later Andrew's sentiments remained unaltered:

'The initial catalyst certainly comes like a thunderbolt,' he says. 'Everything comes into place and there's a channel that's opened up.'

It was all part of the game of evasion Andrew, like all his family, enjoys playing. So did the Princess of Wales who enjoyed acting as go-between and confidential cupid. She teased him, probing to discover his real feelings. She did not have to probe deep – he was making them plain enough.

Flowers and letters began arriving at the little house in Lavender Gardens. So did the telephone calls.

'When he first rang I couldn't quite believe it,' Carolyn recalls. 'He said, "It's Andrew here, Beckwith",' addressing her by a part of her maiden name. 'I was amazed he knew who I was – and that he was a real person! Fergie wasn't in at the time but he said he would call back when he came off watch.'

Sarah responded to the attention. 'If I told her she had had a call from HIM then the sun was shining throughout the week,' she says.

The calls and bouquets were not only for Sarah. Carolyn's romance with old Etonian Harry Cotterell, her future husband, was also progressing. A tall blonde old Etonian six years her junior, Harry ran an enterprising business – a personalized laundry service specializing in shirts which he collected and delivered on the back of his motor bike.

The royal attention was starting to make Carolyn nervous, however. She was worried that her flatmate's romance would soon find its way into the Press and she wanted no part in letting that particular cat out of the bag. So concerned was she that she even refused publicity for her own business, Exclusive Shopping, which, linked to an upmarket travel agency, helped provide a shopping advice service for visiting tourists. Carolyn and her partner Sally Settrington had established a good reputation for rooting out the unusual.

'We were often asked to find the oddest things,' she recalls. 'We were once asked to find a George III free-standing astral globe and we managed to find fourteen in one morning. On another occasion we had a client who was obsessed with the clothes of the Princess of Wales so we took her to every designer who had ever made her anything.'

The service had attracted the attention of the *Observer*'s award-winning feature writer Sue Arnold. Arnold asked for an interview. Convinced that this was simply a ruse to get some information on Sarah, Carolyn – to the annoyance of her partner – refused.

A few days later Exclusive Shopping was summoned to Blake's Hotel in Kensington by an Oriental lady who said she wanted some gifts for her Chinese aunt, her old father and her nephew. The 'Oriental lady' turned out to be Sue Arnold.

Says Carolyn: 'And she genuinely wanted to write about the shopping and it wasn't a back door to Fergie. She had no idea about Fergie.'

Nor did most of her friends, not for sure.

One person who did know what was going on was Paddy McNally – and he was a hard habit to break. The appearance of someone else on Sarah's romantic horizon had not changed his ideas on marriage, however, and that autumn Sarah finally made the decision to bring their relationship to an end. 'I gritted my teeth and swallowed hard,' she remembers.

There was a lunch and a dinner at the Capital Hotel and a couple of other false starts. At last she got it out and told him it was over.

'We were very close,' he said, 'but the parting was amicable. Now it is all over I wish her all the luck and the best in life.' It was a civilized conclusion to a romance that had lasted three years during which time Sarah had embraced all his family – his sons, his parents who live in retirement in a modern house in Marlow near the Thames, his friends. 'Any man who is with her has a fantastic girl,' Paddy added. They remain the best of friends to this day. Sarah continues to remember the birthdays of his sons, Rollo and Sean. McNally was a guest at her wedding – and by the Christmas of that year it was becoming clear that marriage was where Sarah's relationship with Andrew was heading.

'It just got better and better,' Sue Ferguson recalls. 'It completely changed Sarah because it had none of those break-ups or dramas. The more she got to know him the better it became.'

Sarah was now spending almost every weekend with Andrew. They joined a shooting party at Sandringham and then left for the Hertfordshire estate of Alistair Hadden-Paton, an old school friend of Andrew's from Gordonstoun. They spent most of the weekend inside his converted barn, only venturing out for a brief walk on Sunday when they were spotted by some estate workers. A call was made to one of the Fleet Street Sunday papers but the information was dismissed – Sarah, the news editor decided, was merely the cover-up for Andrew's real girlfriend.

From 18 December Andrew's boat HMS *Brazen* was docked at the naval base at Devonport and the couple were almost constantly together. They seldom went out, preferring dinners at Buckingham Palace, where a discreet footman would leave their food on a hot plate in the dining room of Andrew's second-floor apartment. It was six months since their Ascot meeting and the couple were in love.

Shortly before Christmas, Andrew and Sarah decided that their secret should be released to the outside world. The media had not forgotten Andrew and it amused him to see them on the wrong track, linking him to Princess Diana look-alike newscaster Selina Scott and anyone else that fitted what Fleet Street had decided was his type.

It was a game Sarah was tiring of. She wanted to tell her friends and because she was in love she wanted to tell everyone else too.

'We've decided,' she confided to Carolyn. 'It won't matter if people know.' That, amazingly, was easier said than done.

They went to an Elton John concert – Elton is an old acquaintance of Andrew's and played at his twenty-first birthday party

110

at Windsor Castle – and held hands. 'But nobody noticed – and there weren't any photographers!' Carolyn recalls.

On 23 December, however, Britain's tabloids finally caught up with the story. The *Daily Mirror* ran an exclusive story by their exuberant reporter James Whitaker. The headlines blazed 'Andy's Xmas Date' and read: 'An attractive redhead is set to join Prince Andrew for Christmas at Windsor Castle. She is Sarah Ferguson, the new love in Andrew's life and one of Princess Diana's best friends'.

Whitaker, one of the few public schoolboys employed in the popular end of the national press and the reporter who had first revealed Prince Charles's courtship of Diana, had got it right again.

The following day was Christmas Eve and Sarah drove in her blue BMW to Kensington Palace to deliver the Christmas presents she had carefully chosen for Diana, Charles and the princes, William and Harry.

She also had a gift for Prince Andrew and he had been buying presents for her. Just before closing time he slipped into Garrards the Crown jewellers. Diana had told him what Sarah wanted – a twisted Russian wedding ring made from three different coloured golds. Diana had one, Prince Charles had one, which he wore under his signet ring on the little finger of his left hand, and Sarah wanted one. Andrew walked in, ignored the glances of the other customers and asked for the managing director, Mr Summers, by name. He was shown a tray of rings, picked the one he wanted, and left with a big smile and a small parcel.

Sarah spent Christmas at Dummer in a state of agitated excitement. As usual her grandmothers were there and on Christmas Day they telephoned Jane in Australia and told her the news that Sarah was spending New Year with the Royal Family at Sandringham as the special guest of Prince Andrew.

'I got engaged on 30 December, and Fergie was already at Sandringham,' Carolyn remembers. 'Until then there hadn't been any Press near the house. But we had an engagement party at Harry's house and I had to drive to London. I parked my car outside and hurriedly went in.' The *Mirror* story had done the trick. When Carolyn emerged from Lavender Gardens she noticed a motorbike beside her car and when she started the engine, he started his too and drove along beside her all the way to Harry Cotterell's house on the Embankment.

'I was terrified,' Carolyn says. 'I had dyed my hair white so I could put a lavender rinse through it for Lavender Gardens and I had this strange white hair with black bits and I think the cyclist thought I was Fergie with a wig on. Every time I looked out of the window he was right there. But when I got out of the car he realized I wasn't her and just disappeared.'

Shortly afterwards a man approached Carolyn in the street and offered his congratulations. She smiled, thinking it must be a neighbour. He wasn't. It was another newspaper reporter.

Life in once sedate Lavender Gardens had become a commando course of chase and concealment. 'There were funny comings and goings,' Carolyn remembers, 'and strange people knocking at the front door.'

Every morning the two friends drove to work at the same time, carefully taking exactly the same route so that if they needed a getaway, they could change direction and lose their pursuers. 'We had to be clever,' Carolyn recalls. 'It was really amusing going to work with a cavalcade of five or six cars and a motorbike following us. But you never knew if it was going to work.'

It put something of a strain on Sarah's relationship with Andrew. As Carolyn says: 'They were always asking her if she was going to get engaged. How can you carry on a normal relationship when people want a story all the time?'

There wasn't long to go, however. On the weekend of 23 February 1986, four days after Prince Andrew's twenty-sixth birthday, Sarah Ferguson left her hairdresser Michaeljohn in Albermarle Street and caught the shuttle from Heathrow to Newcastle-upon-Tyne. She travelled under the assumed name of

Miss Anwell. Andrew's ship, meanwhile, had docked at Sunderland. The couple met up at Floors Castle, home of the Duke and Duchess of Roxburghe. The Press were about to get the story they were waiting for.

9

Engagement

OVER CHRISTMAS THE ROYAL FAMILY DISCUSSED PRINCE Andrew's romance with Sarah Ferguson. They had not initially thought of her as a candidate for marriage to Andrew, but when they considered it the idea of having her in the Firm, as Prince Philip calls it, looked a most attractive prospect. She came from a suitable background. She had mixed in the edges of the royal circle all her life and knew the ropes. She was down to earth without any trace of the snobbishness they so disliked, and she was probably the first girl Andrew had been serious about who could be considered remotely suitable.

Most importantly the two were deeply in love.

It seemed that almost everyone knew she was about to get engaged except Sarah herself. But the clues were there for everyone to see. She had been treated to certain very public gestures of acceptance by the Royal Family. An invitation to Sandringham for New Year, a February skiing trip with the Prince and Princess of Wales in Klosters, and when Andrew's ship, HMS *Brazen*, had docked in the port of London and Diana had taken Prince William to see him, she had asked Sarah to accompany them aboard.

'Just keep smiling,' she had hissed to her friend in a stage whisper as the cameramen approached. Sarah did. It was all part of her subtle royal training programme.

The Queen liked Sarah. They got along well. Their mutual

enjoyment of country pursuits, their love of dogs and horses, provided them with a common ground.

The Queen Mother liked her at once. 'She is so English,' she declared. The Queen Mother went further and said that any girl of twenty-six would have had previous boyfriends; it was perfectly natural and she thought Sarah would be ideal for Andrew. It was an important show of support because the Nation's Grand Mother can be quite cantankerous.

Prince Philip, when questioned later about his son's choice of bride said, 'I'm delighted he's getting married, but not because I think it will keep him out of trouble because, in fact he's never been in trouble, but because I think Sarah will be a great asset.'

Prince Charles agreed. 'I like Sarah very much. She's a good sort and frankly I think she'd be a great asset to Andrew and to the rest of us – that is, of course, if she'll have him!'

She would. But would he ask? And if so, when and where?

When Sarah arrived at Floors Castle, she still could not quite believe that Andrew was going to propose. Guy and Jane Roxburghe have been friends of the Royal Family for many years and both Andrew and his father Prince Philip, who stays at Floors during the carriage-driving competition, are old friends of this grand Scottish family and Andrew is godfather to the Rox-burghes' youngest son, Edward. Sarah had been invited to a house party at Floors before she became involved with Andrew. She had been there with him several times since.

Yet for all their immense wealth (the Duke is worth over £30 million, while Jane is the sister of the Duke of Westminster, the richest man in England with a fortune estimated in excess of £3000 million), their home is no palace of northern luxury.

'For a start we can't have many people to stay as there are not enough bathrooms,' Janie said. 'The attraction for Prince Andrew is the peace and quiet with no hassles. We usually invite a few other guests and there is lots of telly, fishing and photography.'

It was as relaxed and informal as any ducal home can be and Andrew, still an adventurous schoolboy by inclination, discovered his own private entrance – one of the rooms at the back has wooden steps which lead through a sash window. Originally intended as an entrance into the garden, it provided Andrew with a means of coming and going unannounced.

That weekend in February was not dissimilar to the others Andrew and Sarah had spent at Floors Castle during their brief courtship. They arrived – through the front door. They were given their usual adjoining bedrooms with four-poster beds so high off the ground you almost had to be an athlete to get into them. Fires blazed in the hearths. As important guests they had their own bathrooms and were not obliged, as some are, to run down icy corridors.

There were drinks and dinner and the light conversation of a country weekend. The Castle was swathed in wintry Gothic mist and as bedtime approached the snow started to fall outside. Just before midnight Andrew went down on both knees and asked Sarah Ferguson to be his wife.

Sarah was caught off-guard and, to cover her confusion, tried to make light of it. 'If you wake up tomorrow morning, you can tell me it's all a huge joke,' she said. But she allowed him to fill her glass with champagne and they drank a toast to their future.

In the morning Andrew repeated his proposal.

'It came as a complete surprise to her,' Carolyn says, recalling how Sarah described the weekend afterwards. 'I thought he would ask her – but she didn't.

'I was so happy for her – it was the first time she had ever been completely happy in a relationship.'

But although Andrew had asked and Sarah had said yes, they were not yet in a position to announce their engagement. They did not even tell their host and hostess. 'When they left,' Janie remembers, 'they said nothing and Sarah wasn't wearing a ring.'

By law Andrew could tell no one until he had officially asked permission of the Queen and obtained her consent to marry – and the Queen and the Duke of Edinburgh were not due back from their tour of Australia and New Zealand for another three weeks.

At the end of the weekend Sarah – again posing as Miss Anwell – sneaked into Newcastle airport to catch the evening flight to Gatwick. The false name confused no one. 'She didn't fool us in that fur head band, it was definitely Fergie,' one airport worker declared afterwards.

It was an exultant and exuberant Sarah who returned to Lavender Gardens, content to bask in the heady delights of true love before the responsibilities of the situation settled on her. She left her car parked all over London, collecting dozens of parking tickets, which dropped like early confetti through the letterbox at Dummer. She continued commuting to the little fourth-floor office in St George Street, Mayfair from Clapham and continued work on the book, *Palaces of Westminster*. It was almost impossible to work. The telephone was constantly ringing and if she had to get something done she was forced to put the answering machine on.

The Press were now camped on her doorstep every day, following her every move – to the café across the road, to lunch, to the hairdresser. Once her former boss William Drummond rescued her as she was walking down the street pursued by dozens of cameramen. He gave her a hug and quickly whisked her in through the back entrance of Sotheby's and out of the paparazzi's camera range.

In truth she found the attention exciting and flattering and she kept up a polite banter with the waiting newsmen.

'I'm just a normal working girl,' she protested. 'I do a full five-day week.' To the admiration of her future husband, she never let her composure slip.

'Sarah is very level headed,' Susie Barrantes says. 'She isn't the sort to just drift into situations that are going to put her under a lot of pressure without thinking about it. She's twenty-six, but there's a much older and maturer head on her shoulders.'

However mature she may have been, Sarah has always been

a great talker. She was just not used to keeping her own counsel, especially when the subject in question – her engagement – was something she wanted to shout from the roof tops. She wanted to be able to tell her friends what was happening before they read about it in the papers.

'I thought something was up because she kept losing weight,' Clare Wentworth-Stanley says, recalling the beginning of the romance. 'But she kept a very low profile.'

Playboy Dai Llewellyn, whose daughter Arabella is one of Sarah's godchildren, remembers going to see his estranged wife, the Duke of Norfolk's niece, Vanessa, at her country home and finding Sarah there. 'I had no idea and treated her as I always would, slapping her round the shoulder and asking about her love life. When I got a slightly cold look from Vanessa, I shut up and assumed something had gone wrong. Fergie never said a word.'

On the weekend of 15 March, immediately after the Queen's return from Australia and New Zealand, Andrew arranged to see his mother at Windsor Castle. She already knew what he was going to say and she readily gave her consent.

'She was overjoyed,' Andrew recalled. 'Very pleased and beyond that what else is there? Just that of a delighted parent.' Andrew had already spoken to Major Ferguson, something he found 'fairly nerve-wracking'. The two men had met at the top of the Long Walk at Windsor by the statue of the copper horse.

'We had a rendezvous on the Saturday,' the Major recalls. 'We talked for about twenty minutes. It was short and sharp.'

The following day, while Andrew was performing an official engagement at the All England Badminton Championships at Wembley, Sarah had lunch with her future mother-in-law, the Queen. She then drove to Dummer where she paused for a cheery word with the posse of waiting pressmen, and went inside to tell her stepmother Sue the news.

'Sarah came home on Sunday and told us that Prince Andrew had asked her to marry him,' Sue Ferguson said. 'I wanted to break open the champagne there and then. Sarah told us we mustn't until it was made official on Wednesday. She was terrified even telling us in case something would happen.'

Sarah had already told her mother. She now telephoned her sister Jane at her outback home in Australia. Jane, after suffering two miscarriages and the death after one day of another baby, had at last given birth to a daughter called Ayesha.

Her father had already warned her, whilst on a visit to the Antipodes with Princes Charles, that something was in the air and she had received several excited calls from her sister, telling her of the hundreds of cameramen who pursued her all over London.

Jane says: 'Gosh, one's first impression is, "How lucky, she'll never have to wash her clothes or do any ironing". Then, when it starts to sink in, it is a bit overawing.'

Because Tuesday the eighteenth was Budget Day, it had been agreed with Downing Street that the announcement of the engagement would be postponed until the following day.

It was a delay that was now becoming fraught with embarrassment and, on Sarah's pleading, Andrew agreed that, despite the risk, they had to tell their closest friends. One of the first calls was to her old school friend, Clare Wentworth-Stanley, who was on a skiing holiday.

'We were in Méribel,' Clare remembers, 'and the telephone rang. It was Fergie and she said, "I have something to tell you". When she told me, I couldn't believe it. My first thought was "I'll never see her again, help she's going."'

Janie Roxburghe remembers: 'I was in Barbados when the nanny back at Floors phoned me and said the world's press were on the doorstep. Ten minutes later the phone rang again and this time it was Andrew and Sarah on the line to tell me the good news themselves. They were both bubbling over with joy.'

The next couple of days were madness for Sarah, but she still turned up at her office on Monday morning, pushing through the ranks of photographers. In time-honoured family tradition,

Ronald Ferguson, who was due to fly to Australia on the Wednesday to see his new granddaughter, took Sarah for lunch in the Causerie at Claridges. It was something he had always done on special occasions and when Sarah and Jane were children he would take them there for treats, after they had been to the dentist and sometimes on their birthdays. Then they used to have a competition to see how many times they could go around the laden buffet on the circular table in the centre of the room.

'We used to go round once, come back and go round again,' Jane recalls. Sarah could barely make it round once this time.

That night Sue Ferguson stayed at Sarah's Clapham home, helping her pack and load the car with the belongings and souvenirs she had collected in the five years she had shared with Carolyn.

'I cleared her room and brought everything she didn't need back to Dummer,' Sue remembers. Then the two women met for lunch at the Westbury Hotel, where Sarah introduced Sue to the press as 'my wicked stepmother' – blissfully unaware that at that moment reporters were rifling through the rubbish bin outside Lavender Gardens. They were in luck; one reporter found a crumpled piece of paper covered with Sarah's doodles. They showed a list of the clothes she would be wearing for the week and, in the bottom left hand corner, a sketch of the engagement ring which Sarah had drawn when she was describing it to Sue – a large central ruby surrounded by oval-shaped diamonds, which, as Sue discovered when she saw the engagement interview on television the following day, was an accurate description.

'I helped in the design,' Andrew said proudly. Several jewellers, including Collingwood and Garrard, had been to Buckingham Palace with a selection of rings. None had appealed so Garrard, who had supplied both Princess Diana's and Princess Anne's engagement rings, were asked to make something up. It was ready within the week, in time for the announcement on Wednesday 19 March.

A royal engagement is a public affair, never more so than

in the media-conscious, money-conscious eighties. The British public are Royalists for the most part but they like to see what they are paying for and they wanted to see Sarah. Michael Shea, the Queen's silver-haired press secretary, duly organized for Andrew and Sarah to do a radio interview followed by a television interview with the accredited court correspondents. They would then appear on the front lawns of Buckingham Palace for the official photocall.

At the appointed time the two court correspondents, Anthony Carthew from ITV and Michael Cole from the BBC, were ushered into a downstairs room. The lights and microphones had been set up. There was some trouble with reflection from an ornate mirror over the fireplace and Sarah admitted she had woken with a headache. Carthew and Cole had worked out the questions they wanted to ask and ran them by the hesitant Shea who immediately made some objections to the question about the romance. Experienced reporters know how to get around small problems such as not being allowed to ask the key questions and when they were ushered into the room they chatted casually to make the couple relaxed.

'What did you have for breakfast?' they asked Sarah. 'Sausages, I think,' she answered and the stage was set.

The interview took about twenty minutes. The BBC considered it their best royal interview ever. Andrew and Sarah were relaxed and playful and their loving banter made a refreshing change from the studied formality that characterizes so many of these events.

'We are a good team,' Sarah claimed. 'Very, very good friends.'

It was Sarah's own friends who helped her over the next few months as the pressures of a life alien to her independent spirit yet so exciting built up and the wedding date, which had been set for 23 July, came closer. Instead of hiding herself away in the vast greyness of Buckingham Palace as Lady Diana Spencer had done, Sarah kept on working. 'I enjoy my work enormously,' she said, although the media attention forced her to move her offices

As a child, Sarah spent her holidays on the beaches of Southern England, where she would use her imagination to build cars, airplanes and even horses out of sand. Here she is starting to build a sand car for herself and Jane to ride in. *(Ferguson family album/Obee)*

One o'clock – two o'clock– three o'clock? Sarah blows the petals off a dandelion as she plays the childhood game of telling the time. She was tall for her age and her bright red hair grew in big, unruly curls, which reminded her mother of "the coils of a spring." *(Ferguson family album/Obee)*

The look of total happiness. Sarah Ferguson on the arm of her father as they stand at the altar of Westminster Abbey. She admitted later that she was nervous and her hands were shaking, but the special bond she has with her Dad helped her overcome any nerves.
(Copyright © Alpha London)

Sarah Ferguson, "my little sister" as Jane Makim called her, is now the Duchess of York and pauses for a moment with her new husband on the steps of Westminster Abbey. Her father admitted he had never seen her look so beautiful and everyone agreed Lindka Cierach's dress was quite stunning.
(Copyright © Photographers International Ltd.)

With her great friend the Princess of Wales on the balcony of Buckingham Palace during the fiftieth anniversary of the Battle of Britain fly-past. Princess Beatrice enjoyed herself, too, playing with her mother's black gloves, dancing to the band and chatting to Prince Harry. *(Copyright © Alpha London)*

Yves Saint-Laurent's stunning ballgown teamed with some equally stunning diamonds show the Duchess at her most glamorous for an evening engagement. *(Copyright © Alpha London)*

Sarah has always had great patience with young children and during her tours the visits to hospitals, homes and orphanages are part of the agenda she enjoys most. Here in Australia she tries to get a shy little girl to speak to her.
(Copyright © Alpha London)

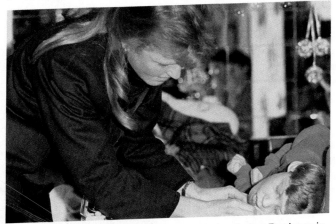

During the working day described in this book, the Duchess is sympathetic with a sad little patient in one of the homes she visits. These trips are harrowing, but Sarah is positive in her approach and turns her emotion to doing something useful rather than just looking on. *(Copyright © Alpha London)*

Sarah at the controls of her fixed wing Piper. You can just see the gold "S" for Sarah painted on the side of the plane.
(Copyright © Photographers International Ltd.)

Sarah with her flying instructor, Colin Beckwith. Sadly, since becoming a mother for the second time, she finds it hard to make much time for flying.
(Copyright © Photographers International Ltd.)

Sarah and Princess Eugenie, who is placid and good and looks very like her mother as a child. *(Copyright © Alpha London)*

The family group, with Prince Andrew left holding the baby. The Duke is not exactly a househusband, but he loves helping with the children at bathtime and reading to them at bedtime. *(Copyright © Alpha London)*

An excited and happy Princess Beatrice claps her tiny hands with glee as she watches the horses during the Windsor Horse Show. Beatrice has always been a happy child and seldom cried even when she was tiny. *(Ferguson family album)*

Sarah sports her new hairstyle on a visit to Inverness in 1991. *(Photo by Dave Chancellor; Copyright © Alpha London/Globe Photos)*

from the fourth floor of St George Street to the second floor of Buckingham Palace (a move, incidentally, which amused her boss, Richard Burton, who frequently popped in to see the young woman who was about to marry a prince but was still his employee).

She continued to enjoy her job. It kept her occupied, gave her a sense of individual achievement. It also provided her with some very necessary income. 'Just because you marry a member of the Royal Family, it doesn't make you rich,' Ronald Ferguson says.

At first hearing, that remark sounds absurd. The Windsors are the richest family in the world. Yet for all their riches the Royal Family is notoriously parsimonious with their money. Because they never have to use it – and the Queen really doesn't carry it – it has no real relevance to their lives and they have no real understanding, in the day to day sense, of its value or what it means to other people. Their fortunes are locked away in trust funds which are administered by professional advisors. If they want something they simply order it and leave the paying to their staff. Andrew is certainly 'rich' – the Queen established a sizeable trust fund for him at the time of his sister Anne's marriage – but not in the cash sense and if Sarah wanted to have lunch at Scott's restaurant with a girlfriend she had to pay for it herself.

The telephone at Buckingham Palace did not come out of Sarah's account, however, and she was constantly on the line to her mother in Argentina.

'We talked about everything,' Susie remembers. 'We had a lot of telephone calls. A lot.'

Susie was also being chased by the media – an experience totally new to her. Just before Sarah's engagement Susie and Hector were in Palm Beach when a film crew came to interview her.

'I'm not nearly as quick as Sarah and I was thinking to myself, "What should I say . . . what should I be saying . . .",' she recalls.

Asked where Andrew and Sarah originally met, Susie replied

she supposed they had met on the polo ground, jokingly adding, 'Doesn't everyone meet at polo?'

It was a remark she has regretted ever since. 'I said it, but I did not mean it to come out as if I was the biggest ya-boo snob and the only thing in the world was polo. After that I decided that was it, and I preferred not to say anything to anybody.'

If Susie wasn't talking, everyone else was and the three months leading up to the wedding passed in a whirl of chattering social activity. Everybody wanted to see Sarah and everybody wanted to invite her out. As she was not yet Prince Andrew's wife she was not entitled to any staff of her own so she enlisted the help of one of her girl friends, the efficient Jules Dodd-Noble, to help her with the mammoth task of sorting out the wedding list.

'I shudder to think,' Jules recalls, 'but I did it on the typewriter. Every time the list changed I had to re-type it.'

Sarah and Andrew were able to invite about six hundred people each. Jules worked on Sarah's list which, given her wide circle of friends and relations, had to be pruned and re-pruned before it finally went to the Lord Chamberlain's office complete with all the current addresses. The wedding list was dealt with by another part of the office, involving Andrew's staff, but the thank-you letters and the selection of possible gifts were done by Sarah.

'We had meeting after meeting at Buckingham Palace,' Jules remembers. 'I helped her set up an office: it was just me helping and we had so much to do we didn't know where to start.'

There were other celebrations going on at the same time. Her former flatmate Carolyn married Harry Cotterell, wearing a Lindka Cierach dress of white lace and there was the christening of her god-daughter, Jane's daughter Ayesha, at Dummer.

It was the first time for over ten years Susie Barrantes had been back to her old marital home and the atmosphere was tense. Ronald Ferguson glared at his ex-wife and she glared at him and everyone smiled sweetly at Jane, wearing one of Sue Ferguson's hats, and clutching the baby while Sarah tried not to steal the show as godmother.

When a member of the Queen's immediate family marries, the invitations are issued on behalf of the Queen by the Lord Chamberlain and the organization and costs of the event are divided between the taxpayer and the Queen. So Ronald and his wife Sue decided to hold a garden party for the people of Dummer village, to which Andrew and Sarah would be invited, and a dinner dance for Sarah's hundreds of friends along with Ronald's polo playing cronies, Sue's friends and the large Ferguson-Wright family.

Ronald decided to hold the dance in a marquee in the centre of Smith's Lawn where the Cartier Polo International would be held the weekend after the wedding. The organization was divided between Ronald and Sue and once Sarah had presented them with a list of the people she wanted to ask, they forged ahead with the plans. Sue Ferguson laboriously wrote the names on almost eight hundred invitations herself and carefully arranged the placements for dinner. Every member of the Royal Family was to be there along with America's First Lady, Nancy Reagan. The Americans saw it as a security nightmare. Ronald Ferguson did not.

'I had tremendous faith in all the people who were behind the scenes. It was a massive security operation and the Thames Valley police were fantastic,' the Major remembers. The Americans did not at first agree. They asked that Nancy Reagan be accompanied by twelve security men. Since the Queen was to arrive from Windsor Castle with a single motor-cycle outrider, Ronald Ferguson foresaw problems. He was right . . .

There is nothing the Queen dislikes more than the presence of too many obvious security men and knowing this, Ronald Ferguson was determined not to accede to the American request. In a heated altercation he informed the head security man: 'This is a private party and a personal invitation from His Royal

Highness the Prince Andrew. It is not extended to twelve body-guards.'

The Secret Service man protested. 'In that case,' he said, 'Nancy Reagan would not be able to come.'

'In that case,' the Major replied in a voice used to issuing orders (he had, after all, once commanded the Sovereign's Escort and had once fined a drummer two days' pay for idleness when he had missed two beats at the Queen's Birthday Parade), 'she needn't.'

'They finally settled on two,' the Major says. 'One at the door and one inside.'

With that situation sorted out, the Fergusons were able to get on with the business of enjoying themselves. The whole evening was organized with military precision and every detail remembered. Sue Ferguson's artistic eye had seen to the flowers and each table had a basket of sweetpeas and roses tied with a ribbon and decorated with a large velvet bumble bee to represent the Ferguson coat of arms. The menus were printed with Sarah's coat of arms and the balloons had the initials 'A' and 'S' and the date, 21 July 1986, printed on them.

The discotheque was run by Sarah's friend, Angus Gibson. It was decorated like a ship. The tented ceiling was set with tiny star pricks of light and the central pivot of the canvas overhead was disguised by a ship's wheel surrounded with hurricane lamps. Around the walls were life belts initialled 'HMS Andrew' or 'HMS Sarah'.

'All the little extra details that Sue had organized were perfect,' Ronald Ferguson remembers. By way of a thank-you he gave her a pair of earrings to wear that night, which he left with a note at the house of the Ranger, Ronald Wiseman, in Windsor Great Park, for Sue to find when she went there to change before the dance.

Sue had spent days working out the seating plan for dinner. Each circular table seated ten people. Sarah was seated with Andrew on one table, Jane on another with her father and the Queen. Alex Makim, in a hired dinner jacket, sat with the grandmothers, Doreen Wright and Lady Elmhirst. His table was one person short.

The missing person was Princess Michael of Kent. When Prince Michael arrived, he was on his own. He had no explanation for his wife's absence, only an apology.

After dinner the main body of the guests arrived – celebrities such as Elton John, Billy Connolly, Pamela Stephenson and Chris de Burgh, skiing chums from Verbier, friends from school days, ex-army polo players, members of the fast Chelsea set. Sarah, in a pastel-pink Gina Fratini gown with flowers in her hair, stayed close to Andrew as they threaded their way through the crowd of guests, kissing and shaking hands. She nodded hellos, exchanged jokes and proudly showed off her fiancé to her friends, most of whom had never met him before.

'He gets on with her friends,' Clare Greenall says. 'He has done right from the beginning. He has a good sense of humour and he's full of fun – you just have to allow him to feel relaxed and he's away. We are all very natural with him.'

Andrew is virtually teetotal. He only drinks when there is a toast to the Queen, and then only the smallest amount of wine or champagne, mixed with Perrier water. Without alcohol to relax him he can sometimes appear stiff and uncomfortable at parties – as can his father-in-law. He had no problem that night, however, as he escorted his future wife through her 'army' of friends.

While the Queen danced with practised precision on the main dance floor, the younger and livelier guests were in the discotheque.

'One doesn't normally enjoy one's own parties,' the Major says, 'but I did enjoy that, even though it did start to pour with rain and got a bit steamy inside. Everyone was in tremendous form. It was a terribly happy event.'

The lead-up to the wedding was one long round of parties and why not? Sarah was popular with the media, she had accepted the jibes about her figure in her usual good-humoured way. She attended openings, galleries, hospitals, fêtes, and even made a trip to Belfast to open a block of the City Hospital.

'Frontline Fergie' shouted the headlines above stories that began, 'Shrugging off the danger, she made a surprise visit to Ulster with her husband-to-be Prince Andrew . . .'

The public couldn't get enough of her, back then in the first flush of a new royal romance. She was spontaneous and fun. And there was more fun to come.

INTERLUDE

The Secret Policewomen's Ball

IT WAS DONE IN INNOCENCE, WITHOUT MALICE AND CERTAINLY without forethought. But when the future Duchess of York and the future Queen of England dressed up as policewomen and, accompanied by four friends, marched into the smartest nightclub in Europe, they caused a sensation beyond anything they expected.

With Andrew out on his stag night, Sarah and Diana decided to hold a party of their own. Sarah, discussing the plans for the evening a few days earlier with Jules Dodd-Noble, suggested a picnic. To the Buckingham Palace chefs a picnic is a moveable banquet.

It was decided to hold their feast in the Belgravia flat of Janie Roxburghe. And to try and ensure that Sarah made it there without being recognized, wigs were organized. As Jules and Sarah went up to Janie's apartment they put them on and joined their waiting friends – their hostess, the Duchess of Roxburghe; Catherine, then married to Prince Charles's long-time friend and former equerry, Sir Winston Churchill's grandson, Nicholas Soames; and the Princess of Wales.

Laughing and joking and sipping champagne, the five got started on their picnic supper: smoked chicken, honey-glazed ham, thin slices of rare beef, salads, strawberries and cream.

They discussed Andrew's stag night. They knew the guest list which included Charles, Guy Roxburghe, David Frost, Elton John and comedian Billy Connolly. They also knew the venue – Aubrey House in Holland Park which, as well as boasting one of the most magnificent gardens in London, had the advantage of being completely surrounded by a high wall with only one entrance which that night was heavily guarded by both plain-clothed and uniformed policemen.

Inevitably the talk turned to disruption. It might have been possible had they been able to slip in through a side door but there wasn't one.

After supper Pamela Stephenson arrived, dressed up in full policewoman's disguise down to the dark stockings and the regulation lace-up shoes, in preparation for the attempted gate crash. Her companion, Renalte, then the wife of singer Elton John, was likewise attired. There was a lot of giggling as they decided that Diana and Sarah should wear the extra two uniforms Pamela had brought with her.

By about 10.30 p.m. the girls were ready to unleash them-selves on an unsuspecting London. Having decided that Aubrey House was unassailable, they settled on Annabel's nightclub in Berkeley Square. Jules sauntered into the outer bar and ordered some drinks as if it were the most natural thing in the world to arrive in a nightclub accompanied by four giggling policewomen.

It was the height of the London season and the bar was crowded with party-goers stopping by for a late nightcap. One of them, restaurateur Nicky Kerman, quicker than most, recognized Sarah and ignoring her whispered 'Shhh' offered to buy the 'policewomen' a drink.

'I don't drink on duty,' the Princess of Wales replied, shaking with laughter as Kerman went ahead and ordered glasses of champagne and orange juice.

At this point a visiting American walked up to the Princess

of Wales, looked her straight in the eye from just a few inches away and said, 'Gee, you policewomen, I suppose you're here because of the IRA.' In all, the incident had lasted ten minutes but the joke was over. It was time to go.

Heading back to Buckingham Palace their detectives heard over the walkie-talkie that Andrew's party was breaking up and that he was also heading home. It was another opportunity to test the success of their disguises and they told the duty policeman that they would take charge of the sentry box. As Prince Andrew came into view, the Palace gates swung shut.

From Andrew's point of view from behind his steering wheel something was clearly wrong. He braked. Police-driver trained, he slammed into reverse gear and with tyres screeching, tore backwards, swung the car round and headed off at speed around the Victoria Memorial.

The policeman with Andrew started shouting into his walkie-talkie, poised to go on red alert. A few hushed words with control assured him nothing was really wrong and Andrew headed the car back to the gates again.

This time it was opened by two bewigged 'policewomen' who stopped him as he drove in. The wigs were lifted to reveal Diana and Sarah. Twenty-four hours later the story was front-page news.

It was Sarah's last bachelor fling. Seven days later she married Prince Andrew and became the Duchess of York.

10

The Dress

IN A FLUSH OF BRIDAL EBULLIENCE, SARAH DECLARED ON THE eve of her wedding that there would 'never be a dress to match it'. It was a boast its designer, Lindka Cierach, had done her best to justify.

Born of a Polish father and an English mother, Lindka was brought up in Lesotho, the one properly independent homeland in southern Africa, 'and lived in the bush until I was five years old'. From that rural springboard she progressed via English boarding schools, a brief spell in Italy and nine months in Paris to a job in the promotions department of *Vogue* magazine. There her talent for making her own clothes ('My mother had some training as a tailor and her talent was very inspirational to me,' she recalls) was first recognized and after a two-year course at the London College of Fashion she had set up in business as a designer.

By the time Sarah came to her she was working out of a small house in Fulham, catering to a keen but not very large clientele drawn from the West London set of upper-middle-class young ladies.

'I developed my business through making dresses for friends,' she says. By chance, one of those friends happened to be Sarah's housemate, Carolyn Cotterell.

'I met Fergie from time to time,' Lindka says, 'but she was seldom in this country so when her engagement came up I had no idea she was considering me. The day after the engagement I was surprised when she rang up,' Lindka recalls. 'I thought, "How nice of her to ring", never imagining she was going to ask me to submit sketches for the wedding dress. But that was exactly what she did.'

She had told Sarah that she could not design 'cold' something as personal as a wedding dress. 'There has to be a liaison between the designer and the wearer,' Lindka explained. She was told to see what she could do, and spent the following weekend in a fluster of excitement and trepidation producing sketch after quickly discarded sketch. Gradually a theme emerged; with a professional's eye to the occasion, Lindka had started off by picturing how the dress's train would look from an aerial television shot. But it was no more than a theme and one that offered many variations.

Instead of the long conversations about styles and alternatives she had expected, at the next call Lindka received from Sarah there was no discussion. Most unusually for a bride-to-be – but very much in character – she did not ask to look at the sketches. She simply ordered the designer: 'Go for it!'

Says Lindka: 'It was wonderful to have so much confidence from her. I think she was under so much pressure that she simply did not have the time to worry about whether she had made the right choice, it was too traumatic. So she relied on her instincts.' So Lindka went for it.

The two met in the attic studio in Lindka's Fulham home. 'We bashed out a few ideas and finally settled on two shapes,' Lindka says. 'After I had done the first one I realized it wasn't right and settled on the latter. We discussed fabrics and styling and because of all her own pressures she let me do virtually what I wanted.' Cost was a secondary consideration (Lindka even then was charging upwards of £2000 for a bridal gown).

The first task was to develop a theme for the beadwork on the train, all seventeen and a half feet of it, which would be seen at its best from the television cameras placed high in the rafters of Westminster Abbey. In consultation with the Herald at the College of Arms it was decided to incorporate the thistles and bees from Fergie's newly created coat of arms into the design, with hearts, waves and anchors to represent Sarah's love for the sailor prince.

Over the next four months the dress started to take shape in an atmosphere of friendly and remarkable informality: when the veil blew out through the attic skylight of Lindka's studio, an assistant was dispatched to clamber on to the roof to fetch it back.

Despite such occasional mishaps, the making of the dress was not a particularly trying task. Lindka, a specialist in delicate beadwork and embroidery, enjoyed her work while the effervescent Sarah proved a reliable sitter. Despite being under 'a great deal of stress', she maintained her weight, allowing the designer to work to 'a shape that remained fairly static'.

Less than twenty-four hours before the actual wedding, however, a major problem presented itself.

'We decided to take the dress for its first walk the afternoon before the wedding,' Lindka recalls. 'My sitting room was exactly the length of the train so there was absolutely no way we could walk in it there.' The dress was accordingly secreted in a waiting car and driven round to Buckingham Palace. It was taken up in the ancient lift to Sarah's apartment on the second floor. She put it on and set off down the long corridor.

As soon as she started walking Lindka knew that something was amiss. 'The train started flipping off and going to one side,' she says. 'I knew the dress was extremely well balanced so I could not for the life of me figure out what was wrong.'

She turned Sarah round and walked her back the other way. The same thing happened. The train kept pulling away to one side. She suddenly realized: the pile of the carpet was catching the train and pulling it off line. If that happened on the red carpet at the Palace it would certainly happen when Sarah walked down the long blue carpet that led to the altar in Westminster Abbey.

There was only one hope and a frantic message of instruction was dispatched to the Abbey. That done, Sarah changed and went round to spend her last bachelor night at Clarence House.

And when she set off down the aisle the following day the train followed directly behind her. The Abbey cleaners had fastidiously vacuumed up and down the carpet all that previous night until the pile stood in upright perfection.

11

Wedding Day

'AT ABOUT MIDNIGHT DAD AND I DROVE DOWN THE MALL just to see what was happening,' Jane Makim recalls. 'It was overawing. There were so many people lying there, some asleep, but most of them awake. I thought, "Gosh, they're all waiting to see Sarah . . ."'

The crowd had been gathering all day, a trickle that became a stream that became a flood, and by nightfall a hundred thousand people had been drawn in to the heart of London.

They came from all corners of the British Isles, from the old Empire and the new Commonwealth and lands without legal connection, now or then, to the British monarchy; an amorphous swirl of creeds and colours and nationalities united in celebration.

London is brought to life by these rites of passage. The mood lightens, spirits rise. There is a feeling of expectancy in the air and even die-hard republicans feel unexpectedly cheerful as they witness the ancient spectacle of the marriage of a monarch's son. It is only a wedding but it is more than that. The Victorian constitutionalist Walter Bagehot called it society's 'theatrical show' and its ritual and pageantry celebrate hope and it was a mood the Fergusons found impossible to resist. It would have been extraordinary if they had.

By royal tradition Sarah spent the night with the Queen Mother in Clarence House, her London residence. The Princess of Wales called by to see her. From her bedroom she could hear the crowds singing her name and her own family formed part of the chorus. As midnight approached, the Fergusons at different times went out to mix with the people gathering to witness the marriage of one of their own.

The Fergusons were staying at the Belgravia Sheraton on the other side of Hyde Park Corner but as Sarah's stepmother, Susan, recalls, 'We felt rather claustrophobic in the hotel — we wanted to be part of the excitement and soak up the atmosphere.'

At first the Major, however, did not. He was tired and, underneath his drilled military demeanour, just a little over-wrought. He had fallen asleep during dinner and insisted that he had to get to bed so Sue set off with two friends. They drove the three-quarters of a mile to St James's Park and then, on Sue's prompting, parked and set off on foot down the Mall.

Her friends kept pointing at Sue and teasingly asking people, 'Do you know who this is? It's Sarah's wicked stepmother!' The crowd waved and hurrahed and offered her drinks which she took.

'We made so many friends,' Mrs Ferguson remembers.

Further along they came upon a party from the Fergusons' home village in Hampshire holding up a big sign that declared, 'We are from Dummer' which they would wave when the Glass Coach bearing Sarah to Westminster Abbey passed in front of them twelve hours later. Among the group were the two daughters of Patti Palmer-Tomkinson who two years later would be caught with the Prince of Wales in the avalanche in Klosters. As a treat the two girls were being allowed to sleep out in sleeping bags that night.

'We all felt as though we were part of one big family,' says Sue, 'and that was an incredible feeling.'

Jane Makim finally cajoled her father into venturing out down the Mall for father and daughter, like Susan before them, decided to get out of their car and walk for a while. Parking places were few and far between in St James's Park that night and when the Major tried to ease his red BMW into a space, 'someone came up behind us and tried to steal it. Dad, naturally, got really irate and the other man got really irate and was trying to crash into our car to force us to move.

'"Oh no you don't, you silly old fool," the other man raged. "I was here first." The exchange got more and more heated and Dad pulled his head back inside the car and said, "If only he knew who I was."

'We both collapsed with laughter at the image of Dad storming out of the car, pulling himself up to his full six foot two inches and telling the man in no uncertain terms who he was and why he was there!'

The Major resisted that temptation and, having at last secured possession of the disputed parking space, Jane and he sat quietly for a moment looking out at the crowd eddying by in the lamplit night.

Recalls Jane: 'Finally Dad turned and looked back at Buckingham Palace and said, "This is all for your little sister, my little daughter." His eyes were quite wet.

'"Tomorrow," I thought, "tomorrow my little sister is going to be a princess."'

The Major's tiredness had left him. He says: 'It was the height of the polo season and I had been organizing matches sometimes twice a day then rushing up to London for the wedding rehearsals and I was exhausted. I remember quite distinctly going to sleep after the first course at dinner that night. My neighbour nudged me and told me the main course was there. I gave a grunt – and stayed asleep until the pudding. But there in the Mall my adrenalin started working. There was a wonderful atmosphere amongst the crowd. Someone offered Jane and myself a drink and my fatigue disappeared.'

Sue Ferguson, further down the Mall, was experiencing the same emotions. 'I was on such a high,' she says, 'that I wanted to stay up all night. I persuaded my friends to take me to Annabel's where we drank a special bottle of champagne. I was so excited I never wanted to go to bed.'

Sarah has always found the excitement of the crowd contagious and irresistible. Shortly after nine o'clock that evening, dressed in a pair of old jeans, she slipped out of Clarence House to stroll amongst the crowds gathered outside. She did not venture very far – that proved impossible. People looked at her, inquisitively at first, then with astonishment, and as the cry of recognition went up she turned back inside again. But she had done it – she had been out and she had joined in.

After a light sleep Sarah awoke to a day bright with anticipation and the rare sunshine of an English summer.

Across the way in Buckingham Palace the Queen was dressing. She had had a long discussion with her couturier, Ian Thomas, and her dresser and long-standing friend, Bobo MacDonald, about how she should wear her pearls. They suggested that she should wear them with the clasp at the side instead of at the back. She informed them that she considered such display ostentatious and that she would rather wear a brooch. 'No,' they argued, 'it looked better without the brooch,' and 'Please Ma'am, wear the hat with the large brim.' They were persuasive; the Queen wore the hat they had suggested and, for the first time ever, the clasp of her pearls at the side. She also chose pale grey suede gloves and handbag instead of the black she usually favours.

Farther west still, the Major awoke rested (he was fast asleep when Susan arrived back at the hotel) and the little Fergusons were in a state of high excitement. It was the first time Sarah's half-brother and sister, Alice, then aged five, and seven-year-old Andrew, and Jane's son Seamus had ever stayed in an hotel and they were 'thrilled', as Mrs Ferguson recalls, 'to have breakfast in their rooms'.

Susan went round the corner to Hugh in Ebury Street to have her hair done, leaving the children in the care of her nanny, Linda, to face some coiffuring of their own. The three – along with the Duke of Roxburghe's seven-year-old daughter Lady

Rosanagh Innes-Ker, the Princess of Wales's niece Laura Fellowes, aged six, Princess Anne's son and daughter, Peter, eight, and Zara, five, and (youngest and cheekiest of the little troupe) four-year-old Prince William – had been chosen as the bride's attendants and shortly after eight o'clock Princess Anne's hairdresser from the Michaeljohn salon in Mayfair arrived to see to their hair.

Back at the hotel Susan changed into the green silk Bellville Sassoon suit dress and jacket she had carefully laid out the night before and went to join her husband, already dressed in his black morning coat edged with silk on the lapels. Sir Robert Fellowes, the Prince of Wales's brother-in-law and now the Queen's private secretary, had sarcastically told him that it looked like the kind of coat a member of Pop, the elite corps of Etonian prefects, would wear. Which is exactly what it was: the Major had inherited the coat, as is the custom with such essential though little used garments of formal dress, from his father who had indeed been a member of Pop. He liked it. And besides, his daughter had ruled that she would refuse to walk down the aisle with him if he followed Fellowes' hint and ordered himself a new one.

That sartorial argument settled, the party set off in the small fleet of Daimlers the Major had hired for the day and made their slow way through St James's Park to Clarence House.

The crowd, now ten deep along the route of the royal procession, waved as they drove past.

'I suddenly felt terribly important,' Sue remembers. 'For me the wedding had already begun and I felt part of it.'

When they arrived at Clarence House Susan went upstairs to help ready the children who had arrived ahead of them while the Major stayed downstairs to talk to the Queen Mother's Comptroller, Sir Alastair Aird, chat to the Lifeguard escort – 'they were all friends of mine' – and then stroll into the garden 'to wait for Sarah to finish getting ready. I was very relaxed.'

Upstairs on the first floor the scene was altogether less sedate as dressers and hairdressers and dressmakers bustled about and the pages and bridesmaids were pushed and pulled into their outfits.

That morning the about-to-be-Duchess of York had woken with a headache. Prone to migraine attacks – she attributes them to the numerous falls from her ponies she suffered as a child – she is usually forced to retire into a darkened room and wait for them to pass. Most fortunately this one passed quickly and she was feeling fine by the time manicurist Beverly Nathan and the beautician Teresa Fairminer arrived to put the finishing touches to her soon-to-be-royal personage.

The dressmaker, Lindka Cierach, who arrived with Sarah's hairdresser Denise McAdam was struck by the 'wonderful atmosphere' at Clarence House. She says: 'It was obviously not the first time I had been there – I had been in and out consulting with Sarah about the dress – but that morning it was different. It had a unique feeling, the most extraordinary atmosphere I've ever felt in my life. Everyone was so happy. And being on the inside and seeing and hearing the crowds in the Mall cheering was a fantastic experience for everyone.'

While Lindka stayed with Sarah, her assistant went to help with the children's dressing, checking their hair and putting on their headdresses. Little Alice Ferguson was delighted to find herself being tended by yet another hairdresser who curled her hair locks with Carmen rollers, something she had never had done before. The bridesmaids' peach satin dresses were carefully hung until the last possible moment to avoid creases and spillage. There was no cause for concern, however – the girls were all very well-behaved, standing as they were told, or peeking out through the window at the crowds below.

The same could not be said of the boys. They were wearing the midshipmen and sailors' uniforms of the Royal Navy in 1782 and as soon as Susan Ferguson darted across from the bridesmaids' room into the page boys' suite she realized that all was not well.

Her son, Andrew, normally the most well-behaved of

children, had tears in his eyes. 'Mummy,' he whispered desperately, 'everything itches, this tickles, and it's too tight and I can't bend my legs.'

An anxious mother started imagining the worst – a page boys' rebellion despite all the careful preparation. The clothes, made by the Savile Row tailors, Gieves and Hawkes, had been fitted at Dummer, where they had been perfect, but they clearly did not fit now. They had been laced too tight. Sue looked across at Seamus, a picture of uncomfortable misery in his Georgian sailor suit.

Electing himself spokesman for the group, Andrew, who was wearing the midshipman's uniform, continued: 'Mummy, Seamus can't breathe. They've made his top too tight.'

Prince William, who was being restrained by his nanny, Olga Powell, seemed happy enough – the undoubted consequence of the extra fittings the Princess of Wales had insisted upon – but it was clearly going to be a problem persuading five-year-old Seamus, used to the unrestricted life of the Australian outback, to behave himself in an abbey filled with two thousand people if he could not breathe.

Abandoning her promise to herself not to interfere, Sue Ferguson turned to the man from Gieves and Hawkes and asked him to loosen the boys' uniforms. He did.

In the stables the grooms harnessed the great grey horses to the ancient, exquisitely maintained carriages of state while the postillions adjusted their livery. In the great kitchens of Buckingham Palace where the wedding breakfast was being prepared chefs gave orders to under chefs who gave orders to cooks and scullery maids while upstairs in the staterooms butlers and an army of footmen went about their allotted tasks to the clatter of crockery and the occasional oath. In the barracks the sergeants barked orders to the men while the officers, in uniforms of red and gold, admired themselves in their mirrors. And in the main bedroom of Clarence House the centrepiece of all this activity was making her final preparations for the greatest day of her life.

Her mother, Mrs Susan Barrantes, was with her. So was her sister, Jane, who kept dashing out with progress reports. Her nails were manicured, her hair was ready, her make-up was on. Denise the hairdresser placed the veil and arranged the headdress of flowers made by Jane Packer. Now, at last, it was time for the dress which had been kept overnight on a dressmaker's dummy.

'We were all anxious,' Lindka recalls. 'I was nervous, she was nervous. A wedding is always public but this had such a grand sense of occasion.'

With Lindka's help Sarah pulled the dress over her head and as she did so she noticed two rolled up messages of luck stitched into the underskirt. One was from her father. The other from her 'wicked stepmother'. Sue had hoped to see Sarah, the girl she had cared for since she was twelve years old, before she left for the Abbey but that moment was denied her.

Mrs Ferguson recalls: 'I was so emotional that I couldn't see reason. I thought it was the most normal thing in the world.'

And so it would have been had Sarah not been marrying into the Royal Family where etiquette and protocol are rigorously observed. It was therefore Susan Barrantes who helped put on the dress.

There were gasps as Sarah descended the Clarence House staircase. 'It was a staggering moment,' says Lindka. There have been times when Sarah's dress sense and style have been subject to criticism. This was not one of them. She looked stunning, and a little nervous – as she made her way down, slowed by the weight of the dress and its train, she was gripping the bannister so tightly that her knuckles went white. Her throat felt dry and when she saw her father, waiting for her at the bottom, she thought for a moment that she was going to burst into fits of giggles – or break down and cry. Fortunately she did neither.

The Major, who is not one given to overt displays of emotion, was 'awe-struck'.

'That dress, the flowers in her hair . . . it was breathtaking, no other word. It was the first time I had seen the dress. I hadn't had any details and I didn't want to know. I was prepared for anything, but this . . . it was the most extraordinary vision. I shed a tear. I thought of saying all sorts of things to calm her down – well, to calm me down – and then I saw the happiness and confidence in her face and said nothing. I knew we were còmpletely under control when one of the assistant dressmakers trod on her train and she swore. I thought: "Everything is under control, we're home and dry."'

Sarah then lifted her dress to reveal the underskirt with its several blue bows containing the good-luck messages from her family. Then she walked out under the striped awning and climbed into the coach, no easy operation with a seventeen-foot train to manoeuvre.

'We had been to look at the carriages the day before just to see how difficult it was to get in and out of them,' says Lindka. 'They look amazing but it is quite different looking at them to travelling in them. They are small and cramped and quite uncomfortable when you are trailing seventeen feet of lace and satin behind you.'

When the operation was completed, Lindka was driven off by car via a back route to the Abbey while the bride and her father set off in the Glass Coach accompanied by eight Lifeguard troopers.

The original plan had been for the carriage to be escorted by police horsemen. The Major had pointed out through the appropriate channels that the Fergusons had served the Royal Family for five generations and that it would be appropriate and fitting if the Sovereign's Escort he had once personally commanded were to conduct his daughter. It was not until after he had broached the question with the Queen herself at a dinner at Windsor Castle, however, that permission was finally given for the most elite and colourful of British cavalry to escort Sarah Ferguson along the Mall to Westminster Abbey.

It was Sarah's first experience of the adulation the British people reserve for their Royal Family on such occasions; of trying to remember to wave but not too much and only from the wrist, not with the whole arm, a technique that takes practice. There is also another small problem to be mastered, as the Major explained: 'It took a while to get used to waving and talking to each other while facing away from each other.'

Half way down Whitehall the Major nudged his daughter and remarked: 'Just look at all those people. Why are they here? All come to see my little daughter.' Sarah hissed back: 'Shut up, Dad.'

At the West door of the Abbey Lindka was waiting. 'Sarah had asked me to be there to help her out of the carriage, which I did,' says the dressmaker. 'When I took her hand it was firm. She was very calm and collected. She let us whizz around and brush out the skirt. Then the train had to be arranged and then the veil which was so light and feathery that it kept blowing as the wind caught it.'

The Major, following on the heels of his daughter's satin slippers, lent a hand in straightening the train. It seemed, he says, 'the most natural thing to do'. It also provided him with a moment of comforting distraction, before he set off on that long walk to the altar.

'We chatted all the way up, personal father and daughter stuff and most of it unprintable, until he got to the archway of the Abbey and realized, "This is serious stuff".' Then, Sarah recalls, 'I was very nervous being up in front of so many millions of people but it was a really special bonding occasion with my father.'

The procession was timed at four minutes. To the people involved it seemed to take much longer. Even the Queen was to be observed glancing expectantly down the nave. Only Prince Andrew, officially gazetted as the Duke of York that morning, appeared confidently unconcerned, smiling broadly when he glanced round to watch his bride's progress.

Susan Ferguson was sitting on the bride's side and directly behind her husband who would be seated beside the former Mrs

Ferguson (the Queen had granted the Major's request for the Sovereign's Escort; his request to break protocol and be seated beside his present rather than his former wife had been refused). She recalls: 'There was an intoxicating smell of fresh flowers in the air and everyone was chattering and whispering and turning around to see who was there' – and wondering, with the time-honoured concern of all weddings, whether the bride had actually made it to the church.

Sue Ferguson suddenly remembered that the fitter from Gieves and Hawkes, when he went to Dummer for the pages' fittings, had mentioned that Prince William and Seamus Makim would be wearing straw boaters which they were supposed to take off as they entered the Abbey. They were only to put them on again when they got into the carriages for the drive back to Buckingham Palace. In the excitement, however, no one had mentioned that to the two boys who, without any instruction to the contrary, kept them on through-out the service.

Up at the altar now, Sarah Ferguson and the Duke of York were being joined in holy matrimony by the Archbishop of Canterbury, according to the liturgy of the 1662 Book of Common Prayer, before a worldwide television audience of two hundred million. She promised to 'obey', because, as she explained, 'I think it is the man's role to be the leader and therefore he will make the final decision – but that does not mean that I am a "yes" woman, I must stress that.' He placed a ring of Welsh gold on her finger. She, more unusually, gave him a wedding ring in return (though, true to royal tradition, he does not wear it).

It was a ceremony both solemn and personal. Royal weddings are often two dimensional in their formality but the Yorks – tactile, overtly affectionate and obviously relaxed in each other's company – are a break from that restraint.

Behind them, the pages and bridesmaids were shuffling and smiling. Prince William pulled faces and fiddled with the dirk in his sock. Sarah's little half-sister Alice was wiping her nose on the back of her hand, while her brother, Andrew, was looking uncomfortably hot in his itchy uniform.

'I kept willing the children to be good,' Sue Ferguson says. 'I kept mouthing to Alice, "Don't do that", and making a movement with my hand across my nose but that only confused her and she looked at me in amazement and said in a stage whisper, "What am I doing wrong?"'

And all the time Jane's Australian husband, Alex Makim, insisted on providing his own running commentary on the service. When Mrs Ferguson, who was sitting next to him, turned away pretending not to hear, he still persisted and even repeated himself to make sure she had heard.

Sue Ferguson kept her eyes on the ceremony. 'Sarah and Ronald were standing so close to me that I could see her hand shaking,' she says. 'And all the time, through my haze of emotion, I could hear Alex saying, "Look at this . . . look at that." I thought: "If he says one more word I'm going to scream." He hadn't got the aura of the moment.'

Immediately after the ceremony, while the bride and groom were preparing to drive back down the Mall to Buckingham Palace in the open-topped 1902 State Landau, Lindka, together with photographer Gene Nocon and his wife Liz were scrambling into the mini-bus that was waiting to take members of the Royal Household back to the Palace. Lindka's work was almost done. Nocon's was about to begin.

Several weeks earlier Prince Andrew had asked Nocon, his friend and photographic advisor, to draw up a short list of names of photographers who had not done a royal wedding before but who would be professional and artistically up to the assignment. Meetings were arranged. The first two cameramen Andrew and Nocon saw were Terence Donovan, a Cockney Londoner, and Scots-born, New York-based Albert Watson. They got the job. Donovan was chosen to do the official engagement pictures while Watson, who made his reputation working for *Vogue* magazine, was given the coveted responsibility of taking the official wedding photographs.

'When I called Albert and told him that he had been selected he was thrilled,' Nocon remembers. 'But then he is that kind of guy. He's thrilled just to wake up in the morning. He's very cool and can handle pressure. He had just the right temperament for the job.'

Watson was meticulous in his preparation and, with Gene's assistance, spent the two days before the event running through the lighting – it involved sixteen flash units and four backups – over and over again. He even insisted on straightening the candles in the chandelier in the Throne Room where the pictures would be taken. There is no margin for error in royal wedding photography, and time is of the essence.

Says Watson: 'We moved into the Palace three days before the wedding to make sure that everything was right. On the day itself I arrived at 9 a.m. to check and recheck and who should walk in but Prince Andrew. I was surprised; it was his wedding day, after all, and the Throne Room is a long hike from his quarters.

'He asked me if we had everything we needed and then told me not to worry, that everything would be all right. I thought that he had got it the wrong way round – that it should have been me saying those things to him.'

When the royal guests arrived back at the Palace they gathered in the Long Gallery to sip champagne and watch the live coverage on a television monitor while they waited for the wedding breakfast to start. Having their photographs taken was not their most important consideration, as Nocon discovered.

He recalls: 'My job was to get people into the Throne Room where Albert was waiting. I had written everyone's name on sheets of A4 paper and put them in place, rather like a dinner party placement, so that when they came in all they had to do was find their names and stand there.

'It didn't work out quite like that, however. I fetched one

person in and put him in his place but as soon as I went out to get someone else, the first person got bored standing there and moved off.'

With fifty-seven members of the Royal and the Ferguson families to organize a feeling of exasperation cum desperation was creeping in.

'We only had thirty minutes for the main picture and this had to be divided into eleven different situations, which meant less than three minutes for each shot,' says Watson.

Nocon gave up with the adults and started bringing in the children and sitting them down, whereupon the adults started appearing and good naturedly shoving their way past each other to their places, with Nocon scurrying behind removing the pieces of paper.

Watson, meanwhile, was up his ladder, checking to make sure that he could see everyone. He could, including the people at the back whom he had placed on a small platform. But if he could see them, not everyone was looking at him. The Royal Family, trained from birth to sense a camera lens, is used to being photographed. The Ferguson family is not. Watson says: 'They were really spaced by the situation and I couldn't get their attention.'

In the end he resorted to squeezing a big, old fashioned bicycle horn with a rubber bulb at the end to attract their attention, while the Queen's then press secretary, Michael Shea, lent his expertise at keeping everyone in their place (Gordonstoun-educated Shea is famous for enforcing discipline at photographic sessions, though on one occasion, having organized a shot of the Queen with all the heads of the Commonwealth, it had to be pointed out to him by his Sovereign that he was still in the picture himself).

'Perhaps the most crazy moment of all,' Watson says, 'was when I saw the Queen, who was no longer needed in the picture, climbing up the ladder and looking through my camera. Prince Andrew told her about the special back I had made for my

Hasselblad and she wanted to see it. And there she was, perched on the third rung of my ladder. This, I thought, is a moment of pure insanity.'

Watson still had to deal with more than a dozen excited young children, a task which would have daunted the most competent of royal nannies. 'They just didn't want to sit still,' he says. 'Prince William was supercharged and his nanny kept coming up to me and informing me that he was sticking his tongue out in every shot.'

In the end Watson's professionalism carried the day. 'He only used two rolls of film and had the pictures in less than five minutes,' Nocon remembers, 'but then he had to do all the individual family groups, which took half an hour.'

Sue Ferguson, having driven back to the Palace with Sir Robert Fellowes and his wife, came through into the Throne Room to see how her children were. She bumped into the Queen who was on her way out. They both laughed. Back in Buckingham Palace and away from the relentless stare of the television cameras, the occasion had taken on the feeling of a small, if rather grand, family wedding. Everyone who was not being photographed stood behind Watson cracking jokes and yelling 'Cheese' to those still in the frame.

Sue noticed that her mother-in-law, Sarah's grandmother, Lady Elmhirst, was holding a very large and less than formal brown handbag. 'Marian,' she called out, 'put your handbag behind you.' She did – the bag is not to be seen in the official photographs.

Sarah's other grandmother, Doreen Wright, suffers from pain in her legs and her daughter, Mrs Susan Barrantes, remembers her concern over her walking stick; whether it was right to take it to Westminster Abbey, whether or not she should have a new one specially for the wedding. A new one was decided on. Like the handbag it does not appear in the official pictures.

On the other side of the Palace gates a more informal celebration was taking place. When the royal procession had made its way back from Westminster Abbey, through Admiralty Arch, down the Mall and on to Buckingham Palace, the vast crowd had been drawn along behind. It was now crushed before the Palace gates, swaying, cheering, waving flags and calling for Britain's newest duke and the Queen's newest daughter-in-law to come out and play the traditional balcony scene. When they made their appearance the cry went up, 'We want a kiss.'

The chants of the crowd carry clearly up to the balcony. The Duke feigned not to hear. His Duchess playfully cupped a hand to her ear and called out, 'What was that?'

The crowd told them again and the couple obliged, provoking a cheer that roared through St James's Park and carried all the way down to Trafalgar Square and back along the Strand.

It was a balcony filled from one end to the other with pages and bridesmaids, Sovereign and sisters, fathers, mothers, aunts and Sue Ferguson, who, unaware of her position as stepmother, had to be prodded on to the balcony.

As the group retired inside again Sarah hugged her stepmother and asked, 'Don't you love the dress?'

After the balcony encore Andrew and Sarah joined their guests for the wedding breakfast – a cold buffet of lobster and lamb cutlets followed by strawberries and cream, washed down with Piersport Goldtropfchen Auslese 1976, Chateau Langoa-Barton 1976, Bollinger champagne and Graham's 1966 port, served by liveried footmen who did not stand behind the chairs but waited to be rung for.

Singularly honoured to be invited to the breakfast Carolyn, Sarah's former flatmate in Clapham (and a new wife herself – she had married baronet Sir John Cotterell's son Harry the previous month) remembers: 'There was a string quartet playing and as we came in we were shown to our table with the minimum of fuss – as the Queen was there, there wasn't a traditional wedding line-up.

'We were seated at a table with the Infantas of Spain. I was next to Harry and I thought to myself, looking around the room, that we were probably the only plain Mr and Mrs there.'

Andrew and Sarah, the Queen and Prince Philip, Major Ferguson and Mrs Barrantes, and Jane Makim were on the top table.

Mark Phillips, Princess Alexandra, the Duchess of Kent and Susan Ferguson were at another table while Princess Margaret was seated next to Jane's husband Alex and, according to the outback farmer, spent most of the meal chatting to him about the kangaroo problem in Australia.

The pages and bridesmaids were on their own table and placed at each setting was a Biggles bear complete with flying goggles and jacket which it was hoped would keep them amused until, one by one, the children were called up by name to receive their special wedding gifts from the new Duchess: cuff-links for the boys, bow brooches for the girls.

The selection of wedding cakes is peculiarly royal. There is the ceremonial one made by the Palace chefs and a display outside the Bow Room of those baked by various catering firms and one from each of the catering corps of the three armed forces. It was the five-tiered, 240-pounder baked by the three chefs at HMS *Raleigh*, the Navy supply school at Torpoint in Cornwall, that Sarah and Andrew, hand in hand, cut with the Duke's ceremonial sword.

Yet away from the television cameras and with the shouts of the crowd outside drowned by the chatter from the 140 guests, it did take on the feel of a more intimate occasion and the sense of friendliness and family feeling is echoed by other guests. Says Sue Ferguson: 'You forgot you were in Buckingham Palace with the Royal Family, you forgot all the foreign royalty and liveried footmen – it was like a family wedding.'

The formalities completed, Carolyn and Mrs Barrantes accompanied Sarah upstairs to the suite of rooms on the second floor that was now her London home to change out of her wedding dress and into her going-away outfit.

'She was very excited – ecstatic,' says Carolyn. 'She couldn't believe it had really happened. We helped her get dressed while Lindka fussed over the dress, Denise brushed her hair out and Teresa Fairminer touched up her make-up. We talked about the Azores where she was going for her honeymoon; it was too soon to talk about anything that had just happened. She kept saying, "I just can't believe this, I'm so happy!"'

The pictures were now ready for selection. As soon as the photographic session was completed, Nocon and Watson had slipped out of a back door, driven up Park Lane with a policeman as escort to the Crawford Street laboratory, handed in the film and then joined Watson's assistants at Joe Allan's restaurant in Covent Garden to wait the hour-and-a-half for the colour negatives to be developed. At 2.30 they were back at the Palace.

The Duke and Duchess took the contact sheets of pictures and scanned them quickly on Andrew's light box. 'Make sure we are all smiling,' Andrew instructed Nocon who then cut out the approved photographs and handed them to Roger Eldrich from Camera Press, the agency charged with their worldwide distribution.

Says Nocon, 'Albert and I gave a sigh of relief and then I rushed downstairs to get the going away pictures for their own personal album.' This informal collection of black and white snaps would be Nocon's wedding present to the couple. The album also contains photographs taken by Andrew's celebrity friends recording what they were doing on the wedding day.

'The wedding present was a great success,' says Gene. 'The final picture in the album is of Sarah's father and half-brother, Andrew Ferguson, running outside into the road outside the Palace to wave them off. It seemed a fitting end and it was a great shot.'

The Major explains: 'I took Andrew outside. We stood staring at the crowds, saying nothing. I felt myself gripping Andrew's hand so tightly I must have hurt him.'

Other guests were now drifting out of the Bow Room, where

they had been drinking champagne, coffee and eating slices of wedding cake, and made their way downstairs for the departure of the bride and groom.

Says Sue Ferguson: 'We all went down a bit too early as everyone thought they would leave long before they did' – the Queen included. Everyone started jostling for the best vantage points, then changing their mind, and all long before the couple were ready. And while the adults engaged in their version of musical chairs, the children started running around, grabbing handfuls of rose petals from the silver bowls being held by footmen, throwing them into the air, shrieking with laughter, then running back for more. When the newly-weds eventually came down the wide staircase there was a cheer. The guests, grabbing handfuls of the confetti the children had left, showered it over the couple as they drove off in a carriage resplendent with a large teddy bear – placed there by the Princess of Wales and Princess Margaret's son, Viscount Linley – and festooned with a papier mâché satellite dish bearing the message "Phone Home", courtesy of Prince Edward. Their guests ran after them, under the archway and into the forecourt of the Palace. Even the Queen broke into a regal trot as she hurried after the couple. Then they were into the street and away to the Azores for their honeymoon.

Ronald Ferguson saved the occasion on video. He had had all the television coverage taped professionally. 'I expect one day when I am in my dotage and hobbling from room to room I'll while away my days watching the re-runs on TV.'

12

Life Together

WHEN PRINCE ANDREW STARTED COURTING SARAH HE USED to tease her about her social life, about how many appointments she had squeezed into the day and how many cocktail parties she would be going to that evening.

Brought up in the closed environment of a palace and a member of a family that is always very selective in its choice of friends, Andrew's social circle was a limited one, confined to the people he was introduced to as a child, a few chums from his Gordonstoun days, and some fellow naval officers. Sarah's lifestyle was very different from his own and he found it hard to understand how she could have so many friends and knew such a large and varied number of people.

Outgoing, loyal, and with an easy and embracing social manner, Sarah has always found it easy to make friends. She comes from a large family (her uncle, former cavalry officer and one-time butler, Brian Wright, has counted twenty-one first cousins) and she takes a warm interest in the relations of those she loves. She insisted on taking her octogenarian grandmother to Ascot, for instance, much to her delight.

She made a point of introducing Andrew to her friends – old flatmates, friends from school, colleagues from her days in public relations – and on his wife's prompting his evening entertainments broadened to include a wide variety of people ranging from such society stalwarts as the Greenall brewing family through to showbusiness folk like Scottish comedian Billy Connolly and his wife Pamela Stephenson, the Frosts, Elton John and Michael Caine.

The showbusiness connection was originally forged by Andrew. Since his marriage, acquaintanceship has grown into friendship and the Yorks are now regular dinner guests at, for instance, the Chelsea home of David Frost and his wife, Lady Carina, daughter of the Duke of Norfolk. It is a lively crowd which shares Andrew's and Sarah's love of boisterous good fun.

At a joint birthday party for Andrew and Australian comedian Barry Humphries (their February birthdays are two days apart), hostess Pamela Stephenson with Sarah and Elton John's manager John Reid went upstairs and wiggled into tight gold lamé dresses and blonde wigs. Hobbling back downstairs, Michael Caine helped them into a large 'sardine can' box which he covered over. Then, with Elton John tinkling away on the piano, the Duke of York and Barry Humphries rolled back the lid – and out leapt the three 'mermaids' singing Happy Birthday.

As Reid said to friends: 'Andrew's face was a picture.'

More conventionally, the Yorks have been to stay at the Jersey home of Carolyn Cotterell's mother and at her family's estate in Herefordshire. Carolyn admits she was nervous at first 'but he is such good fun and now, when they leave, I always feel, "What a shame". It is very informal and the detectives help with the washing up.'

Clare Greenall who has known Sarah all her life but only met Andrew recently is also impressed.

'He's full of fun,' she says. 'You just have to let him relax and he's away. He talked about everything and anything,' she says. 'People think they have to talk to him about the helicopters or the Navy, his subjects, but he is perfectly happy to talk about something quite different.'

Marriage has certainly matured Andrew. He is still very aware of his royal position but he has learned to adapt to situations.

'He's a charming bloke and much less insecure than he was,' says a friend.

Someone who knows the Yorks well puts it succinctly. 'Andrew is the nice guy that's been trying to get out.'

The Yorks do a fair bit of entertaining themselves 'at home' where they give dinner parties for eight and sometimes ten people, assisted by their cook, Mandy, and Terry the butler.

'Prince Andrew is a very good host,' Clare Greenall says.

After aperitifs in the drawing room the guests – perhaps including the Connollys and David and Lady Carina Frost – go through into the dining room for dinner.

'Everything is just right and not overdone,' Clare says. 'You are waited on at table but other than that it is not grand.'

If Connolly is there he will amuse the other guests with tales from his days of wild excess. Sarah, never at a loss for words, holds her own and Andrew also joins in. Says photographer Terry O'Neill: 'He's quick witted with a great sense of humour. He's as sharp as a tack.'

'Sarah is a good actress,' her sister Jane says. 'She has a fantastically mobile face and can bung on different characters when she is telling a joke.' 'My face and eyes tell a story,' Sarah admits.

She also likes charades, a major plus in a family addicted to that clownish game of mime which they play frequently during their extended family holidays at Balmoral and Sandringham. Andrew's and Sarah's dinner parties are a little more sophisticated but they enjoy telling jokes and 'mobbing each other up' and their parties are light-hearted and enjoyable affairs whether they are in Buckingham Palace or at their new home, Sunninghill Park.

The house, designed by Professor James Dunbar-Nasmith, head of architecture at Heriot Watt university and Edinburgh College of Art, is five miles from Windsor Castle and down the road from Lowood House, the Duchess's childhood home. The professor's firm, Law and Dunbar-Nasmith, has done work for the Royal Family before, designing a staff wing at Balmoral and a kitchen for the Queen Mother at Birkhall, her stone manor house on the edge of the Balmoral estate. They were not controversial projects. Sunninghill Park is.

Reputed to have cost £5 million, it is a gift from the Queen and is built in a modern ranch style which has attracted some criticism. It has been called 'Dallas Palace' and 'Southyork' after the Southfork ranch in the television soap opera.

Initially the interiors were to have been decorated by the American firm of Parish-Hadley. The Duchess had become enamoured of their country style when she visited the Connecticut home of polo player Henry de Kwaitkowski who had given Sister Parish carte blanche to create a home for him out of an old stable block. Sarah liked the comfort of the house, the big, squashy sofas and the unexpected appeal of the rooms, which offered an exciting alternative to the frilly, chintzy look that has become the hallmark of English interiors and which Sarah dislikes.

Sister Parish prepared some practical additions to the house. 'Do you know, that in the plans there are four children's rooms and a nurse's room and only one bathroom,' she shuddered, adding that in the original plans there was not even a nursery kitchen.

Sister Parish got no further than making these revisions. There was the logistical problem of employing an American firm to work in England with local workmen and materials. And there was public opinion which thoroughly disapproved of such a high profile contract going to a foreign firm. Parish-Hadley's contribution was reduced to a couple of rooms and the very English Nina Campbell, whose style of contrived clutter Sarah admired, was chosen instead.

Nina's brief was to create a comfortable and original look for the house. That she has done – for all the criticism it has attracted, Sunninghill is an imposing, almost magnificent residence.

There is a thirty-five-foot-high, white-painted entrance hall that sweeps up into a small glass dome in the ceiling, a minstrel's gallery and rustic beams complementing the natural stone floors.

The family bedrooms are upstairs. The Yorks' suite is thirty-five feet long with bay windows overlooking the back garden. One of the two master bathrooms doubles as a security shelter with a heavy, steel-framed door. The other is twenty feet long with a circular tub with a wooden surround set in the middle of the white marble-floored room. There are dressing rooms with built-in wardrobes and spring-loaded drawers that open at a touch.

The guest suites are on the ground floor. The guests' bathrooms have white units, including bidets, and bear the Campbell hallmark of panelled wooden surrounds.

The huge kitchen area is American farmhouse style with a central worktop. In keeping with this ecological age, the refrigerators are ozone friendly and the stove is an old-fashioned Aga.

The five acres of partially wooded garden have been carefully landscaped. Some of the trees were planted by the Duke himself. There is an outdoor swimming pool and tennis court.

The overall effect, as one guest observed, is 'safe from criticism and censure and yet there is, somewhere within the depths of the sofas and overstuffed turban padded bolsters, a little whoopee cushion just waiting to get out'.

The decoration carries Nina Campbell's stamp of casual elegance. It also bears Sarah's touch – giant stuffed teddies jostle for position on the sofas and one of the rooms is decorated in her own tartan.

Mindful of the controversy that had surrounded its construction, Sarah suggested that a select number of pressmen should be allowed in to see the finished product. Andrew vetoed the idea (though inevitably some unauthorized photographs taken by a workman found their way into popular print). He did not want strangers tramping around his new home, which is a gift from his mother and not the taxpayer. Sunninghill is a private residence, not a stately home waiting to throw its doors open to the public; like all the members of the Royal Family, Andrew values his privacy.

Sarah may have broadened his circle and he thoroughly enjoys the mix of showbusiness and aristocratic friends she has assembled, but it is only his own relations who are allowed to share his private confidences. Being royal has its obvious advantages but it is also a barrier, as Sarah has discovered. There is a predictability to her life that can be claustrophobic at times, says Sarah. 'If someone invites you to do anything, you can't because six months ago you agreed that on a certain date at a certain time you would be at a certain place.' There is also the formality. Just as everyone calls Andrew 'Sir' (Sarah included when first she lunched with him at Windsor), her friends must now curtsey to her and call her 'Ma'am'.

The new Duchess objected to this imposition of protocol. It made her feel unnatural. She says: 'At the beginning I thought, "Don't do that, you don't have to do that to me." And then I was told I had to accept it. It's very difficult . . .'

For someone who had lived the life of a modern, independent woman since leaving school, these restrictions were irksome. As she says: 'I'm a spontaneous person. I have to be controlled but I like to be free.' As a member of the Royal Family, however, her independence and spontaneity are limited. She must always watch what she says and does, which for her is sometimes very difficult. 'I love being straightforward and frank,' she explains, 'then everyone knows where they stand.' Her honesty has got the Duchess into trouble on more than one occasion, but it is not something she complains to her girlfriends about. Only with the Princess of Wales can she be completely at ease.

'They are both in the same situation so they can talk to each other about things they wouldn't mention to anyone else,' says Clare Greenall.

'The Princess of Wales has helped her more than she has been given credit for,' Clare Wentworth-Stanley says.

Sarah, in her turn, has been a support to the Princess of Wales.

As Diana's father, Earl Spencer says: 'The two of them are great friends. Sarah's arrival made things much easier for Diana. She was so thrilled when Sarah and Andrew got married. After all, Diana was the one who brought them together.'

If there is one thing both dislike, though, it is being compared with each other, but Sarah values her friendship with Diana and the two women remain close, though with young families and the constant round of royal engagements to fulfil, they do not see quite as much of each other as is sometimes supposed. As Carolyn Cotterell says: 'Their lives take them in a million different directions. Geography doesn't always allow them to be together but they are close.'

The Duchess also gets on well with the Princess Royal and when circumstances bring them together, they take pleasure in each other's company. They have some friends in common – Patrick Lichfield, for instance, whose former wife, Leonora, is one of Anne's ladies-in-waiting – and the Princess, though hardly the most demonstrative of people, is sympathetic to the plight and problems Sarah faced, coming from the 'outside in'. Sarah has a well-developed sense of duty which Anne recognizes and she likes her sister-in-law's obvious devotion to Andrew whom she once considered the least interesting member of her family.

The respect is mutual. Sarah likes Anne, values her opinions and appreciates her gestures of friendship.

For all that, and despite the attentions of ladies-in-waiting and equerries and servants, Sarah's position can, because of being royal and also because of her husband's job, be a lonely one.

As a serving officer in the Royal Navy, Andrew is away for long periods at a time. Sarah tries to be philosophical. 'I knew when I married into the Navy I was going to have separations,' she says. 'I'm in full support of his career and I think it is important a wife remembers that and is always there smiling. I'd be wrong to say there aren't days when I'm lonely, but more often than not I just get on with it.'

Once asked how far he hoped to go, Andrew replied that he

wanted to be an Admiral – 'doesn't everybody?' He has recently been serving as Flight Commander aboard the lead ship of the Nato Standing Force *Atlantic*, advising the captain on all matters to do with aviation and with responsibility for all members of the force that carry helicopters.

It is an important job and one he takes great pride in. But it can take him away to sea for months on end. 'And that,' he says, 'is terrible. You are going away and leaving what you love behind. But you just have to take it otherwise the Navy could not exist.'

In his absence Sarah is left to run the household and shoulder the royal responsibilities. Says Jane Makim: 'She just has to get on with her life and when he's around he's around.' That is why she was so determined to keep up with her old friends.

When Sarah first disappeared through the portals of the Palace it looked as though contact might be lost, as if the demands of royal life would swallow her up.

Ros Duckworth, the Fergusons' old housekeeper, wisely let matters take their course. 'I made no contact with her at all for the first two years,' she says, 'as I thought it was much better to back off a bit.' Others were not quite so sanguine.

Clare Wentworth-Stanley admits: 'I didn't understand the pressures. But she had taken on something far greater than any of her friends had except the Princess of Wales.

'We talked about it amongst ourselves and I moaned that I never saw Fergie and when I rang up she was never there. It was just the thought of losing her. Then I spoke to someone who had been through a similar experience with another member of the Royal Family and he explained that the same thing had happened to him and I had to be a bit patient until she had sorted her life out and then she would come back.'

Clare and Sarah's other friends heeded that advice and, as predicted, she was soon on the telephone to them, inviting them round, organizing lunches, accepting dinner party invitations.

'She had a lot of learning to do and it took her a while to adjust,' Clare continues. 'But now I feel secure in her friendship.

She is still a good friend.' As she is to all the people she knew before. And remarkably, and despite the elevated position her marriage has placed her in, all her friends agree on one point – that she hasn't changed, that she is still the exuberant, open and warm-hearted woman she always was.

It is being herself that has caused Sarah some of her problems. She is still enthusiastic, still impetuous, still reflexive in her reactions to people and events. She laughs easily and heartily and her facial gymnastics are as uncontrived as they ever were. She has none of the calculated solemnity that has been the public hallmark of the Royal Family since the reign of George V and her natural good humour is sometimes seen as a lack of decorum.

Andrew has offered what advice he can but it is difficult for him to comprehend fully the pressure his wife has sometimes been under. As one friend of the Duke observes: 'Imagine what it is like being married to a man who has never eaten a Big Mac, been into a pub or been shopping in a supermarket.'

'I don't mind criticism but I hate inaccuracy,' he says. Given the smoke screen of official platitudes behind which the Royal Family is hidden, inaccuracies are inevitable. And Sarah hates the criticism.

Diana before her suffered terribly from some of the things that were said about her in the early days of her marriage. There were times, she admits, when she did not want even to go out, and the Queen took the extraordinary step of summoning the senior editors of Britain's newspapers to Buckingham Palace and asking them if, out of consideration for the Princess of Wales' mental health, they would order their reporters to ease off.

The Duchess of York has the defence of greater maturity. It can still wound, however. During a trip to New York in June 1990, Sarah amused a group of New York socialites by dubbing their dog 'Sir Rutherford' with a table knife. It is the kind of jape the Royal Family, and Princess Margaret in particular, has always played. But when the story leaked out she was blasted again, and wished her high spirits had not got the better of her.

It is criticism like this that so infuriates her friends and family. Says her former employer William Drummond: 'I remember saying to her at the beginning when she was flavour of the month and the Princess of Wales was being accused of being too thin, "They'll turn on you eventually so be prepared." I've sat in on dinners when her name has come up and I usually let people get deep in and then I say, "Have you ever met her? Have you ever seen her?" Usually they haven't. I suppose the media must be partly to blame for this because everybody who has met her is bowled over by her.'

The loyalty she commands amongst her friends is remarkable. She is also very well regarded by her new family who admire her tenacity and the enthusiasm she brings to her work. Her public image, however, does not always mirror this private approval.

The Duchess of York is nothing, however, if not determined. It is the word that sums her up best. Says Carolyn Cotterell: 'She is a very definite, strong person. She is a real professional and she will polish up the bits she thinks are necessary.'

13

Duchess at Work

BUCKINGHAM PALACE IS AN INTIMIDATING PLACE TO ANY newcomer.

Long, wide corridors lined with Victorian cupboards and cabinets of china and covered with dark red carpet, worn in places and well hoovered, yet seemingly always deserted. Green silk wallpaper hung with oil paintings depicting British battle victories. The occasional travelling trunk tagged with a coloured label and printed, HRH The Duke of York, Canada. An old rocking horse minus its plastic harness waiting dolefully outside the lift doors for a small rider. The pervading atmosphere is that of a gentleman's club on a wet afternoon; quiet, understated and slightly faded.

Inside Sarah's offices, however, all is bustle and activity and it is from this corridored world that the Duchess of York runs her royal life. The routine, like the Duchess, is hectic.

'It's like a railway station – people are constantly coming and going,' says Jane Makim.

From the moment Sarah gets up until the moment she sinks into bed again at the end of the day, she is answerable to someone or something. Even the suite of rooms which she calls her London apartment lacks privacy. Once the old bachelor quarters of Prince Charles and then Prince Andrew, they are pleasant, but hardly private. There is no front door to close on the world. Instead

163

there are interconnecting doors, two of which lead on to the corridor.

It is easy to understand why Prince Charles found excuses to go hunting twice a week during the winters of his bachelorhood and play polo every day during the summer. It would be easy to be overcome by the red-carpeted gloom, 'working above the shop' as Prince Philip accurately calls it.

On the doors are small brass card holders holding typed notes (in case there is any doubt about the occupants of the rooms), 'The Duke and Duchess of York, Dining Room'.

Buckingham Palace has never been thoroughly refurbished or modernized and the rooms retain their original proportions. The furniture looks as if it has been there since the beginning. Nothing is built in. There are no fitted cupboards; everything is stowed in free-standing wardrobes made of sturdy oak or mahogany. They line the corridor outside the Yorks' quarters.

In the bedroom is a massive gilt painted wardrobe reminiscent of a grand French hotel, not a home. It does not provide storage enough and everything spills out into the corridors: suitcases, hat boxes, Wellington boots, Sarah's dresses which are kept in cupboards carefully labelled 'Wardrobe B' or 'Wardrobe C' to help her dresser, Jane Andrews, in her search for the correct outfit.

There are also chests of drawers containing nothing more complicated than a selection of the Duchess's coloured velvet hairbands.

The Duke's clothes are in a large dressing room, lined from floor to ceiling with yet more wardrobes in which are hung his suits, spare uniforms and ceremonial robes. They are cared for by his valet, Michael Perry, who has been looking after Andrew since he was a nursery footman and Andrew was a naughty child. Perry has a passion for motorbikes and can sometimes be spotted leaving Buckingham Palace in his biking leathers.

When Princess Beatrice is in town, she too spills out into the corridor, rushing from one room to the other with nanny in hot pursuit. She pounces on the drawer that contains her mother's hairbands and grabs one, brandishing it with delight, held high above her head.

Further down the corridor are the offices of the Duke and Duchess's half-dozen staff, including their Equerry, until recently Major William McLean.

Charming, intelligent and above all diplomatic, McLean doubled as a private secretary and was genuine in his respect for the young couple. He, more than any other of their staff, cared for the Duchess's image. He knew her strengths and her weaknesses and how best to handle them.

During one American trip, she was exhausted and bored and simply did not wish to meet any more people. She slumped in a back room and announced she had had enough for the day. It was McLean who firmly told her that this would harm no one but herself and she had better get out there and meet the people. She duly did and did it cheerfully.

Equerries are seldom seconded to the Royal Family for more than two years. McLean has now returned to his regiment, the Coldstream Guards, and his office is now occupied by Captain Alexander Buchanan Baillie-Hamilton of the Black Watch.

Opposite the Equerry's small room is the large office of the private secretary, once used by the Queen's Mistress of the Robes, the Duchess of Grafton, when she had to stay overnight at the Palace. The main office, occupied by the Yorks' private secretary, retired naval Captain Neil Blair, is decorated with an incongruous beribboned border and has an en-suite bathroom with a huge old-fashioned bath. A mahogany desk dominates one corner and a circular table is placed in the centre of the room. Here all the correspondence relating to the working life of the Duke and Duchess is dealt with.

Beyond this suite of rooms are the offices of the lady clerks. There are two, sometimes three, working full time under Lynn White, the Comptroller, who oversees the offices and all the running expenses of the Yorks' life. There is also the Duchess's personal secretary, Jane Ambler, who acts as the buffer between the Duchess, as all her staff call her, and the outside world. Jane spends most of her day scuttling from her office to Sarah's private rooms with lists and telephone messages, leaving the huge amount of administrative work to be dealt with by the other secretaries.

As Sarah carries out her official duties she has the support of several ladies-in-waiting. They are her companions and assistants who accompany her on royal engagements and they divide the workload between them. Helen Spooner was chief lady-in-waiting and worked for the Duchess on a full-time salaried basis while the others – Jocelyn Floyd, Carolyn Cotterell, Sarah's close friend and former flatmate, and Lucy Manners, the Duke of Rutland's niece – act on a part-time basis. They receive no salary, but are reimbursed for all out-of-pocket expenses and are given a petrol allowance for travelling from their homes to the Palace and a small allowance to cover the costs of tights and shoes – these wear out faster than anything else during royal walkabouts.

All the ladies-in-waiting have a highly protective attitude towards the Duchess and consider their position a great honour, which, in the courtly world of royal life, it is. Before her appointment Carolyn Cotterell, for instance, swore she would never become a lady-in-waiting, insisting, 'I'd really mind if I wasn't up to the job.'

Both Carolyn and the eldest of the group, Jocelyn Floyd, who is in her early forties, have children – Carolyn's eldest, Poppy, is a godchild of the Duchess and her youngest, Richard, is a few weeks younger than Eugenie. Both Carolyn and Jocelyn live in the country so are unable to give up very much of their time. Apart from Jocelyn, who worked at Buckingham Palace for the young Lady Diana Spencer before she got married, all the girls have known the Duchess for some time.

Twenty-eight year-old Lucy Manners, daughter of the Duke of Rutland's brother Lord John Manners, has known Sarah for ten years and combines her royal duty with running a small but successful interior designer business in South Kensington, Lucy Manners Interiors. She is fun, attractive and much in demand. She has dated Princess Margaret's son Lord Linley and other elegible bachelors amongst her set. Although she loves the round of London life, she is often seen out hunting with the hard riding and socially exclusive Belvoir, which conveniently happens to belong to her uncle, the Duke of Rutland.

Helen Spooner, who was the first full-time lady-in-waiting appointed, worked for the Duchess for three years before a long illness forced her to take life more easily. (She has now returned to public relations and runs her own company with offices in Fulham.)

Helen first met Sarah when they both worked for Durden-Smith Communications in Knightsbridge. Sarah was just twenty and full of life and considered Helen a bit of a 'goody goody'. It was Helen, a more mature and conscientious twenty-one, who complained to Durden-Smith that her co-workers were getting irritated by Sarah's constant telephone calls – and that 'they have nothing whatsoever to do with business.'

That incident proved no barrier to their subsequent friendship, and nowadays Helen has a good laugh, with Sarah joining in, about the time she 'spilt the beans' on the future Duchess of York.

It is obviously important to have a good working team and Sarah has been fortunate. But working for the Royal Family is not always all it is cracked up to be. Some of Sarah's staff have found her too demanding, and sometimes inconsistent, especially in the early days, frequently changing her mind and often at the last minute. In royal life where everything has to be so ordered, indecision sends waves reverberating down a long column of people. If Sarah should decide at the last minute to have lunch out instead of in, the chauffeur has to be summoned, the policeman brought off his other duties, appointments slightly altered to make more time and the venue she has decided to visit checked for security purposes. Because of this, the Duchess finds there is little room in her life for spontaneity, something she misses very much.

'I think she longs to be able to do something ordinary like just eat out of a saucepan,' Jane Makim remarks. 'Her life is constant and she longs to be able to get right away.'

'You don't presume on her time,' Carolyn Cotterell says. 'She has to be at so many different things. She is such a caring person, she hates it if people think she's too important to be bothered with them, but she's so busy I can't even imagine what it's like to be like that.'

Few people can, except the Duchess's immediate staff, particularly her personal secretary, petite Jane Ambler. Twenty-nine-year-old Jane was already working in the Duke's office at the time of his wedding and has stayed on since. When Helen Spooner fell ill in 1989, Jane took over Helen's duties and now does all the Duchess's personal work. Jane's Cambridge graduate husband Christopher runs his own advertising company which is just as well – Jane's hours are long and the pay poor, although the prestige and the travel and being 'in the know' provide their compensations as they do for all employees of the Royal Family.

One of Jane's main tasks is to juggle Sarah's daily diary. Private correspondence, lunches, dinners, birthdays, holidays, restaurant bookings and social engagements are Jane's responsibility and she answers all Sarah's personal telephone calls, either putting them through or – more often than not – dealing with them herself. Some of Sarah's girlfriends complain they do not like communicating through an intermediary, but that, like it or not (and Sarah didn't) is an inevitable part of royal life. Even the Duke liaises through Jane. 'Hold on a moment,' she will say, 'I've got the Duke on one line and the Duchess on another.'

All this activity and organization is to a purpose. Up until the Queen's generation royal ladies did very little. Nor were they expected to, and apart from the occasional charity engagement they lived a life of leisure befitting their position.

Charity work is still the main channel for the activity of the women in the Royal Family but now it is approached as if it were a full-time job which is exactly what it is. The Duchess of York is patron or president of over twenty charities and she takes a direct and active interest in them all. Even if she only goes to three functions and a couple of private meetings per charity each year, the number of appointments adds up to over a hundred. On top of that there are her official tours and such essential royal appearances as Remembrance Day.

'There are not enough hours in the day for me,' is her constant lament. 'I don't think people realize just what I do put into the day.'

At one stage shortly after her marriage the Duchess was having a particularly hard time from her critics. She was accused of being a 'parasite' who spent all her time on holiday. The charge upset her deeply.

'What can I do,' she said, 'Andrew tells me to take no notice, but he's away on his ship, not in the midst of things.'

In desperation she asked her Equerry to speak to the Princess Royal's private secretary, Lieutenant-Colonel Peter Gibbs, to enquire if there were any requests Anne was unable to fulfil, that Sarah could reasonably do instead.

Nowadays Sarah does not have the time for such worries. She is rather more discerning about what she does and anxious to avoid making the mistake of taking on too many charities without being able to get to the heart of any of them. The bulk of her charity commitments is never witnessed by the public or recorded by the press. She may visit a charity's headquarters to meet the administrative staff or go to a hospital to meet patients, but these trips are private.

So too are the meetings she holds several times during the year. Representatives of the charity concerned are invited to Buckingham Palace to meet her in her office, which doubles as a dining room. These informal gatherings allow the Duchess to be briefed on the progress being made and to discuss future projects and ideas.

One charity with which she is particularly involved is the Motor Neurone Disease Association. Motor neurone disease is an incurable affliction of the neurones which eventually leads to total incapacity and death. David Niven died of it as did Sarah's trusted friend, the author Sir Robert Cooke.

'I commissioned a book from him, *The Palace of Westminster*,' she says. 'But almost as he signed the contract with my former boss, Richard Burton, he was diagnosed with motor neurone disease. Over the months we worked together, I witnessed the disease progress. At first he could manage the six flights of stairs to my tiny office, but as the illness and the paralysis got worse we had to meet downstairs. Every time we met I saw how much more disabled he was and it shook me terribly. After his death I asked his wife if there was anything I could do to help and she asked me if I would be the Royal Patron of the Motor Neurone Disease Association.'

To discover what progress was being made in the search for a cure, the Duchess organized a meeting at Buckingham Palace of half a dozen eminent researchers including Dr Clifford Rose from the Department of Neurology at the Charing Cross Hospital. She was a few minutes late for the meeting but she dispelled any irritation they might have felt by shaking everyone by the hand then honestly explaining that she had just received a telephone call from her mother in Argentina informing her that her stepfather, Hector Barrantes, had been diagnosed as having cancer of the lymph gland and was being flown to the United States for treatment. Before she opened the meeting she asked Dr Clifford Rose about the cancer. He could offer no instant reassurance. She thanked him, steadied herself for a moment and then turned to the business in hand.

The group around the dining table listened as Peter Cardy, the director of the Motor Neurone Disease Association, explained to the Duchess with the aid of a model brain exactly where the disease is located. Jane Ambler, meanwhile, at the mahogany sideboard, poured coffee into white china cups with the royal cypher on the side.

Sarah remembered the remark David Niven once made: 'It's awful, I can no longer tell a joke – but I keep remembering them.'

The Duchess's knowledge of the condition was fairly extensive and if she did not understand something, however simple, she was not afraid to ask.

'If I don't ask,' she said, 'I'll never understand and therefore won't be any use.'

'I spend a lot of time talking to people with the disease,' she says. 'It's such a difficult subject to understand that it discourages a lot of people. When we are having meetings I'm not afraid to ask questions, but there is no guarantee I'll understand the answer. If I don't, I don't go on about it, but wait until I can get someone to explain it again. That way I don't keep breaking up the meeting by asking stupid questions.'

The concentration of the group around the mahogany table was broken only by the occasional clatter of the Guard changing and the odd muffled cry from a tourist far below in the street.

'What would happen if I got motor neurone disease?' Sarah asked.

The group became attentive.

'When I'm trying to raise funds,' the Duchess explained, 'I say to people: "Imagine sitting there with your brain alert and your body not responding to any of its messages." How would they feel? My main problem as patron is to raise enough money to help sufferers and to fund the research.'

During meetings Sarah never consults her watch. She dislikes clock-watchers whom she considers rude. Instead she has a carriage clock placed on her desk, which she can glance at from time to time without being obvious. The only things she has before her on the table are a diary and a leather-bound memo pad, on which she makes hurried notes.

Dr Clifford Rose was drawing the meeting to a conclusion by informing the Duchess of the progress being made in America and how they had a national brain week to raise money and awareness of the problems.

'Why can't we do it here?' she asked. 'Let's do it!'

On this enthusiastic note the group took their leave. The meeting had been useful, informative and a success.

It is the enthusiasm that is such an intrinsic part of Sarah's nature which allows her to participate so successfully in charity work. 'To work with people who are less fortunate than myself puts life into the right perspective,' she says.

Charity work, especially amongst the helpless, is an area where the Duchess can refocus and utilize her abilities in a thoroughly constructive way. It also helps her allay any sense of guilt she may feel about her own happiness.

'I am so lucky,' she says, referring to her marriage. 'I haven't done anything. I was just there.'

Only a few years ago she was just an ordinary working girl on the look-out, like any other ordinary working girl, for happiness and a husband.

'I try so hard not to take too much for granted,' she always says. And she means it.

It is when Sarah is working on behalf of her children's charities that she is most mindful of her own good fortune at having two healthy ones of her own. Action Research for the Crippled Child is another charity particularly close to her heart. 'I look at them and realize how lucky I am,' she says. 'There are so many little children whose lives are blighted by illness or disability and so much of it is avoidable. That is why I'm so interested in Action Research, which uses its resources to try and prevent as well as seek a cure.'

She likes visiting research projects around the country and, as dealing with people has always been her strong point, she thrives on chatting to complete strangers about even stranger subjects. Before her marriage she could not have imagined she would ever be discussing topics such as Molecular Haematology – the study of blood diseases – with learned professors of medicine, when a few years ago she had never heard of the word and a few moments before never met the person. But as her old boss, Neil Durden-Smith always pointed out: 'She can talk to people she doesn't know about anything and everything.'

'I love working,' Sarah explains. Sometimes, and despite those criticisms to the contrary, she overburdens herself, which can cause confusions in her itineraries and she sometimes finds herself with a fourteen-hour day. Even Andrew complains.

'There are many conflicts in Sarah's life,' he says. 'She has a house and family to look after, and not only her own staff and office to run, but also mine while I'm away, not forgetting her own royal engagements.'

The energy she inherited from her own mother and the brisk efficiency of her father combine to make Sarah the woman she is. Even during her pregnancy she worked hard and only a few weeks after the birth of Eugenie was up and chairing charity meetings, having working lunches, and setting up new projects.

Because Sarah is an achiever, she is not content just to be wife of the Duke of York. She sees her position as an opportunity to make up for lost time. She wants to be well read, well informed and a credit to her husband. And she wishes she had applied herself more during her school years when, according to her father, 'she didn't do a stroke of work.'

'There is so much I want to do, so much I want to say,' she admits, 'but I have to control myself. I have to say, "Hold on a minute, steady on . . . you can't do that . . . yet."'

During her first pregnancy she sat down at the dining room table with 'a big pile of scrap paper' and created Budgie the helicopter. In retrospect it was not the luckiest thing she has ever done and it led her into another chapter of controversy.

It was a creative work which told the adventures of a naughty helicopter, presented as two illustrated books for children. The idea, she says, came not from a book published in 1964 called *Hector the Helicopter* which she had never heard of, but from her own experiences whilst learning to fly.

'I used to walk into the hangar and all the helicopters and aeroplanes of the Queen's Flight were enormous and seemed to have characters of their own,' she explains. 'My little helicopter just looked like a naughty boy who would have a catapult in his pocket, his cap on wrong and his socks always falling down.' The Duchess named her helicopter Budgie and, like the teddy bears, dogs and ponies of her childhood, it assumed the character of her imagination.

'She's a good writer', her former boss Durden-Smith says, 'not the greatest speller in the world, but a good writer.'

The idea of writing a book about her helicopter was not all Sarah's, however. Over lunch with American literary agent Mort Janklow, the Duchess and the former poker-playing New York lawyer 'fleshed out the idea'.

'We discussed the obvious possibilities – royal gardens, royal mansions. It was on the day she had acquired her helicopter pilot's licence and she started telling me about Budgie the helicopter,' Janklow says.

The Duchess's association with the mild mannered, tough dealing Janklow proved lucrative. He sold the American rights to *Redbook* magazine for £80,500 while the English rights plus an exclusive interview were bought by the *Daily Express* for £126,000.

The Duchess of York's ultimate aim is to raise £250,000 for various charities through her books, and it provoked an outburst of tabloid outrage. She was accused of cashing in on her position, of not instantly handing over all her royalties.

The Royal Family's financial affairs have always been and will remain a private matter. Every member makes regular and occasionally generous contributions to charity – but how much and to whom is never made public. As the newest member of this most public yet conversely most secret of families, the Duchess had ingenuously put her head above the parapet of fiscal obscurantism – and her critics started blasting away like Italian hunters on a sparrow shoot.

To make matters worse there was the inbroglio with the *Daily Express*. Part of the deal was a series of exclusive interviews with the Duchess. The newspaper, which had invested well over £100,000 in the project, decided she was in breach of her contract when she first gave a television interview to Sue Lawley and then publicly announced that she was expecting her second child – on the very day the *Express* had stated that she was not, based on what she had exclusively told them. Furious, the newspaper decided to delay payment of any further monies.

It was a serious public relations setback for the Duchess and provided her with a painful object lesson in one of the fundamental rules of royal life, which is never to mention money.

Simon & Schuster, her publishers, decided against the option on the further adventures of Budgie, leaving her time to concentrate on another project. On Janklow's suggestion, she has chosen to write about 'royal mansions', starting with Queen Victoria's home, Osborne House on the Isle of Wight.

Sarah has read Queen Victoria's diaries which she found 'fascinating'. 'I hope my Beatrice edits my diaries one day,' she said, 'as Queen Victoria's did. They might be worth a fortune!'

Much of the historical work on the Osborne House project is being done by a researcher – Sarah, given all her other commitments, does not have the time. She does however have access to everything and the book will have the benefit of near unlimited access to the royal archives and private papers.

Sarah's ambition is to find a niche for herself within the working scope available to members of the Royal Family. She does not want to be patron of dozens of charities just for the sake of it. She would rather channel her interests. 'What can I do?' she says. 'Anne has the Third World and Diana has Birthright. I need to be involved too.' She is and increasingly so. And by drawing on her own interests she is finding direction for her energies.

'There is work to be done,' she says, 'and I am pleased to be doing it. God must have put me in the right place at the right time, because here we are. I realize I have this great opportunity to go out and help people and I intend to do just that.'

14

A Day In The Life

The alarm rings at 6.30 a.m. Dummer is already awake and the clatter of buckets from the stable yard and the muffled whinnies of her father's polo ponies can be heard through the dark of early dawn. The Duchess of York's circumstances may have changed dramatically, but the sounds of her childhood home where she has spent this past night remain familiarly the same.

Downstairs in the large farmhouse kitchen warmed by the Aga cooker in the corner Major Ronald Ferguson, always an early riser, is making a cup of bergamot-scented Earl Grey tea for his daughter. There are children's paintings on the wall, a dancing mechanical flower on the window sill.

Sarah — her father always calls her GB but refuses to reveal what it stands for — comes in in her dressing gown and, just a little bleary-eyed, sits down at the long table covered with a patchwork design, child-proof plastic cloth, bids the Major as cheerful a good morning as anyone can manage at 6.30, and opens her attaché case.

There is a busy day ahead and she has some reading to do. The notes, prepared by her Equerry, have been put together with a timed agenda, the relevant correspondence and a small CV on the people she is scheduled to meet. The details have been typed out on Buckingham Palace-headed foolscap paper and photographically reduced to a convenient handbag size.

Just before seven o'clock Princess Beatrice, who sleeps in a large old-fashioned cot in the little room at the top of stairs, starts to stir. Yesterday was nanny Alison Wardley's day off and she will not be back at Dummer for another couple of hours.

Sarah puts her notes aside and goes upstairs to get her daughter up and dressed. Beatrice is standing up, holding on to the side of the cot, smiling and cooing as babies, royal or otherwise, do. There is a single bed in the room for nanny. On the dressing table are wicker baskets full of cotton wool balls and baby wipes.

Once Beatrice is dressed – dungarees are favoured down on the farm – Sarah takes her down to the kitchen, before hastily pulling on a pair of jeans herself in readiness to move the cows and horses out of the paddock in front of the house for the helicopter that is coming to collect her.

At 7.30 the telephone rings. An officer from the Queen's Flight at RAF Benson in Oxfordshire is on the line to inform the Duchess that it is too foggy for the helicopter. A call is put through to Buckingham Palace to Helen Spooner, the lady-in-waiting for the day. When she is told of the fog she puts the contingency plan into action. The Royal Mews is informed that it will now be driving to Crawley after all.

At 7.50 Helen gets into the Duchess's chauffeured black Ford Sierra and sets off on the one hour and ten minute drive down the M3 motorway to the Fergusons' family home in Hampshire.

One of the four police officers who take it in turn to act as the Duchess's bodyguard is already at Dummer. He spent the night in the little bungalow in the stable yard which Sarah and her sister Jane used to use, first as a playroom, then, in their teenage years, as a discotheque.

It is now almost 8.15. The royal party is due at the Crawley Drugs Advice Centre in Surrey at precisely ten minutes past ten.

Sergeant Graham Ellery, the police officer on duty, telephones the Crawley police and informs them that, because of the weather, they might be a few minutes late.

Then, just as the back-up plan which would have involved a drive across three counties is about to be put into operation, RAF Benson phones back to say that the fog has lifted and that, yes, the helicopter will be able to land after all. It is back to plan A.

The Duchess, impatient and keen not to waste a moment, goes out to move the animals from the landing strip, leaving Beatrice eating her breakfast in the company of her mother's four-year-old half-sister, Eliza, and under the watchful eye of Susan Ferguson and the Fergusons' nanny who, coincidentally, is also named Alison.

Beatrice is going through that awkward but flattering stage when she cries when her mother leaves the room. When Sarah comes back in again, kicking off her Wellington boots at the doorway, Beatrice bobs up and down in her high chair and laughs.

It is now almost nine o'clock. A blue van loaded with fire-fighting equipment which is on duty when a helicopter of the Queen's Flight is due to land, takes up its position by the front field. A few minutes later Helen Spooner arrives from London. She says 'Good morning' to everybody, bobs the polite curtsey of etiquette to the Duchess and goes to telephone to the Duchess's personal secretary, Jane Ambler, at Buckingham Palace. She then discusses the daily 'Fergie' story in the newspapers.

This morning it is a front page article which suggests that, because of a scheduling mix-up, the Duchess might undiplomatically find herself in the company of Carlos Menem, the newly elected President of Argentina, when she visits Uruguay in a few days' time.

Helen makes several calls to the Foreign Office, whose business it is to monitor all important people members of the Royal Family may meet. With Britain's relations with Argentina still officially estranged, any impromptu meeting with Menem could clearly cause some embarrassment.

The Foreign Office assures Helen that it will check out the situation when Buenos Aires wakes up and will keep the Duchess informed through her Equerry, Major McLean. The Duchess is still a little anxious, however. She is going to Uruguay as unofficial patron of the all-girl crew aboard the yacht *Maiden* which is competing in the Whitbread Round the World race. Diplomatic incidents are not supposed to be on the agenda.

She goes upstairs to change, making a mental note to remind Bill McLean to brief her on the situation later in the day. Upset by the tabloids' inaccuracies, the Duchess tries to avoid reading them, and concentrates on *The Times* and *Independent*. She misses out on the gossip about her friends, but is filled in on any stories concerning herself or her family by Helen or Geoff Crawford, her amiable Australian press officer.

It is now 9.15 a.m. At the Palace a dresser and hairdresser would be in attendance as they are for all the women in the Royal Family. At her father's home she takes care of those matters herself. She takes her olive green Saint Laurent suit out of the wardrobe and unpacks her Manolo Blahnik brown suede shoes and pale tights which are in a bag embossed with her and Andrew's intertwined initials.

She brushes her long hair and ties it back with a brown velvet ribbon that matches the collar of her suit. No detail has been forgotten by her dresser, Jane Andrews, who packed the outfit for her. Jane has even selected some green earrings that tone with the inset panels in the suit. The Duchess applies some light make-up to her freckled complexion which, she says, looks best when she has a slight tan, puts her brief for the day in her handbag, and goes downstairs to say goodbye to Beatrice who is now in the care of her nanny Alison, just arrived back from her day off.

She says goodbye to her family and the Dummer staff. She was once the boisterous younger girl of the house. Now she is the Queen's daughter-in-law and, by the conventions that govern such matters, the female members of the Ferguson household – cook Anne Baldwin, Maria and Mrs Brown – curtsey respectfully.

Outside the front door Major Ferguson is waiting to accompany his daughter on the short walk across the lawn to the field where the helicopter is waiting. Helen and the duty police officer, Graham Ellery, hang back; the Major might not see his daughter for some time and appreciates a few private moments with her.

As they approach the crewmen salute the Duchess. She responds with a cheery 'Hello', has a brief conversation about the flying conditions, then climbs quickly aboard. They have a busy day and she is anxious to get it started.

The take-off is immediate and during the short flight to Crawley Sarah again goes over her brief. She is due to answer questions on drug-related problems and to meet several patients at the drug rehabilitation centre before going on to Chichester to visit two schools for children with physical problems which cause learning difficulties.

Down below, three counties roll away. There are no traffic jams at five hundred feet and the royal day is back on its tight schedule. The noise inside the Wessex helicopter makes conversation difficult. Sergeant Ellery looks out of the window. Sarah and her lady-in-waiting go through their notes a final time.

On touchdown at the West Green playing fields in Crawley the royal party is met by Mr Pegler, who used to be the Labour Mayor of Crawley. It is the duty of the Lord Lieutenants of the counties, as the Sovereign's representative, to welcome any official royal visitors. Pegler, the Deputy Lord-Lieutenant for West Sussex, is standing in for the Lord Lieutenant, Lavinia, Duchess of Norfolk, who is ill. He introduces her to the reception line of local dignitaries. Hands are shaken, greetings exchanged, curtsies and bows acknowledged and ten minutes later the Duchess arrives at the Crawley Drugs Advice Centre.

She is escorted there by police motorcycle outriders and her drive is expedited by the police officers stationed at every junction to stop the traffic. Sergeant Ellery sits in front with the driver, while Pegler and the Duchess go over the programme in the back. Behind the royal car, which has been loaned by the Lord Lieutenant for the day, are two more police cars. This is more than just a convoy of privilege. Security is and always must be a consideration for the Royal Family and the motorcade moves quickly to minimize any risk.

As soon as the car carrying the Duchess stops, the policeman springs out and opens the passenger door to allow the royal party out. Mr Pegler presents the Duchess to Mrs Moffat, the Mayor of Crawley, and to Mrs Clay, Chairman of the local branch of the Association for the Prevention of Addiction.

Mrs Clay escorts the Duchess around the centre and introduces her to all the relevant people, which she does with great alacrity. It is now 10.25 and although the Duchess has already been up for four hours, the real business of the day is only just beginning. It is a tiring schedule, with an early rise and a late evening, but the Duchess of York is one of those people who, when the occasion requires, is able to shrug off fatigue and go into what she calls 'action mode'.

When Mrs Sandy, the centre's organizer and counsellor, leads her into a room full of people she has never met before, she smiles brightly.

According to the agenda she is supposed to meet and chat with small, informal groups. Instead everyone is clustered together in one large horseshoe-shaped assembly. Necks crane forward. Hands are waved for shaking. It is the kind of situation the Princess of Wales, when she first joined the Royal Family, used to dread. Sarah, on the other hand, thrives on it. When she was working in public relations for Neil Durden-Smith she was always delegated the task of taking charge of any new arrivals at a party because, as her former boss explains, 'She was so good at it – she had an uncanny ability to make even the most awkward person feel at ease.'

She still does and for ten informal minutes she chats away amiably to the gathering – about drugs and the problems of rehabilitation and the damage that addiction to substances, both legal and illegal, can cause – before moving upstairs to talk to some of the clinic's more problematic patients.

It is now almost 10.50 and Mrs Clay, who is aware of the tight royal schedule, breaks the meeting up by saying a few words of thanks and inviting the Duchess to open the centre by unveiling a plaque and signing the visitors book.

Mrs Sandy presents her with a posy and a book on the history of Crawley and the Duchess makes a short speech, without notes, thanking everyone before moving to the entrance to say her final farewells.

Outside a crowd has gathered and Sarah moves professionally along the line of waiting onlookers, chatting and collecting flowers. The Royal Family enjoys the informality of these walk-abouts and Sarah, despite being a newcomer to the Firm, is particularly adept at them. She avoids shaking hands and instead entertains the crowd with cheerful banter explaining that if she did, her hands would probably drop off by the end of a day.

It is now 11.00 and exactly on schedule the royal car drives off. Even before the car is out of the drive Sarah is discussing the thank-yous. It is the lady-in-waiting's job to write to all the people concerned and to send the thank-you notes for any official flowers or gifts received. This can involve a dozen or more letters for each visit, a total of thirty or forty over the day. They will be written that evening – a tiring responsibility for any lady-in-waiting anxious to get off home to her family (though no lady-in-waiting would ever admit as much).

The weather has brightened now and it is turning into one of those clear autumnal days. Looking out of the helicopter window, Sarah remarks that it is perfect for flying and wishes she were piloting herself instead of riding as a passenger.

There is no time for that, however. She is on her way to Chichester and St Anthony's, a school for children with learning difficulties. There are more notes to be read, more names to be memorized.

The Duchess is fortunate in having an excellent memory for names and faces; an attribute, she says, 'I inherited from my mother'.

It is quickly put to the test. A child runs out of a waiting crowd, meets her and then doubles round the back and meets her again ten minutes and hundreds of faces later.

Sarah remembers the child's name and asks her how she managed to get around the crowd so niftily. She has only to look at something once to be able to recall most of the detail.

On arrival at St Anthony's School on the outskirts of Chichester eight local dignitaries, including the Mayor and the High Sheriff of the county, are there to be greeted before the Duchess meets anyone directly involved with the school – at the end of the line-up she is introduced to the Headmaster, Mr Turney, who is to guide her around. His task is complicated when six-year-old Gemma Oakley and seven-year-old Shelly Robertson present a posy.

The usual form is that one or two children present a posy – carefully wired and the stems covered in foil so there is nothing protruding – then step back to allow the royal visitor to proceed. Today blonde Shelly decides the presentation will be her job and hers alone. And having done it, she insists on keeping a hold on the Duchess's gloved hand and guiding her around the school.

Sarah, amused, does not object. Shelly has helped break the ice. And, by talking to this new, unscheduled addition to the royal party, she is able to learn more about the school. The Duchess is comfortable with young children and knows how to talk to them.

'Hi,' she says. 'I'm married to Prince Andrew and he's the Queen's second son.' It seems to work; the children, who were not quite sure who she was when she arrived, laugh.

Shelly pulls her along the school corridor into a large gym. The Duchess sits down on a wooden bench; Shelly and Gemma snuggle up on either side of her to watch the country dancing display by some of the other children. They then lead her into a classroom where children are learning to read and write and show her a Ladybird book of the Royal Family with pictures of their homes.

'That's my house,' Sarah says, pointing to Buckingham Palace. She shows them a picture of the Queen. 'She lets me live there,' she adds. She points to the sentry box and says: 'And this is where the soldiers stand.'

Before she leaves Sarah accepts a large teddy bear that one of the pupils, a fourteen-year-old boy named Darren, has made for Princess Beatrice. She thanks him and asks him how he has made it and how long it took, and congratulates him on his skill. She hands the bear to Helen Spooner, who tucks it under her arm along with the posy of flowers.

The half-hour visit has been easy and pleasant. The Duchess's presence seems to have cheered everyone up. Royal visits break the everyday routine and give both pupils and patients the opportunity to concentrate on something different, something special, which is a therapy in itself.

Bidding farewell to her hosts, the Duchess gets into the car followed by Helen, with teddy bear and flowers. A police escort takes them five minutes down the road to Fordwater, another special school, this one for children who have very severe learning difficulties including deafness and blindness.

On the short drive Sarah again compares notes with Helen on who they will be meeting next. A large press party including a couple of photographers from national newspapers awaits their arrival and Sarah seems pleased to see them.

The London-based papers often send a reporter and photographer on these regional royal visits, but it is usually, as she acknowledges with a wry smile, to capture her making a silly face or bending over in an unladylike manner, rather than to report on the job in hand.

That does not bother her. It never really did. It is the other, more personal criticisms which upset her.

At Fordwater there are another half dozen people waiting to

meet her including the headmaster, Mr Rendall, a charming man who shakes the Duchess's hand enthusiastically, then leads her into the modern school buildings. He explains to her that this particular school is funded by the local education authority and specializes in teaching children who otherwise might be in hospital. Their ages range from two to nineteen and all are handicapped.

In the special class the Duchess talks to a child I shall call Josie, a beautiful little girl aged about five who is strapped into a chair with a little play tray attached. Josie was a normal child until she was sexually abused and beaten up by her mother's boyfriend. She has not recovered; her mind is unbalanced and she is forced to live her life in this specially designed chair. She is now staying with foster parents. Her presence at the school is not publicized for fear that her natural mother might reappear to demand custody.

The Duchess, pregnant and emotional, is clearly upset. She bites her lip. At least, she will tell Helen later, the child is now being looked after, but how sad, how terribly sad . . .

She is impressed with the staff and teachers at the school, who are affectionate and caring. Both she and Helen find these visits very humbling. They make personal problems seem very small indeed.

In the deaf and blind class the Duchess kneels down to talk to a little boy. She lets him feel her long hair and the soft velvet of her jacket collar. He is deaf and blind, but he knows she is a woman and he has been told that she is someone special. Through the headmaster Sarah asks him to say her name in sign language and she takes off her leather gloves so he can hold her hand and feel her warmth.

These are poignant moments – for these few minutes Sarah is able to forget that she is a duchess. It is as if there is no one else there, only a woman who is a mother herself and a young handicapped child. Then the royal party moves on again. It is Helen Spooner's responsibility to keep a watchful eye on the schedule and throughout the visit Sarah will glance around at her lady-in-waiting who is never more than a step behind to check on the timings. Should any unexpected hitches arise, Helen will tell the Duchess's office at Buckingham Palace so that the people waiting at the next engagement can be informed of the delay.

But tight though the timing is, everything is going according to schedule today. Sarah's last duty is to open the scented garden at the back of the school by unveiling a plaque. This she does, once again removing her gloves and making a speech, again without notes. The garden, she says, is a wonderful idea. It is set in a courtyard and filled with lavender, honeysuckle and other heavily scented flowers and herbs specifically selected for the appreciation of those who cannot see.

She asks two children, waiting to give her a posy, what their favourite flowers are. After some deliberation and a few giggles they agree on roses and she then plucks them a rose each out of her bouquet.

It is 12.45 and in five minutes the royal helicopter is due to take off from the nearby field. Meanwhile the Duchess is happy to talk for a few moments longer. She will probably never meet them again, nor they her, but both will carry away lasting impressions from the day – the Duchess has been visibly moved by what she has seen and her natural exuberance is momentarily muted.

After saying goodbye and waving to the crowd, the royal convoy sweeps out of the school grounds and back to the helicopter. There is a special goodbye for the Deputy Chief Constable, Mr Dibley, who is leaving the force, and the Duchess wishes him a happy retirement before clambering back into the helicopter followed by Helen, bouquets and one teddy bear.

The chauffeur will distribute the flowers – apart from the official bouquets which, because they are wired, do not last long – to the local hospice or hospital; the gifts will be taken back and kept until Christmas when they will be given to the Sick Children's Trust or another of Sarah's charities. The Duchess wants to keep the teddy bear for Beatrice.

Half an hour later the helicopter lands on the closely cut lawns of Buckingham Palace. The Duchess, followed by Graham Ellery and Helen Spooner, climbs out, thanks the crew and then goes into the Palace (which at that stage was still her home).

An ancient red plush lift with folding metal gates and mirrored walls carries her and Helen to the apartment and offices on the second floor at the front of the building.

Back in her apartment the Duchess changes out of her formal clothes into a calf-length suede skirt, boots and a cream blouse. She feels more comfortable – and always has – in loose casual clothes than the formal, fashionable garments she is expected to wear on her official engagements.

It is still only lunch time and once changed she pushes the bell which warns her personal secretary, Jane Ambler, that she is ready to have what they call 'lunch on the run' – a sandwich or, in Sarah's diet-conscious case, a salad – eaten without formality or footmen at the dining-room table which doubles as her desk.

Jane curtsies to her employer on entering the room with a wad of notes under her arm, including the morning's messages and the list of urgent phone calls. The Menem problem luckily seems to be receding – it looks as though the Argentine President never intended to be in Uruguay after all.

Glancing at her watch, Sarah makes a quick call to Castlewood House. While the Duchess was in Chichester, Beatrice was being driven by a Personal Protection Officer and nanny Alison to the country house on the edge of Windsor Great Park which Sarah and Andrew rent from King Hussein of Jordan.

Assured that Beatrice is fine, Sarah is ready for her next meeting – with her publishers who are there to discuss a new project. But first she gives Jane Ambler a list of things to do for the next hour. Chaotic in youth, Sarah has become remarkably well organized. She writes everything down on large foolscap sheets of paper kept inside an elegant leather case and during the meeting with her publishers she refers to her foolscap notes and makes more.

After exactly an hour they are ushered out and interior decorator Nina Campbell comes into the sitting room to discuss the latest designs for Sunninghill, the Yorks' new house. Nina is enthusing about a marvellous table she has found. The formalities are slight; although their relationship is never more than employer and employee the two women like each other and enjoy an easy comradeship. Sarah enjoys chatting with her – she is always keen to know who in her old, pre-royal crowd, is doing what – but today the schedule is tight and the visit is kept short.

Jane Ambler sees Nina out and Helen Spooner comes into the room. Helen has just completed typing out twenty blank thank-you letters for the day. She signs most of them. There are, however, a couple for the Duchess to sign and add a small personal note. Helen also brings in the draft programme for an impending visit to Houston and they talk that over for a few minutes before she says goodbye and goes home to her Kensington flat and her investment banker husband, John. She has been on duty since seven o'clock this morning and it is now early evening.

The Duchess, meanwhile, has an appointment to see her gynaecologist, Anthony Kenney, and just before six she leaves Buckingham Palace for the short drive to his Wimpole Street surgery. He gives her a routine examination and sends her round to Harley Street for a scan, standard procedure for someone of her age and stage of pregnancy.

All the other patients have gone and Sarah is ushered straight in. She reminds the nurses doing the scan that she most definitely does not want to know the sex of the child she is carrying.

Half an hour later – even something as personal as a visit to the doctor is worked according to schedule – she is driving back to the Palace through the rush-hour traffic for her next appointment.

Hurrying into her apartment she is told her next lady-in-waiting, Lucy Manners, has arrived and is reading through their schedule for the evening – the premiere of *A Chorus of Disapproval*.

Lucy, niece of the Duke of Rutland, waits in a small office at the end of the corridor. Prettily decorated with patterned linen curtains and wallpaper, it is used by all the Duchess's ladies-in-waiting. After making one final phone call to the cinema organizers to check nothing has altered in the evening's programme, Lucy goes to the Duchess's private apartment and knocks on the bedroom door.

The Duchess shouts a cheery, 'Hi.' Lucy enters, says, 'Good evening Ma'am' and curtsies.

Although Lucy has known Sarah for over ten years and the two women are close friends, royal protocol demands this formality at the beginning and end of each meeting. The bedroom is crowded. Lee from the Michaeljohn salon is waiting to brush through the Duchess's hair while her young dresser, Jane Andrews, is assisting with the Gina Fratini gown she is wearing this evening. A creation in purple organza with large black spots, it fits the Duchess perfectly and Jane is pleased with the way her mistress looks.

Sarah is on the telephone. Jane is used to dressing the Duchess while she chats on the telephone; this is often the only opportunity she gets in a day to make calls. There is only time for two tonight, one to the Duke and one to nanny Alison Wardley to see how Beatrice is. Then it is downstairs with Lucy Manners to the car.

Chauffeur Paul Bishop has been waiting in the central courtyard for half an hour. He has been warned the traffic is bad tonight. His information is accurate and as the royal car with the Duchess, her Personal Protection Officer and Lucy Manners moves out of the Mall into Trafalgar Square, their progress is almost halted in the jam. A police escort of four motorbike outriders fails to make much impression on the London traffic, but they arrive at the Curzon Cinema in Shaftesbury Avenue with minutes to spare.

Tonight's performance is in aid of the Newspaper Press Fund and the Children's Unit of the London Hospital and, as at all royal premieres, there are large numbers of people to meet, ranging from the usherettes, ice-cream sellers and cinema manager to the stars of the film. Sarah smiles as she steps out of the car into the barrage of camera flashes and television lights.

William Heeps, the official Chairman of the Newspaper Press Fund, has the duty of looking after the Duchess. He leads her down the official line-up which has been agreed with Jane Ambler beforehand.

The Duchess is enjoying herself. She is introduced to Prunella Scales, Jenny Seagrove and Gareth Hunt who are in the film and spends several moments talking to the movie's director, Michael Winner. When she enters the auditorium the audience stands and applauds. It is approaching the Cinderella hour by the time the film ends, the presentations have been made and Sarah has made it home to Buckingham Palace. Over a light supper of cold meats and salad in her private dining room, she and Lucy glance at the programme for the last time and discuss who should receive thank-you letters the following day.

By now even Sarah is exhausted. She has been up for seventeen hours, met over a hundred new people, shaken over fifty hands, made two impromptu speeches and travelled across three counties and into London.

The day that began as so many days used to begin in the family home of her childhood, has ended in the palace of her future.

15

Fashion and Beauty

SARAH WAS NOT DESIGNED TO BE A CLOTHES HORSE. NEITHER nature nor inclination had fitted her for the role. She was never unduly interested in what she wore.

Nor was she possessed, as is her sister-in-law the Princess of Wales, of that unaffected knack of turning a neck scarf or a man's shirt worn loose over a pair of leggings into a fashion statement and a style. When Sarah wore the same ensemble the effect was altogether different. She was, as her mother, the inherently elegant Susan Barrantes, bluntly describes her, 'a super scruff'.

It is an opinion shared by her one-time boss, fine art dealer William Drummond. He would often arrive in his Covent Garden gallery to find her 'wearing her father's old shirts, the sort without a collar and with double cuffs which she held together with safety pins.

'One day I particularly remember she was going to go and have lunch with Diana at Kensington Palace and I spotted those dratted safety pins. I said, "You really can't go out like that, let me give you mine." I then took out my own cufflinks, put them in her shirt and sent her off.'

But if that worried her friends and her family it did not concern Sarah. She was never very interested in clothes. As Drummond observes: 'She bought what she liked and wore what she liked.'

Which is where the problem began. For what Sarah liked the British public (or at least the fashion writers who claim to represent it) did not. No female member of the Royal Family in the modern age has had to endure the sartorial abuse that has been directed at her. She feigned not to notice. When that defence was breached, she pretended not to care. But she did. She sought to assuage the criticism by trying first one style and then another and ended up with a mishmash which only exacerbated the situation.

'I dress for Andrew and only for Andrew,' she defiantly declared. That may have been true – but she was listening to everyone.

Marina Killery, a friend of the Duchess's who runs her own successful millinery business in Holland Park, recalls going up to Sarah's Buckingham Palace apartment in those early, troubled days. The bedroom was full of people offering their different advice.

'She became confused,' Marina says. 'There were too many differing opinions and she wasn't sure what to do, which is quite out of character because she normally knows exactly what she wants.'

Sarah had been caught in the long reflection cast by Diana and the light hurt. It was not what she deserved. It was certainly not what she expected. Before, in her pre-royal days, amongst her own set, no one had told her she was badly dressed, that she walked like a duck, or that she had untidy hair. No one really cared. Why should they have? By the standards of her own crowd, Sarah was as well presented as anyone else.

As children she and Jane favoured jeans, though they had to put on dresses when they went to polo. Their father insisted on that. 'He used to hate us wearing jeans,' Jane says. 'We were forbidden to wear jeans outside Dummer. And if people came for lunch we had to wear a skirt. He also hated us wearing black.

'Dad is very good with clothes, though. He's got good taste. He used to send us shopping to find what we liked and if he approved he would buy it. He liked colourful clothes. He liked us to wear bright colours. And it's stuck, too. I never wear black, for instance.'

In what might be interpreted as a small rebellion against the restrictions imposed during childhood, Sarah does. Her step-mother, Sue, remembers thinking that the Major, when they first started walking out together, was too unbending in his attitude towards teenage dressing and would take her young charge on shopping expeditions.

'She was about fourteen and wanted to be grown up,' Sue recalls, 'so Ronald sent me off to London, telling me I was only to spend a certain amount.'

On the train they made a pact – that anything Sarah saw and liked Sue would buy and then take any blame by assuring the Major that she had chosen it.

They went to Knightsbridge and the newly opened Fiorucci boutique which specialized in Italian-styled casuals – usually in denim. Sarah picked out a denim skirt with tassels and embroidery. It cost £30, a hefty sum in those days.

Sue knew the Major would disapprove 'but I said, "Of course you can have it" – I always gave in – "and although it cost £30 let's pretend that it only cost £15 and I'll pay half".'

The young Sarah was thrilled. The Major did not approve. But Sarah still owns the skirt and sometimes still wears it.

It was the beginning of a style. Before her marriage designer outfits were beyond her budget and although she had friends in the fashion business – her flatmate, Carolyn Cotterell, worked for knitwear specialist Edina Ronay while another friend, Viscount Linley's former love, Susannah Constantine, was PR to Alastair Blair – she was not interested in going to the sales or persuading her girlfriends to organize discounts. Rather she shopped when and where she saw something she liked.

It all came together in a style Ralph Lauren calls the 'Prairie Look'; calf-length skirts, chambray dresses, crumpled boots, frilled shirts and patterned cardigans. And it worked.

Fresh-faced, with hardly any make-up but the all-year suntan that came with her winter in Verbier, summer on the Mediterranean lifestyle, she varied it with tight leather trousers worn with frilly blouses and big buckled belts. On the ski slopes she epitomized the wild frontier look in her Davy Crockett hat and her all-in-one ski suits worn over a frilled blouse she had bought in the Antiquarius antique market in the King's Road.

At work she played with a variation of the style, often topped with the kind of large lambswool wrap which became so fashionable. Neil Durden-Smith, the Duchess's former employer at Durden-Smith Communications does remember, however, having to tell her off once or twice.

'Originally she was a bit of a casual dresser,' he recalls. 'She always looked good but I had to tip her the wink that a little bit smarter might be the answer. She took the hint and bought herself a couple of office suits and some smart dresses. It worked. She looked smashing. She is a very good-looking woman and in my book she should never change.'

But change she did. With the most unfortunate consequences. As the newest member of the Royal Family, fashion, which had been of such little consequence before, became the subject of long daily conversations. Outfits had to be carefully matched to each occasion. Decorum and suitability was a constant consideration. It was a problem outside Sarah's range of experience or interest. As the Fergusons' former housekeeper, Ros Duckworth, observes: 'She is an outdoor sort of person, much happier tramping across fields with dogs than choosing materials. It must be a total nightmare for her now, having to think about clothes all the time.'

Her engagement suit got her off on the wrong foot. Just before her betrothal was announced, it belatedly occurred to her that she did not have anything suitable to wear. Susannah Constantine promised to help and introduced her to Alastair Blair. Although a relative newcomer to the world of haute couture, Scots-born Blair had quickly established a reputation as one of the up-and-coming young designers. He was reluctant to take on the assignment; trained under Dior, he had little faith in the quality of English workmanship and liked to get his couture clothes made up abroad where, he believes, the finish is better.

There was no time for that however, and, having accepted the commission, his small team of dressmakers had to work right up to the last minute to finish the navy crepe suit with its long skirt and fitted jacket with wide padded shoulders.

The result was not up to his exacting standards and the Duchess belted the suit too tightly, making it look as if the shoulders of the jacket were too big.

It was a foretaste of things to come. There was the less than flattering outfit in horizontal hoops by Oxford graduate Paul Golding she wore at Royal Ascot in 1986. 'Too brassy,' the fashion writers trumpeted. There was the time she chose to wear a Zandra Rhodes ballgown in fussy chiffon. The internationally renowned Zandra responded tactfully to this choice with the statement: 'I feel very honoured that she likes my dresses.' The fashion writers were less diplomatic. They thought it was a mistake, and they didn't hesitate to say so.

The harder Sarah tried the more strident was the criticism. Opening the newspapers became a daily ordeal.

Even her hair became the subject of adverse comment.

It is the first thing everyone notices about her, as Susie Barrantes remembers: 'She had enormous great big red heavy curls which, when you pulled them away from her head, sprang back as if they were coiled on a spring.'

'As a child,' says her sister, 'she was constantly being teased about having red hair, being called Copper Nob or Ginger Nut or Ginger Nob. I always thought it would be lovely to have red hair but she hated it.' It has stood her in fine stead ever since, though. The first thing that attracted Prince Andrew to her was, he says, 'her red hair'.

And so began Sarah's flirtation with hair styles which, it has been said, was her biggest fashion mistake. Overdressing, overcrimping and overdoing her hair took away from a look which was, at its best, tumbling and natural.

Now with both hair and clothes Sarah has taken on board some of the more pertinent remarks and made some subtle adjustments. Her hairdressers, Nicky and Rupert, from John Frieda's salon in Mayfair, have developed a more natural look. Like her royal sister-in-law, she developed a working relationship with several young fashion designers like Alastair Blair and Lindka Cierach, who made the wedding dress and still contributes to the Duchess's wardrobe. Tactfully she has tried to not patronize the same outfitters as the Princess of Wales (though at the beginning she followed her friend's advice, even borrowing some of her clothes). Instead of Anna Harvey of *Vogue* magazine, Sarah got some initial introductions from Lucy Dickens of *Brides* to designers like Catherine Walker of the Chelsea Design Company and Suzanne Schneider of Sujon. She has also worn outfits by Gina Fratini, David and Elizabeth Emmanuel and Arabella Pollen. On the advice of her mother she has tried the Argentine designer Roberto Devorik who made Mrs Barrantes' wedding outfit, while her stepmother suggested Bellville Sassoon.

With the exception of Lindka Cierach, however, she has not been notable for patronizing new fashion talent. But then that is not the role she sees for herself.

'Clothes are a business to her,' Lindka says. 'She's on show all the time but her life is certainly not clothes.'

Fittings and design discussions are brief and businesslike. 'Because time is always short we try and squash several dresses into one session,' says Lindka who designed all Sarah's Ascot outfits in 1987 and several of the ones she wore during that year's tour of Canada.

Hats have become something of a 'Fergie' trademark. There was her Davy Crockett skiing cap. There has been her association with Marina Killery who makes a witty line in headgear which appeals to the Duchess. One was shaped like a Christmas pudding, complete with a sprig of holly which she wore at Sandringham.

Another was a fake fur hat in the shape of a curled up cat complete with pink ears which she wore to church at Windsor one Christmas.

When it comes to making hats for more official occasions Marina adopts a more conventional approach while retaining the flair of individuality. Traditional straw hats are decorated with silk flowers and, sometimes, real leaves dipped in preserving chemicals. Instead of a hatband she will twist the stems around the crown.

'These are not hats, they are works of art,' says Sarah, who is not timid about allowing Marina's unique style loose on the world.

When Marina is designing a hat for a particular outfit she makes several sketches and selects swatches of appropriate material for Sarah to chose from before she takes them round to the Palace. She likes to have two fittings but, because of the Duchess's hectic lifestyle, this is not always possible and she frequently has to finish her creation without ever seeing the outfit it is going with. Marina recalls the time she was preparing the millinery for Sarah's visit to Mauritius. While she was fitting the hat David Emmanuel was pinning a frock on the far from stationary figure of their royal client while Sarah talked on the telephone and gave instructions to her secretary, Jane Ambler. (This ability to do several things at once is nothing new: as Neil Durden-Smith recalls, 'She had the rather enviable reputation of being able to type a letter. smoke a cigarette, drink a cup of coffee and talk on the telephone, all at the same time.')

One of the problems of fitting clothes, however, is a fluctuating figure. 'A woman,' says the Duchess of York, 'should have a trim waist, a good "up top", and enough down the bottom.' Maintaining that 'good womanly figure', as she calls it, has not proved easy, however, and Sarah has spent half her life working on her weight. It has taken her down some bizarre dietary avenues.

She has, she admits, tried almost every slimming method,

from near starvation to pills and into regimes many nutritionists would dismiss as quackery.

Only now, fifteen years after the puppy fat of adolescence first put her in a health farm, has she found an efficient and effective way of sustaining that shape she regards as ideal.

Small-boned and with delicate hands and shapely ankles, Sarah is not as Rubenesque as she sometimes appears in photographs. But she does have a propensity to put on pounds quickly in just those areas she makes specific reference to. It caused her discomfort as a schoolgirl, embarrassment as a teenager, and was the subject of some light-hearted teasing when she was in her twenties.

When she became engaged she insisted, in a television interview screened on the eve of her wedding: 'I do not diet.'

That was not quite true. Even as a young girl her father was worrying about his younger daughter's weight fluctuations and when her mother, Susie Barrantes, came over to England on her periodic visits, one of the first questions she would ask was, 'What shall we do about Sarah's weight?'

After one such discussion it was decided that Sarah should spend two weeks in the Forest Mere health farm in Hampshire. It was an unusually draconian solution to an ordinary teenage problem but the young Sarah raised no voice of protest. She went and she enjoyed herself, swimming in the pool, playing tennis and subjecting herself to the various available treatments.

It provided no cure to what was becoming a minor obsession, however, one that was exacerbated by the comparison with her mother and her 'disgustingly' slim sister. Sarah went on a permanent diet. There was nothing particularly unusual in this. Slimness has become a fixation and most of Sarah's friends shared this concern.

'We were always on diets,' her flatmate, Carolyn Cotterell, remembers. 'It was usually a question of losing weight to try and fit into a special dress for a party.'

During the five years Sarah and Carolyn shared a house they

never gave a dinner party. Socially they were in great demand, were usually out, and only met for the occasional meal of cottage cheese and lettuce. Carolyn says: 'Weekends were a disaster and during the week we always starved. We were all Monday dieters.'

Sarah's anxiety then was as nothing compared with what she felt when she moved out of Clapham and into the spotlight of royal life. She was not prepared for the torrent of comment that flowed her way. Much of the criticism grossly exaggerated the difficulties but that was hardly a comfort to a young woman already unsure about her figure. She responded, she says, by 'trying everything', including appetite suppressant pills.

She flew to Paris to visit diet specialist Marcel Diennet in his elegant consulting rooms on the Avenue Foch. After that it was back to the diet sheets and off to Switzerland to visit the Aaba health hotel high in the mountains of Klosters, where she was recommended a slimming drink made from 140 different herbs. She worked out in the fitness centre, took jacuzzi baths, had electronic massages and submitted to a spartan diet of white fish, spinach, celery, tomatoes, apples and glasses of ginseng and water from a nearby artesian well. Back in London she took a course in the Alexander technique, an 'alternative' method of correcting poor posture.

Much of this could be classified under the heading of pleasurable indulgence and, despite what she or the tabloids may have thought, her figure remained attractively constant during the first eighteen months of her marriage. When she was carrying Princess Beatrice, however, it ballooned. Like many first-time mothers, she let appetite dictate. She put on more than three stone. Her hands and feet swelled and though she did not develop toxaemia, a careful watch had to be kept on her blood pressure. At the birth of her daughter she topped the scales at over fourteen stone.

It was not only her figure that had suffered. Her hair, nails and teeth needed attention. Her hair, she confesses, 'fell out in chunks' afterwards. Her nails became brittle and split. Few of the royal ladies wear nail varnish. Sarah does and regularly treats herself to a manicure and pedicure.

When Jane Makim stayed at Buckingham Palace, teams of people were coming in all at once to attend her sister: 'There was Ali, the lady who massages oils into her hair, and someone else doing her feet. Denise the hairdresser was there too. So was Prince Andrew.'

Sarah enjoys a naturally good complexion which requires little make-up. Even on formal official engagements she makes do with only a light dusting of blusher. But she does not like being pale and pasty and for many years has been topping up her mountain suntan under UVA sunbeds.

There are a few occasions, however, when that healthy looking bronze glow needs highlighting and then the services of a professional make-up artist are employed. She usually uses Teresa Fairminer, who did her wedding make-up. Teresa's discretion has assured her of continued favour.

'After the wedding I was asked to do a book but they asked me to keep quiet and I have,' the beautician says. 'I did not think Diana looked her best when she got married, but Sarah did.'

Sarah did some boasting after the birth of Beatrice. She took great pride in telling her girlfriends how she had lost twenty-eight pounds 'for Drew', one of the names she called her husband.

'I starved myself,' she said. 'Nothing else was going to work in a short time so I ate almost nothing.'

She went on to explain: 'At breakfast I have fresh fruit and at lunch I have raw vegetables with just a little protein, like cheese or meat. I have fruit again for tea, and then back to raw vegetables for dinner. It sounds boring – but it works.'

In addition she took up jogging when she went to stay at Balmoral, gradually increasing her pace around the grounds as her strength built up. And in the company of Diana she went swimming in the local Craigendarroch Hotel pool which the other guests were politely asked to leave while the royal pair put in their lengths.

But if getting the weight down was one battle, keeping it off was another and her quest for the ultimate easy diet continued. She tried Joseph Corvo, a former miner from Yorkshire who uses massage on key pressure points, and Scandinavian-born Gudrun Johnson, who claims to be able to determine energy levels, mineral deficiencies and food allergies. To bring the body's system into balance she uses a course of homeopathic pills and potions. She then prescribes a regime of food combinations which are supposed to stimulate the body to lose weight. 'Protein and starches in the same meal have a bad effect on the stomach,' Gudrun insists. 'That is why so many people feel tired and bloated.'

The system which, when Sarah first embraced it, was outside the ken of the British Medical Association, is certainly unconventional. But it seems to have worked for the Duchess: during her second pregnancy she retained no water, kept her figure, felt energetic and looked marvellous.

'It's all down to Gudrun,' she says.

In 1988, when the Yorks were on a visit to Australia, Sarah was given a copy of Callan Pinckney's best selling book, *Callanetics*. When the official part of the trip was completed, Sarah joined her mother and her sister Jane for a holiday on the island of Bedara off the Queensland coast. She started doing the exercises every day, as Jane recalls.

'Mum and I took it in turns to narrate to her and she did them religiously. She insisted on doing them vigorously. She lived on ginger tea and fruit and she became extremely strong.'

Callan Pinckney recalls: 'As soon as she got back to England she got in touch with me and invited me over to Buckingham Palace to supervise her exercise programme. When I arrived she had already begun dieting. But she still needed shaping up.'

The three hour track-suited sessions would begin at seven o'clock in the morning. The two got on well together. The Duchess was impressed by the way the older woman enjoyed life. Pinckney, in her turn, treated the Duchess like any other pupil, 'barking orders' and refusing to let her give up 'when the going got tough'. Both agreed that exercise can be 'hard work and boring' but the results, if quickly achieved, make it worthwhile.

'The Duchess is a very determined woman,' the instructor says. 'By the end of it she had lost about ten inches all over.'

During her second pregnancy she continued with Pinckney's programme, putting in forty minutes a day. 'I couldn't do the tummy exercises, of course,' she says, 'but I did a lot of swimming – up to a hundred lengths a day.'

The regimes have brought their rewards. She has made a habit out of the discipline required and the achievement is an enviable one. It has given her energy and strength. It has also given her, Callan Pinckney says, 'a figure that ninety-nine per cent of women would envy'.

And as a result, her clothes look better on her too. Edina Ronay provided her with a more tailored look. Petite, blonde and the daughter of the Good Food Guide's Egon Ronay, Edina made her name producing a very successful line in handknitted sweaters. When Ralph Lauren cornered that upmarket ethnic look Edina, who claims to have pioneered the style, switched into off the peg well-cut clothes with skirts and little jackets in bright colours offered at a reasonable price. They suited Sarah.

The only concession Edina has to make for her is to lengthen her skirts. 'Anything too short is hopeless,' she explains, 'as she is always getting in and out of cars.' She adds: 'I get upset when her fashion sense is criticized because she looks great when she is understated and she looks great in tailored clothes.'

Perfect tailoring, in the power-dressing mode, is the hallmark of Yves Saint Laurent's clothes and he provides the Duchess with her smartest dresses. When she first wore one of his couture creations – an evening gown in cream satin overlaid with black lace – questions were asked. Saint Laurent is a French fashion house and the Princess of Wales, fashion pundits claimed, has never patronized a foreign designer (the Chanel dress she wore when she arrived in Paris on her official visit in 1988 excepted).

Then there was the price. Sarah's evening dress cost over £20,000 and how, the critics wondered, could she afford it. The answer is, of course, that for the sake of publicity, top couture houses are prepared to offer certain favoured clients clothes, if not for nothing, then at a very substantial discount. The Duchess of York falls into this elite and enviable category and, after a few visits to Saint Laurent's Paris salon where she was pinned and measured by an army of *vendeuses*, she was able to collect almost a complete wardrobe ranging from ballgowns and cocktail frocks to smart business outfits.

The complement to couture is, of course, jewellery and as a member of the House of Windsor Sarah has acquired a number of admirable pieces though, by royal standards, her collection is still a modest one.

In her bachelor days she wore the type of jewellery typical of her social circle. Gold Rolex or Cartier watches, the Cartier 'slave bracelet' – a narrow band of gold set with small gold screw – large earrings and necklaces from which would hang either a small diamond or gold initials. Sarah wore a Rolex, a present from her former boyfriend Paddy McNally. On her necklace were the initials 'GB', the nickname given her by her father. She also liked fun, individual pieces like brooches in the shape of teddy bears, Christmas trees and bees (the bees form part of her father's and now her own coat of arms).

When she became engaged to Prince Andrew she was introduced to a different type of personal adornment. As well as her ruby and diamond engagement ring, as a wedding present he gave her a pearl necklace with geometric diamond pendant.

Other members of the Royal Family made their contribution. Diana presented her with a pair of diamond and enamel heart earrings. The Queen and the Duke of Edinburgh gave her a necklace consisting of twelve diamond clusters with matching earrings and ring, a modern suite from Garrard which cost £60,000.

Like the Queen and the Queen Mother, Sarah loves brooches. The Queen lent her one of her bow-knot brooches when she attended the Highland Games whilst on the Scottish part of her honeymoon. Mounted by Garrard in 1953 with diamonds first supplied by Queen Victoria, it is part of a set of three, one of which the Queen Mother often wears. And Andrew, after the success of the engagement ring, designed a brooch of gold and diamonds with an intricate tear-drop ruby with the outline of a bee as a first anniversary present.

For the first time this century, none of the Yorks' wedding presents were put on public display, so the full extent of Sarah's jewel box remains to be seen. For day-to-day wear Sarah, like most of the young women in her set, enjoys costume brooches which she buys from Butler & Wilson in Chelsea.

She also patronizes Kiki McDonough, who runs her own business from a small shop in Belgravia, and specializes in dramatic modern pieces in gold and semi-precious stones. Another jeweller Sarah uses is Theo Fennell, an old friend. And through her friendship with Cartier's glamorous Pilar Boxford she has a choice from that wide-ranging collection. She has received several gifts from Cartier, including two Panthere watches with gold bracelets that ripple like animal skin.

It is not the individual components, however rich and expensive, but the sum total that makes up a style. The most expensive dress or the most glorious jewel can lose its point if the combination is wrong and there have been times when the Duchess of York has chosen to ignore the oldest fashion maxim that a little is a lot – and a lot is too much.

The picture is not quite as dire as has sometimes been painted, however. In simple, well-tailored outfits complemented with a few carefully chosen pieces of jewellery, her hair flowing naturally, the Duchess of York shows herself to fine advantage. She is always elegant on the ski slopes and, despite what her father may have thought, in the informality of denim suits.

Sarah is no Diana. But nor would she want to be. She has a style of her own: casual, informal, or tailored. And as the Duchess constantly says, 'Andrew says it's okay, and if Andrew says it's okay, it's okay, OK?'

16

Challenge

SARAH HAS ALWAYS RESPONDED TO A CHALLENGE. WHEN SHE was a child her mother took her skiing in France or Switzerland every year with her sister. Too small to manage alone, but anxious not to be left behind, she insisted on balancing between her mother's legs as they plunged together down the slopes, whooping with delight. When she was old enough to manage on her own, she would face straight down the mountain and take off, never bothering to put her skis in the trusted 'snow plough' or even to turn to lessen her speed as her instructors had taught her.

It was the same with horses. Once astride her little pony she would head it straight for the largest fences. What she lacked in style she made up for with determination. She was almost fearless in the face of any physical challenge. And overcoming it, as she would explain years later, was 'fun'. 'I'm very athletic,' she says. 'I'm an outdoors person and very adventurous.'

This determination to prove herself, to herself and her family, reasserted itself on the eve of her wedding to Prince Andrew. She announced she would like to learn to fly because, she explained, 'Flying is his life and I want to be part of his life.'

It turned out to be rather more technically complicated than skiing or riding, however, and according to her instructor, Colin Beckwith, 'She needed quite a lot of encouragement.'

'I'll never be able to fly this thing,' she said, looking at the array of dials on her Piper Warrior. Colin reassured her. 'One of my immediate feelings was that she felt she had bitten off a bit more than she could chew,' Colin says. 'But she was really keen and wanted to do it.'

They settled into a routine. In the mornings Sarah and her instructor would start with technical work. She took copious notes in her exercise books and at the end of the day packed everything into a small attaché and took them back to Buckingham Palace to study.

'She got tired,' Colin recalls. 'She would actually say if she had had enough. But she was always very determined and always wanted to know how she was doing.' After each lesson he was required to write up details of her progress, which the Captain of the Queen's Flight looked at before he, in turn, wrote a report for the Queen (these confidential assessments are now in the royal archives).

Practice was the hardest thing for the flying Duchess to fit in. Still a newcomer to royal life, she had official engagements to attend. She was house hunting. She was also facing the problem of adjusting to her new role.

Her friends and even her family saw very little of her during this period. 'She was simply too busy so we left her alone,' says one. 'We knew she would call us as soon as she could.'

Flying became a release. She started enjoying that strange feeling of freedom that pilots find up in the sky. Because the work demanded such concentration, she was able to forget everything else and immerse herself completely. Even the zealous attentions of the royal press corps (Colin counted fourteen cameramen at one time) did not disconcert her.

Because of the security demanded by her royal status, certain restrictions were placed on the Duchess. She was not allowed to fly solo cross country, only on the home circuit. 'I don't think she minded,' Colin says. 'The object, after all, was to fly and it did not particularly matter where she flew.

'She knew she could do it perfectly well and if she asked me what to do I said to her, "Sarah, I'm not here!" I was quite rude to her at times in order to make her think for herself.'

Andrew came to the base several times. Beckwith found him most appreciative.

'It's the best thing she's ever done,' the Duke told Colin, adding, 'Thank you for looking after the wife during the week.'

On their last flight together Sarah and Beckwith flew over Andrew's naval base in Devon and along the coast to Lyme Regis. They circled Chideock Manor, the house rented by the Duke and Duchess, but only used on a couple of weekends. Flying over the craggy Devon coastline, Sarah was enthralled and later used it as an inspiration for her Budgie books.

Having mastered fixed-wing flying, the Duchess then moved on to helicopters. It is a more complicated discipline. It is also more dangerous. But Sarah thoroughly enjoyed handling the Bell Jet Ranger with its customized registration G-DOFY (for Duchess of York) and got on well with her instructor, thirty-six year-old former Navy pilot Kevin Mulhearn, whom she nick-named 'Spotty' ('It's lucky he has a sense of humour,' she quipped). 'There was lots of silliness and fun. The helicopter became a human being. I used to get into the machine and say to Kevin: "Let's take Budgie for a spin".'

Her helicopter lessons were memorable for their spontaneity. 'We would go up having been told to do a particular circuit and once we were up and away we'd feel sure Budgie would want us to go left instead of straight on so off we'd go. We made it all very enjoyable.'

The Duchess still enjoys flying with Mulhearn, now a pilot with British Airways, whose youngest daughter, Stephanie, is just a few months younger than Princess Beatrice.

He says: 'The Duchess enjoys flying and doesn't do it just to keep her licence valid. She flew right up until the last recommended moment with her second pregnancy which is three months before the birth and flew again as soon as she could afterwards.'

The Duke of York is proud of his wife's success and when he presented her with her 'wings' at RAF Benson, where she gained her helicopter licence in December 1987, he made a short speech. He praised her skill in obtaining the licence in forty hours' flying time.

'It is amazing how well Sarah has done,' he said. 'When I learned to fly my instructor told me to forget girlfriends, home and everything like that and concentrate on flying. It was easy for me closeted away in Cornwall. But Sarah had a lot of other pressures. I am constantly surprised by her.'

17

Motherhood

THE DUCHESS OF YORK, BY HER OWN ADMISSION, IS NO earth mother. She subscribes to the old-fashioned precept that children have a time and place – and not all the time and not all over the place.

She was not, she says, 'the maternal type'.

The baldness of that statement does not mean that she is not loving or that she does not care very deeply for her two children. She does and very much so. But by dint of position and inclination she is – and intends to carry on being – a working mother. She believes that by keeping herself active and involved she is able to contribute more to her family.

She explains: 'It's better to be together with a child for several concentrated hours rather than for a whole day with possibly both of you being unhappy.'

She admits she did not appreciate how time-consuming motherhood is or how hard it would be to combine it with the obligations of being royal. For unlike most working mothers, who according to Yale University child psychiatrist, Kyle Pruett, make a point of giving their children nearly an hour's concentrated attention every day, her schedule can be a block of solid bookings for up to six months in advance.

It is a strain the Princess of Wales sometimes found difficult to cope with. Distressed and exhausted, she was loath to leave five-month-old Prince William crying with his nanny and arrived fifteen minutes late at the Albert Hall Remembrance Service – and, to make matters worse, after the Queen.

The Duchess of York, who had her first child when she was almost twenty-nine as opposed to Diana's twenty-one years, is practical about the situation.

'I'm just so glad I have found a good nanny,' she says.

Her name is Alison Wardley. She has worked for Sarah since Princess Beatrice was born in August 1988 and, according to friends of the Duchess, is 'fantastic'.

Nannies, those foundations of Victorian childhood, still play an important part in the upbringing of royal children. All the Queen's children were placed under such surrogate care. So are her grandchildren. But while the appearance may remain the same – big prams, starched uniforms, little charges dressed in White House coats with velvet collars – the methods have changed with the times. The royal nannies are no longer the unquestioned mistresses of their nurseries. They are younger and both Diana and Sarah and, to a lesser extent, the Princess Royal, spend far more time with their children than the Queen ever did (Charles and Anne used to see their mother only briefly in the morning and then again just before they went to bed).

As a child, Sarah had been looked after by a Princess Christian-trained nanny. It was to that famous Manchester college that she returned when she was looking for someone to look after Princess Beatrice.

Alison, from Withington, Manchester, was only twenty when she accepted the job and the only student in sixteen years to gain a distinction in the college exam. It is a hard and varied course that includes lessons in subjects that would have horrified 'Alah', the nanny who first looked after the Queen. As well as learning such conventional skills as nappy changing, childcare and nutrition, the two-year course provides lessons in self-defence – and students must know how to dress their charges and themselves in bullet-proof vests.

The principal, Miss McRae, insists that her girls wear uniforms, do not smoke or drink – certainly never on duty – and do not have overnight visits from boyfriends. She also trains them how to handle the press and how to avoid attention if their charges are in the public eye.

Sarah and Andrew wanted someone discreet, competent and adaptable, the very recommendations Alison brought with her from the Harrogate family for whom she first worked after leaving college.

'She is the best,' said Susan Lancaster who employed Alison for a year. 'She is so professional – but when she's off duty we respect her privacy and she respects ours.'

'Alison is very sweet-natured and natural and Beatrice is very attached to her,' Jane Makim says. 'Alison also knows when to make herself scarce' – something some nannies find hard to do.

Jules Dodd-Noble and the Duchess have holidayed together with their nannies and children in the mountains of Klosters. Jules' daughter Eliza is five months older than Beatrice and Jules was impressed with how Alison handled the baby, the situation and the Duchess.

'The Duchess likes things done properly. She has very high standards,' Jules says. 'She's practical and matter of fact. She knows what she wants and has clear ideas how the baby should be brought up.'

So too has Prince Andrew. He believes in the importance of routine. Says Jane Makim: 'One day Sarah and I were bathing Beatrice when Sarah had to go downstairs for something. I was just sitting there playing with Beatrice, enjoying her because she's such a responsive child and very quick and mature for her age. We were splashing in the bath – she loves water – when Andrew came in and said, "Have you washed her hair yet? Have you washed her with soap?"

'I said, "No, I was just playing with her."

'"Oh my goodness," he exclaimed, "you must wash her first." He took off his watch and started washing her and it was not until he was finished that Beatrice was allowed to get back to splashing the water and playing.'

Like all good nannies, Alison is willing to adapt her routine to fit in with the child's parents. She was not so keen, however, on having to accommodate the ideas of Prince Andrew's former nanny, Mabel Anderson, who helped out when Alison had her holidays. Mabel, who started out under Helen Lightbody, had cared for all the Queen's children and some of her grandchildren. And while she was noticeably more lenient than the formidable 'Mrs' Lightbody (the Mrs was a courtesy title afforded the senior nanny), she insisted on still enforcing some time-honoured nursery traditions.

She once worked for Princess Anne at Gatcombe Park looking after Peter Phillips, but could not accept the informality of the place. Where once a nursery footman had stood to attention when she came in there was now a row of riding boots, and instead of a chauffeur from the Royal Mews she had to rely on a groom in a Land Rover.

Anne realized a younger nanny would be more suitable and duly employed one. Mabel then went to help out with Beatrice where she worked alongside Alison. There was a difference of opinion, as there usually is when the old comes up against the new.

Mabel, for instance, believed in potty training from the earliest age. Alison, in keeping with more modern thinking on the subject, does not and it was sometimes a case of one day on, one day off. In spite of their differences, however, Alison speaks highly of Mabel, understanding the attachment Prince Andrew has for her and how important that is to the Duchess.

Certain aspects of child rearing are more important to the Duchess than others. Memories of her own childhood and the way her mother raised her and her sister Jane are firmly implanted in her mind. Susie Barrantes often tells the story of how, when Sarah was little, she was so restless she would not sit on her pot so Susie tied her to the table leg. Sarah recounted this story on television in America on a visit to promote her Budgie books and the interviewer, Barbara Walters, was horrified at what she considered the barbaric methods used by the English to control their children.

'Sarah has strict ideas about bringing up children,' her father barks when asked. Sue Ferguson is more forthcoming and explains that Sarah is a traditional sort of mother. No dummies are stuck in her babies' mouths and there is no leaving them in front of the television. But with two permanent nannies, Alison and, since the birth of Princess Eugenie, Caroline Grinnell – also from the Princess Christian College – and Karen Black as a relief nanny, there is no need to resort to the dumb nanny of television.

Alison and Caroline both work five-day weeks, doubling up on three of them. For the first six weeks of her children's lives she also had a maternity nurse, Mrs Esme Tudor, an old friend of the Ferguson family, to help.

This traditional sense of order is reinforced by the cosy decorations in the nursery. Beatrice's babyish daubs hang in frames alongside the collages Alison, who is very artistic, has made and the original drawings for *Budgie the Helicopter* by artist John Richardson. Most of the nursery furniture – scaled down tables and chairs, chests of drawers and toy chests – is white, with designs from Beatrix Potter's *Peter Rabbit* books painted on the backs and sides. Characters like Peter Rabbit and Jemima Puddleduck in pastel pink, blue, apple green and primrose adorn everything from the smallest, chintziest armchair to the four-poster cot. Clusters of Peter Rabbits scurry around the little tabletop. Tiny chairs with 'Beatrice' and 'Eugenie' painted on the back complement the range – all from the children's furnishers Dragons in Walton Street. (Sarah is particularly fond of Beatrix Potter's characters. When she had Princess Eugenie she presented both the hospital staff and her visitors with tiny Peter Rabbit badge-brooches.) And for Beatrice's second birthday party the tiny tots who were invited to lunch were requested to dress as rabbits, while the nannies were asked to come as 'grumpy Mr McGregor' – a character from *The Tale of Benjamin Bunny*.

Although sometimes reluctant to say so, Sarah takes an appreciative pleasure in motherhood. 'Children', she says, 'are great and enhance people's lives . . . especially ours.'

She is not, however, the 'mummsy type' who drools over babies.

'She is rather like me,' Jules Dodd-Noble confirms. 'She is not that into babies, but absolutely adores Beatrice and misses her when she's parted from her.'

When Beatrice was six weeks old the Duchess left her in the care of Nanny Alison and flew to join her naval husband on an official tour of Australia. It provoked the most severe and enduring criticism she has ever had to face. It was a decision she still has to defend. She firmly believes, however, that she did the right thing.

It has been the fate of all royal children to be parted from their parents for long periods of time. The Queen, for instance, left Charles when she went to Malta to join Prince Philip when he took command of his first ship, HMS *Magpie*, again when she and her husband went on an official tour of Canada and the United States, and yet again in 1952 when Princess Elizabeth and her consort set off for a trip to East Africa, Australia and New Zealand – a tour that was cut short by the death of King George VI. No one suggested that the little prince should have accompanied his mother on those journeys and Sarah had no intention of breaking with that precedent.

Little babies, she feels – and many professionals will agree – are better left undisturbed in the first few months of their lives so they can get used to a routine and familiar surroundings.

Betty Parsons, the doyenne of antenatal teachers, came out of her semi-retirement to help Sarah through the birth of her first child. With her cheerful, no-nonsense approach, she has given several generations of royal ladies – including the Queen – the benefit of her sound and practical advice. She offers such gems as 'doggie, doggie, candle, candle' (a mixture of puffing and blowing) to assist her 'Mums' with their breathing during labour pains and tells them 'to pick up your surfboard and ride' the pain, while focusing on a spot on the wall to aid concentration. Now in her seventies, Betty has more energy than most people half her age. The secret, she says, is being able to relax and she showed Sarah the trick of relaxation and breathing. 'Drop your shoulders,' she would say, 'and breathe.'

The Duchess liked Betty. 'She's just like a mum,' she says, and saw her half a dozen times before the birth of Beatrice. 'I teach my mums not to have very high expectations about childbirth,' Betty says, 'and then if something goes wrong they do not feel they have been a failure.'

Betty instilled confidence in Sarah, who accepted the Parsons creed – that there is no blueprint for birth, that she must go with her own individual pattern. They discussed breast feeding and natural childbirth, neither of which, Betty insists, a woman should be made to do – and the Duchess did neither.

Betty is equally adamant on the subject of carting young babies around.

'To take a six-week-old baby to the other side of the world, into a different time zone and a climate of heat, dust and flies and then leave it with a nanny would have been mad,' she says. 'Small babies need a routine. And as for bonding . . . it is a fashionable expression, but some babies end up being smothered rather than mothered.'

Sarah says: 'I thought it was more important to be with my husband. It was his turn and I think that was the right thing to have done. I'm very old fashioned, but he comes first.'

Andrew fully supported the decision to leave Beatrice at home. 'What would we do with her if she were here?' he said in Australia. 'When would we see her? Beatrice is much better off at home where things are stable, there is a routine and no constant upping and changing or haring around the countryside.

'It would have been possible to bring her here, but it would have made life so complicated and disjointed it never would have worked.'

Paediatric consultant nurse Christine Bruell, who has advised several members of the Royal Family on nutrition and the general wellbeing of tiny babies, concurs. 'A little baby needs security and familiar surroundings to help it settle. If the Duchess had taken Beatrice to Australia she wouldn't have been with her anyway. She couldn't exactly strap the baby to her tummy while doing a walkabout.'

When Sarah and Andrew became engaged they were asked if they wanted a big family and replied they thought it would be fun to have a few. 'Numbers and size and all the rest is still way in the future,' Andrew said.

It was not that far in the future. Fourteen months after her marriage, in November 1987, Sarah became pregnant. It was one of the worst kept royal secrets for years and during a skiing trip to Klosters in the January of the following year the *Sun* newspaper and not the Palace made the announcement.

Sarah was staying with Clare, wife of brewery heir Peter Greenall, in their mountain home, one of four private apartments in the Walsarhof Hotel in the village of Klosters. She was looking forward to a break. Instead she found herself being chased over peak and through valley by pursuing cameramen. It was like being engaged again, with complicated plans hatched to escape the attentions of the press corps that had descended on the little village.

The two detectives had their work cut out. Clare suggested a difficult run where the Press would have some trouble following. 'I don't mind, I'll try anything,' the Duchess said and sped off over the snow pursued by French and German papparazzi with walkie-talkies.

'We did once try to get rid of them,' Clare recalls, 'and it was very satisfactory. The skiing in Klosters wasn't very good, so we decided to go somewhere else.'

Two days later Sarah and Clare were spotted in St Moritz by

an astonished reporter who noticed British tourists looking in disbelief at the well-wrapped figure of the Duchess skiing down the main street.

The Duchess's two detectives became involved in this high altitude game of cat and mouse. Clare tells how they made their escape from Klosters by sending one of the detectives down to the railway station early one morning. He parked his car at the second stop along the line and waited.

'We managed to creep round the back of the station without anyone seeing us, got on the train for one stop, got out again and transferred to his car!'

During the first few months of her pregnancy, the Duchess felt fine. She had no morning sickness – 'It's all in the mind,' she doggedly claimed – and felt quite energetic. Eschewing royal tradition, she stayed with her own specialist, rather than switching to Sir George Pinker who, as the Queen's surgeon gynaecologist, normally delivered royal babies. Some years previously her GP, Michael Gormley, had recommended her to talented young obstetrician Anthony Kenney. They had always got along well and she decided to remain in his care.

'He doesn't take himself seriously, but he takes his patients very seriously,' one of his anaesthetists says. Kenney, who lives at Kingston-on-Thames in Surrey with his wife Tricia and five children, is a consultant at St Thomas's Hospital in London and conducts his private practice from the Churchill Clinic in Lambeth and from his rooms in Wimpole Street. He believes in using all the modern obstetric technology now available – monitors, ultrasound and epidurals.

He warned the Duchess about her weight and he warned her not to do too much. But he did not force her to stop skiing – he knew better than to do that – merely advising her to be careful.

'I'll be skiing in Klosters,' she said, 'but only on powder and I'll be resting. I can't wait to be able to lie in bed and not have to get up for anything.'

She was being careful on that fateful day in March when, after a tumble in the morning, she decided to stay peacefully with Diana in their chalet while Prince Charles and his party, which included Patti and Charles Palmer-Tomkinson and former Equerry to the Queen, Major Hugh Lindsay, went out on the slopes again in the afternoon.

Charles and his party in the company of ski guide Bruno Sprecher were skiing off-piste on the notorious black Wang run. They were caught in an avalanche. Patti Palmer-Tomkinson was badly injured, suffering several severely broken bones. Hugh Lindsay was killed. It was traumatic.

As a registered guide Bruno Sprecher faced criticism for failing to dissuade the group from skiing down the Wang run when an avalanche warning had been given. Charles, in an unprecedented statement, absolved Sprecher from any blame, accepting full responsibility himself.

The tragedy caused the Queen concern and the families of the victims terrible anguish. Charles remained philosophical.

'We shall all miss dear old Hugh quite enormously,' he wrote in a letter. 'But the reason I survived and he didn't is just one of the wonders of our existence.'

The accident had a double impact on the pregnant Duchess. Not only was Hugh Lindsay a friend, but Sarah his wife, who worked in the Buckingham Palace press office, was six months' pregnant.

'The Duchess was devastated,' Betty Parsons remembers, 'and did everything she could to help.'

It added to Sarah's other problems. If she did not suffer from the morning sickness that had so upset her sister-in-law Diana, she admits she dislikes 'the whole thing about pregnancy'. The weight gain, the discomfort, the restrictions on her hyperactive lifestyle, the waiting.

As Carolyn Cotterell observes: 'It was a difficult time because she is action all the time. She likes to be on the ball, doing things all the time and when you are told you can't do this and you've got to stop doing engagements – now – and you've got to sit down it can be very frustrating.'

There was also the fact that before she actually had one the Duchess, as she admits, 'never liked babies much. And I felt fat and ugly during my first pregnancy.'

Her sensitivity was understandable. Everything she wore and did was criticized. Her fashion sense – or lack of it – was attacked and she was constantly being compared with the Princess of Wales – something she hates.

Then her 'darling Dad' was discovered to have been patronizing the Wigmore Club, a West End massage parlour.

When there is a scandal involving a family or friends, the royals close ranks. The Royal Family carries on as if nothing had happened. The subject is never mentioned in public. In private support is given.

'Sarah told me to hold my head up high,' Ronald Ferguson remembers. 'She reminded me of how awful she had felt when she came back from Los Angeles to the barrage of press criticism. Her support was a great source of strength to me, but it was her I had let down.'

Sarah told her father to pull himself together and warned him she did not want to have to say it twice. The bravado she showed her father, however, concealed her real feelings.

'It has broken him,' she would say quietly.

'She was terribly worried about him,' Jane Makim remembers. 'I was too. He used to ring me up in a real state and I'd then ring Sarah and ask her what on earth was going on – there were so many different stories. It must have been very hard for Sarah, but she held her head up high and said, "Well, he's my Dad".'

If it was a difficult time for Sarah, it was also difficult for Andrew. He was about to leave on a six-month out-and-back deployment on board HMS *Edinburgh*. They were sailing from Portsmouth to Sydney, and the highlight of the trip was to be the bicentennial naval review in Sydney during September. He was leaving his very pregnant, very distressed wife and he did not like it. His concern for his wife was heartfelt. He did everything he could to comfort her. They spent a few days together in Craigowan Lodge on the Balmoral estate and he got her a lovable scrap of a dog – a Jack Russell puppy named Bendicks – to look after her while he was away.

Only a couple of months before, Sarah had admitted quite happily that she did not know if Andrew would be around for the birth and was anxious he was seen not to be having any preferential treatment. Now she wanted and needed Andrew at her side. Kenney, who was concerned about the additional pressures being placed on his patient, was sympathetic. He intended to induce the baby, partly to ensure Andrew could be there, but mainly because of Sarah's discomfort.

'I had swollen ankles and hands,' Sarah says. 'I didn't have toxaemia, but I had high blood pressure.'

High blood pressure combined with excessive weight gain can be dangerous to the unborn child and Kenney watched his patient very carefully. Sarah had ballooned to over three stone above her normal weight and she could not stop eating. Even Andrew joked about his wife being 'a bit of a lump'. Sarah herself confessed she 'felt like an elephant' and that she was fed up with the waiting.

She was not the only one. The Queen, stopping to chat with well-wishers outside a London hospice, admitted that she too would be relieved when the baby arrived.

'These wretched babies don't come to order, they come when they are ready,' she said.

On Monday 8 August 1988, it was. Andrew, who had arrived back from Singapore on compassionate leave the previous morning, drove his wife from their temporary home at Castlewood in Egham to the fashionable Portland Hospital in London, arriving just before 10 a.m. Once she was safely installed in her second-floor suite overlooking the mews at the back, the five strong medical team – the Queen's physician and head of the medical household, Sir John Batten, gynaecologist Anthony Kenney, paediatrician Barry Lewis, anaesthetist Dr Tessa Hunt and the Duchess's family physician, Dr Michael Gormley – took control. They also had the assistance of the midwives and nurses attached to the hospital. When a royal birth is imminent, nothing is left to chance and the entire Portland Hospital was on red alert.

At 8.18 p.m. the Duchess gave birth to a six pound twelve ounce baby girl. It was an auspicious date for stargazers. The Chinese believe all the eights – the eighth day of the eighth month in the 88th year of the century – to signify as much good luck as any day can bring.

It was a short labour for a first birth, lasting just under five hours. Even so Andrew, who had been at his wife's side throughout, had thoughtfully turned the clock to face the wall so she would not notice how long it was taking. According to paediatrician Barry Lewis, 'the birth went very well. There were no problems. She is a beautiful baby.'

The birth of the fifth in line to the throne was announced in a short typewritten message pinned to the Buckingham Palace railings. A twenty-one gun salute was fired by two army units in Hyde Park in celebration of the event.

Almost thirty years before, Andrew's birth was heralded in the same effusive sentimental way. British society has changed since 1960, but a great deal – some think too much – has survived.

'There was far, far too much fuss made about the baby,' Sarah said afterwards, but that was outside their control. The guns fired and the newspapers printed special editions (the *Sun* put on an extra 20,000 copies a day in the week of the birth). Thousands of letters and cards of congratulation from all over the world poured in. Once again Sarah's 'efficient friend', Jules Dodd-Noble was able to help her out.

'There were boxes of mail and the corridors of the Portland Hospital were filled to overflowing with congratulatory flowers and gifts. Each was carefully recorded by her lady-in-waiting, Helen Spooner, who presented the Duchess with a daily list. Remembering the strict lesson her mother had taught her, Sarah sat in bed with her writing case and personal notepaper and cards spread on her knee and replied to everyone.

The letters, written on a small card (Sue Ferguson had sensibly advised Sarah to get some cards designed for this very purpose) were in her own rounded hand. Irritatingly for her, one of these notes fell into the hands of the *Daily Express* diarist, who duly printed the part of it which read: 'Baby Yorklet is a wonder, All love, Andrew, Sarah and Baby Yorklet.'

'Baby Yorklet' she was for the next two weeks until it was announced that she would be called Beatrice (meaning 'bringer of joy') Elizabeth Mary of York. The name Beatrice was last used in the royal family by Queen Victoria for her ninth and final child. Elizabeth is an obvious choice; it is the name of the present and previous Queen. Mary, the name of the Queen before that, was actually chosen because it is the middle name of Sarah's mother, Mrs Susan Barrantes.

The christening was held in the Chapel Royal of St James's Palace rather than Buckingham Palace. The venue was the personal choice of the Duke and Duchess; Sarah's passion for anything Victorian (which dictated the choice of the name) was fuelled when she discovered the Chapel Royal was where Queen Victoria and Prince Albert were married in the days before royal marriages were public affairs. In keeping with the baby's title, the christening was performed by the Archbishop of York, Dr John Habgood.

Peter Palumbo is an old Etonian and a half-blue for polo at Oxford. He was none the less a controversial choice as one of the five godparents. A multi-millionaire, he is Chairman of the Arts Council and owns islands in the Hebrides. His ideas on architecture had brought him into direct and public conflict with the Prince of Wales who denounced the office block Palumbo proposed building at Mansion House in the City of London as 'a giant glass stump'.

Palumbo was Sarah's choice – because of his close friendship with her family and because of his deeply-held religious beliefs.

Palumbo claims his apparent serenity and inner strength come from his deep Christian faith.

'I felt at one moment I was destined for the church,' he says.

The other godparents were more predictable. Viscount Linley, son of Princess Margaret and the only member of the Royal Family, was an obvious choice. First cousin to Prince Andrew, he is close to both the Yorks and has known Sarah for several years through mixing in the same social circles. Two of the three female godparents reflect Sarah's personal friendships. Carolyn Cotterell and Gabrielle Greenall are close friends and Sarah is godmother to Gabrielle's daughter, Katherine and Carolyn's daughter, Poppy. The Duchess of Roxburghe, the third godmother, has known Andrew since he was a child when they used to accompany each other to dances, and her son Edward is Andrew's godchild.

A second baby presents far fewer problems. Parents know what to expect and tend to be more relaxed. Andrew and Sarah were no different. This time, however, they were determined to keep the news of Sarah's pregnancy to themselves until they were ready to make the announcement.

'It was my secret and I was determined to keep it,' Sarah said at a Foyle's literary lunch held to mark the publication of her two children's books, held on the same day as the announcement. 'I only told my best friend Carolyn (Cotterell) – apart from Andrew, of course. I am very pleased the news didn't leak out.'

Determined to avoid the fuss that had accompanied her first pregnancy, she ignored it almost completely and carried on with her life as usual. She travelled to Switzerland for Bruno Sprecher's wedding, which coincided with her own thirtieth birthday. She made a 12,000 mile dash to Uruguay to re-start the Whitbread Round the World yacht race and to see her mother who came across the River Plate from Argentina. She made an official visit to Texas on behalf of the British Opera Festival.

She then took Princess Beatrice and Nanny Alison Wardley to Australia for a short holiday with her sister Jane, whose marriage was in difficulties. It was an opportunity to introduce fifteen-month-old Beatrice to her cousins, eight-year-old Seamus and three-year-old Ayesha, Sarah's god-daughter.

According to Alex Makim there was another reason why Sarah took the child and nanny with her. It was, Makim said, because she was worried about a kidnap threat contained in a note made up of letters cut from a newspaper and pieced together – a report Buckingham Palace refuses either to confirm or deny.

Lizard Island, their holiday retreat on Australia's Great Barrier Reef, is not an obvious place for kidnappers. It is patronized by the rich and discreet. There are no cars, no telephones, televisions or discos, just beaches and the occasional big-game fisherman. The northern-most part of the necklace of resort islands that wind up the Barrier Reef, twenty of its 2500 national park acres are occupied by thirty luxury suites, each costing at least £300 a night. The holiday was an opportunity for Jane to discuss her marriage problems and to tell her sister that she felt there was no future with Alex.

Family problems have dominated both Sarah's pregnancies, and no sooner had she returned from Australia than she received a call from her mother in Argentina to say that Hector Barrantes had been diagnosed as having lymph cancer and was on his way to have treatment in New York. Sarah was extremely fond of her stepfather, and, typically, flew to New York a few days later to visit him in hospital, leaving Beatrice behind with the nanny.

At the end of July 1990 Sarah received a telephone call which made up her mind to visit Hector Barrantes again. The doctors who kept the Duchess informed had warned her that he had only days, or at best weeks, to live. She had to go to Argentina. Hector loved children and had asked Sarah to bring the new baby Eugenie and Princess Beatrice to see him. She could not refuse, but first she had to ask the Queen's permission as no member of the Royal Family had visited the Argentine since the Falklands War. The Queen understood Sarah's concern and told her to go at once. It meant missing the Queen Mother's family birthday celebrations and it meant missing her husband, who would be at sea when she returned, but she had no choice. Sarah stayed at El Pucara, with the children, nanny Alison and a policeman, for just over a week, during which time Hector recovered enough to drive around the ranch with her and watch her out riding with her mother, sometimes with Beatrice held tightly in front of the saddle.

Two days after the Duchess left, Hector died at the Mater Dei Hospital in Buenos Aires, where her mother believed he was only resuming his treatment. Susie was devastated. This was the man who had asked her to travel to the end of the world with him. She had given up her marriage and her children and now he was gone. Sarah could only offer her love and support, which she did, allowing Jane to take over when she flew in from Australia.

Beatrice has quite a busy social life of her own. As her mother says: 'She comes up two days in the week to play in London to be a London girl and then weekends are spent with me at home.'

When Beatrice is in town she attends the tea parties given by Sarah's large set of friends for their children. Jenny Elias, whose husband David originally took the house in Verbier with Paddy McNally and whose son Alexander is a few months older than Beatrice, is one of the set. Debbie Bismarck, wife of the London-based Bollo, a descendant of the Iron Chancellor who united Germany first time round, has two boys Nicolai and Tassiloe. Beatrice was one of the fifty tiny tots who attended their joint first and third birthdays.

Most of Sarah's married friends have children of similar ages – Pam and Billy Connolly's daughter was born in the same hospital as Beatrice only weeks before. Her closest friend Carolyn Cotterell has a daughter, Poppy, and a son Richard, only five weeks younger than Eugenie. Jules Dodd-Noble's two daughters are almost the same age as the Yorks' children and Clare Greenall's youngest son, Toby, is four months younger than Beatrice. They all live an active social life. Either Alison or relief nanny Karen accompanies Beatrice to the parties while a discreet detective remains in the kitchen amongst the jellies and cakes.

The hospitality is reciprocated. To celebrate Beatrice's first birthday, Sarah decided to organize a spectacular children's party in the garden of Castlewood House. Her vivid imagination set to work and she decided on a theme of ragamuffins and dragons – ragamuffins for the children and dragons for the nannies. There were special invitations with a Roald Dahl-like figure on the front, and the garden was transformed into a fairground with a hot-dog stall, a fruit stall where the children could help themselves, and an old-fashioned bicycle with ice-cream in a cold box on the front. The ketchup bottles and the mustard jars were catering size. There were straw bales for the children to sit on and an inflated rubber castle for them to bounce in. The policeman on guard duty organized races and there was a hoopla stall.

The best thing of all was the jelly pit, where the children could grab handfuls of jelly and eat as much as they liked.

The Queen, who arrived before the rest of the guests, complimented her daughter-in-law on the arrangements. As she was walking around the garden with Sarah and Sue Ferguson she asked how many children were coming. At least one hundred had been invited, but just as Sue Ferguson was about to reply she got a sharp kick on the shins from Sarah who hastily replied there were just a few friends. Worried that the Queen might think the whole thing quite extraordinary, Sarah decided to play it down.

The Queen, however, was there to enjoy herself. She consented to give the prizes for the best ragamuffin costumes. The son of Geoff Padgham, Sarah's detective, won the prize for the best boy, while the girls' prize went to Arabella, daughter of the Duke of Norfolk's niece, Vanessa.

'Beatrice had a wonderful time sitting on a bale of straw getting ice-cream all over her,' Sue Ferguson recalls. Beatrice wasn't the only one to enjoy herself. Unencumbered by frills or bows normally worn to parties, the tiny guests ran riot around the stalls, in the bouncy castle and into the jelly pit.

At one end of the lawn there were outsize cardboard figures of Terry, the Yorks' young butler, in striped trousers, and Alison the nanny in a Princess Christian uniform. In place of their faces were large holes so anyone could put their head through and take on the disguise. The idea – Andrew's naturally – was to throw crazy foam pies at whoever was behind the cardboard cutouts.

First in were Sue and Ronald Ferguson and Prince William and Prince Harry took great delight at throwing pies at them. All the adults had to take their turn, including the Prince and Princess of Wales.

Gene Nocon, Andrew's photography mentor, was on hand with a Polaroid camera to record the moment for posterity (private view only) and gave a photograph to each victim.

The party was a huge success. With democratic forethought, Sarah had carefully mixed the guests – her friends, the Royal Family and the policemen who look after them along with their wives and children. It was, Andrew admitted, just as much a party for them as anyone else. The mix worked. Sarah still was a 'party star' as Neil Durden-Smith used to call her.

Andrew had played his part. He is very good with children (Sarah calls him 'brilliant'). He is also good with adults. Once all the children had gone Andrew, Sarah and the Fergusons climbed into the rubber castle and bounced up and down, laughing and shouting like the tots before them. There was still the clearing up to be done, however, and with the command his position affords Andrew organized everyone into groups to clear up the mess.

Sue Ferguson says: 'There was never any question of leaving it to the staff – it was all hands on deck.'

At the time of the party Sarah was expecting again. The pregnancy was unplanned. She had just recovered her figure. She was enjoying Beatrice more and more. She would have been quite happy to concentrate on her husband, whom she seldom saw.

Andrew was delighted, however. And Sarah resolved to keep a tighter rein on herself this time round. She was determined not to balloon up 'like an elephant' again and she didn't.

She got up early every morning, sometimes before six, and spent forty minutes doing callanetics and then, if she had time, swam one hundred lengths. She also followed Gudrun Johnson's diet as closely as she could and cut down on her intake of alcohol, drinking only the occasional glass of wine or champagne but usually sticking to mineral water.

She stuck to it even though she found it difficult.

'I love food,' she said. 'And you need it in this job, so it's hard for me to do without it. But I will.'

She refused to ease up on her work. As she says: 'I don't think you would relax if as soon as you walk out of the door everyone gets at you.'

When Sarah finally went into Portland Hospital on the appointed day, Friday 23 March, she knew the baby was in the breech position (its feet were facing down and its head hadn't engaged), so it would have to be induced, but she was hoping Kenney would be able to turn it. He couldn't and Andrew only just arrived in time, having driven up the motorway from Plymouth where his ship, the frigate HMS *Campbeltown*, had just docked.

The baby was born by Caesarean section just before 8 p.m., four hours after the Duchess had arrived at the hospital from Buckingham Palace. Once again a notice was pinned to the railings of Buckingham Palace which read: 'Her Royal Highness the Duchess of York was safely delivered of a daughter at 7.58 today. Her Royal Highness and her child are well.'

It was signed by Mr Anthony Dawson, physician to the Queen, Mr Anthony Kenney, the Duchess's gynaecologist and Dr Michael Gormley, the personal physician of the Duchess.

Sarah was exhausted afterwards and had to stay on in hospital for several days longer than she had planned.

This time round, however, she knew what to expect and

with the confidence born of experience enjoyed her expanded responsibilities, forming a close and instant bond with her new child.

'Eugenie,' she says, 'is more tearful and not quite as placid as Beatrice but you never get two the same. She has a pale face and red hair.' According to Andrew she also has Sarah's glint of determination in her eyes.

Beatrice took to her sister at once. 'She loves her and opens her arms to her and giggles and laughs,' the Duchess says.

Inevitably the Duchess received a large number of baby clothes on the birth of both her children – it is the new and eminently more practical practice amongst her set to send clothes rather than flowers. And her stepmother, Sue, looked out some of Sarah's own baby wear – little smocked dresses with mother of pearl buttons down the back – and dusted off the old Ferguson family pram, a large, old-fashioned Silver Cross. But Sarah also enjoys shopping herself, at Patrizia Wigan's shop in Chelsea or at the clothes sales organized by her old school friend Pandora Delevingne. She particularly favours modern and 'romperish' outfits for her daughters like Osh Kosh dungarees with pink and white stripes and little mini dresses.

At night, however, Beatrice wears traditional nightdresses from the White House or Anthea More Ede in Kensington. And on more formal occasions, like a visit to Windsor Castle to see 'Ma'am' (the nickname by which the Queen's own family sometimes refer to her) both girls are dressed in the seemingly timeless style of old-fashioned button shoes, woolly tights or short socks and smocked frocks, many of which are from Sue Ferguson's Beloved range. They are, after all, the grand-daughters of the Queen, and as with all royal children, they do on occasion have to dress the part.

There is more to growing up than the maintenance of outward appearances and the Duchess is keen for her children to enjoy as rounded a childhood as possible. Sarah herself was brought up in a free and easy atmosphere where she was allowed to follow her own interests and she is determined that her own offspring should be allowed the independence to be themselves and develop their own characters. 'You can certainly advise your children and bring them up in a certain way, but you don't really have any control,' Sarah says. Andrew agrees. 'You just have to hope and pray that they follow the right course.' Both Beatrice and Eugenie mix with children from outside the laager of royal life and there are plans for Beatrice to attend a local school near the Yorks' new home in Berkshire. With the ambition common to all mothers – and perhaps with a retrospective eye on the gaps in her own schooling – she wants the girls to have a good education while at the same time ensuring that they acquire the athletic skills like riding and skiing that will stand them in good stead for the rest of their lives.

As Diana has discovered, raising children at the fighting end of a press photographer's lens can be problematic. But this difficulty aside, Sarah is enjoying motherhood – much more than she ever thought she would. As she says, 'Having children has made me much more responsible.' It has added an extra dimension to a life already amply blessed.

When she and Andrew held their house-warming at Sunninghill Park in October 1990, they invited two hundred guests. The party, by poignant coincidence, fell on the same day as the memorial service for Hector Barrantes. There was no question of cancelling – Hector, a big man who loved life, would not have wished it. Instead, Sarah persuaded Elton John to play a selection of his haunting ballads, including 'Candle in the Wind', 'Song For Guy' and 'Daniel', in musical memory of her stepfather.

The Duchess of York was born in a house just three miles away from Sunninghill Park, but the journey from then to now has covered a distance far greater than she could ever have imagined.

On Thursday, March 19, 1992, Buckingham Palace announced: "Last week lawyers acting for the Duchess of York initiated discussions about a formal separation for the Duke and Duchess."

Behind that terse statement which, by poignant coincidence, was issued on the sixth anniversary of their wedding announcement, lay several months of increasing tensions between Sarah and her sailor prince.

She had seen little of Andrew in the five years of their marriage. In 1990, for instance, he only spent 42 days at home. When he was there he was morose and uncommunicative, preferring to spend his days on the golf course, his nights slumped in front of the television watching films on video.

She, all the while, was having to deal with a torrent of abuse from the British press and public which had made a national pastime out of criticising everything from her clothes and her hair style to her walk, and, above all else, her ebullient behaviour. The Duchess, so the complaint went, simply wasn't royal enough for the Queen's second second.

Underlying all this was the heavy breath of rumour linking Sarah to Steve Wyatt, the handsome 35-year-old adopted son of Texas's natural gas multimillionaire Oscar Wyatt. Sarah and Steve had been an "item" in the gossip columns since they met in the autumn of 1989 while the five-months-pregnant Sarah had been on an official visit to Houston.

Wyatt, a socially ambitious young man with a mother rich enough to afford such ambitions, paid for Sarah to holiday in Morocco. He had invited her to his mother, Lynne's, birthday party in the south of France, and she had accepted. He had been a guest at Sunninghill, Sarah's Dallas-style home near Windsor. When a set of photographs showing Sarah and Wyatt together fell into the hands of the press, her marriage was subjected to the closest scrutiny.

Wyatt's influence on the Duchess was apparent to everyone who knew her. Following his example, she became interested in meditation, pyramids, exercising with rubber bands, and other quirks of New Age mysticism. He gave her the spiritual support she so urgently needed as the pressures of her royal life mounted.

The fact that Wyatt also happened to be a friend of Andrew's was conveniently ignored as the rumours gathered force. But if there was more smoke than fire to their relationship, it was a situation that nonetheless proved to be a destructive catalyst to a marriage that had been drifting erratically towards the rocks for many months.

Sarah was desperate for her husband's support in her battles with the old guard of Buckingham Palace, who treated her with barely disguised contempt. She wished Andrew would take a greater interest in their two daughters. She looked to him to protect her from the media's onslaught. Andrew, however, left her to deal with her problems by herself. Programmed from birth to keep his emotions under tight control, he didn't even notice when she cut off the long red locks that had been her most noticeable trademark.

"He didn't say whether he liked [the haircut] or not," Sarah told me sadly, "so it probably means he doesn't like it."

Andrew had failed her. Yet, by the perversity that governs relationships, even royal ones, the announcement that the Duke and his Duchess were negotiating their separation actually drew the couple together again. They stayed under the same roof at Sunninghill—a house, incidentally, that Sarah dislikes—and continued to act as if they were still happily married, attending a party given by rock star Elton John and dining together in the romantic setting of the Waterside Inn just outside London. It was as if the announcement had released the pressure.

Sarah is confused about her future. In her effort to escape the gilded cage, she has only succeeded in focusing more unwelcome attention on herself. Needless to say, the Queen was hoping against hope that, even at the eleventh hour, the couple could patch up their marriage.

Of one thing Sarah is certain, however, and that is her role as a mother. She could yet be stripped of her title—Her Royal Highness—though certainly not at once. She cannot be deprived of her daughters, Beatrice and Eugenie, however. She would not stand for that. The Queen, who remains very attached to her daughter-in-law and continued to invite her to take tea with her at Buckingham Palace, would never suggest that she should be.

As Sarah told me: "My children are my world. They are the only thing in my life that is a hundred percent safe and loving and wonderful."

INDEX